SEP – – 2005

TAKING YOUR
BUSINESS TO

THE ~~NEXT LEV~~EL

A~~N ENTREPRENEUR'S GUIDE TO~~P
SUCCE~~SSFULLY GROWING YOUR BUS~~INESS

D1411279

Published by Sourcebooks, Inc.
P.O. Box 4410, Naperville, Illinois 60567-4410
(630) 961-3900
Fax: (630) 961-2168
www.sourcebooks.com

Originally published in 2001 by McGraw-Hill Ryerson Canada
Second Canadian edition published in 2004 by Eastleigh Publications, a division of Eastleigh
Management Services

Library of Congress Cataloging-in-Publication Data

McGuckin, Frances.
  Taking your business to the next level : an essential step-by-step success plan /
Frances McGuckin.
      p. cm.
  Rev. ed. of: Big ideas for growing your small business. 2001.
  Includes index.
  ISBN 1-4022-0393-4 (alk. paper)
  1. Small business--Management. 2. Small business--Growth. I. McGuckin,
Frances. Big ideas for growing your small business. II. Title.

HD62.7.M394 2005
658.02'2--dc22

2005003352

Printed and bound in the United States of America
DR   10   9   8   7   6   5   4   3   2   1

MORE PRAISE FOR
TAKING YOUR BUSINESS TO THE NEXT LEVEL

"This new book will be an invaluable resource...it provides you with practical advice on how to plan and overcome growth problems...the added bonus being the tips throughout each section that suggest innovative ideas to use within your business."   MOCHASOFA

"Everybody writes books on starting a business but no one seems to bother actually showing how to run one. McGuckin does so admirably with a series of amazingly detailed lessons on managing business growth."   *THE PROVINCE*

"Her easy-to-read book is a refreshing, insightful, step-by-step guide for anyone looking for the right way to grow a small business."   *CARIBOO ADVISOR*

"No small business would be complete without this second book, *Taking Your Business to the Next Level*, from bestselling author Frances McGuckin. Easy to read and understand, it contains the formula for making your business successful."

CRAFTLINK CONNECTIONS 2004

"This book is well thought out and presents a no-nonsense approach...she'll help you get out of your rut, move on, and take your business to new heights."

OFFICE@HOME MAGAZINE

PRAISE FROM HAPPY READERS

"Her latest book, *Taking Your Business to the Next Level*, is wonderful—filled with new ideas for the small business person. Thank you for your wisdom, Fran."

BARBARA PELLEY, VALLEY WOMEN'S NETWORK

"*Taking Your Business to the Next Level* is fabulous and totally relevant to issues that our business faces. The tips are a great touch; it's much easier to read that way when I am pressed for time."

LISA AND DEREK RICKWOOD, OWNERS, RICKWOOD'S MENSWEAR
(Real Life story, Chapter 6)

"As well as a great ideas book to guide you through growing your business, I refer to *Taking Your Business to the Next Level* as an everyday manual for help with writing those formal business letters, approaching the media, planning a presentation, guiding me through the things I should be doing and how to succeed at them, and the pitfalls to avoid. I took some advice from your wonderful book and got a whole-page exposure in the *North Shore News*! Thank you! It is an easy read for a busy professional and a 'must-have' book on the daily reference shelf in every small business."

LORNA STEWART, PIE-ONEER, ACME HUMBLE PIE CO.
(Real Life story, Chapter 9)

"We read *Taking Your Business to the Next Level* and saw ourselves and all the pitfalls within the book and realized that we were no different from anyone. It made us refocus and not give up; we had made common mistakes and we realized where we could change, reinvent the business, and be successful. It gave us all the skills and techniques to do so."

JIM AND LINDA KURTZ, WEGO TOURS AND TRAVEL
(Real Life story, Chapter 14)

"Four of us met for three months once a week and reviewed a chapter of *Taking Your Business to the Next Level*. It's too easy to get caught up in the work and not working on the business. The book is a good reminder to keep focused and be accountable. It was invaluable that way. I get something from the book every time I read it. It focuses you on fine-tuning your business and policies and brings you back to the reality checks."

VICTORIA BIGGS, UNIQUELY YOURS FURNITURE ON CONSIGNMENT

"Just finished reading your wonderful book *Taking Your Business to the Next Level!* Truly a helpful and straightforward book for entrepreneurs. A bit of an eye-opener as well!"

"I just finished reading your book, and it was great! Your book helped me to realize that I still have a few areas to work on before I am ready for a large retail business."

"I have just finished *Taking Your Business to the Next Level* and would like to thank you for producing such a good resource for small business. I have already taken some of your suggestions and put them into action."

"Your book is my inspirational source! Before, I planned my business in a one-dimensional way. Now, I use multidimensions. My business is starting to grow like crazy. Your title is perfect. Thank you for writing such a great book!"

DEDICATION

To my incredible 96-year-old mother,
Emilie Gisela Shaw,
who has shown me that if you
stay positive and busy, you can overcome
all the curveballs that life throws at you.
So this book is devoted to her, because
her strength and determination, courage and
sheer stubbornness, persistence and perseverance
are a daily inspiration, not just to me,
but to friends and family universally.

I love you, Mom.

TABLE OF CONTENTS

FOREWORD xii

ACKNOWLEDGMENTS xiii

PREFACE TO NEW EDITION xv

INTRODUCTION xvii

CHAPTER 1: Are You Taking Care of Business? 1
    Where are you now? 2
    You are your business 3
    Business is all about service 5
    The top ten mistakes in growing a business 7
    Take the test: The "Where Am I Now?" questionnaire 10

CHAPTER 2: Do Your Entrepreneurial Skills Need Fine-Tuning? 17
    You're the boss 18
    The Eight Essential Entrepreneurial Skills 18
    How to survive and succeed in a changing world 22
    Your golden box of opportunity 23
    The A to Z entrepreneur 27
    Take the task test 29
    Entrepreneur or operator? 30
    Getting by with a little help from your friends 32
    What do you really want to do? 33

CHAPTER 3: Are You Organized—Or Out of Control? 37
    Get organized 38
    Organize for the "Five Fs" 43
    Organize the office: Manage time 44

Organize your files 45
Utilize your filing system 46
Organize your computer 47
Organize your email 48
Organize and master time 48
Organize a monthly routine 50
Organize the home office 52
Plan to stay organized: a checklist 56

CHAPTER 4: Are You In Control of the Financial Reins? **59**
What does accounting tell you? 60
The six-step accounting cycle 61
What are source documents? 64
The general ledger—your business "bible" 65
Financial statements—your business health barometer 67
Design an informative chart of accounts 68
How to analyze an income statement 69
Know your break-even point 73
How to decipher a balance sheet 79
The balance sheet shows... 81
Increase your gross profit margins 82
Is your overhead out of control? 84
Plan for your future. 85

CHAPTER 5: How Else Can You Increase Your Profits? **89**
Increase profits by increasing efficiency 90
Take a systems inventory 90
Is your inventory under control? 93
How to count inventory 96
How to cost inventory 99
Are your customers paying you? 101
Set credit policies 102
How to use credit applications 103
Monitor accounts receivable 105
What if your customers don't pay? 107
Improve your administrative efficiency 109

CHAPTER 6: Are You Ready for Growth? **111**
Did your plan go to plan? 112
Use the six-step growth analysis plan 113
STEP 1: Evaluate where you are now. 114
STEP 2: Decide whether you are ready to grow 116
STEP 3: Set goals. 119

STEP 4: Plan how you will grow 120
STEP 5: Plan your financing needs 122
STEP 6: Compare progress to projections 126
Grow your business by exporting 128
The benefits of incorporation 132
The downside of incorporation 134
"Going for growth" action plan 135

CHAPTER 7: How Do You Find—and Keep—Good Help? **139**
Are you ready to be a boss? 140
"I can't get good help these days!" 142
How do you hire the right person? 144
How to recruit the perfect candidate 145
Wading through the résumé pile 148
The art of successful interviewing 149
Reference checks 150
Your responsibilities as an employer 152
How much does an employee cost? 153
Make your employees "LIFERS" 155
Employee theft—an employer's nightmare 158

CHAPTER 8: How Do You Grow and Maintain Your Customer Base? **163**
Are you missing your market? 164
Understand the components of marketing 164
Revisit your marketing plan 165
Reevaluate your marketing plan 166
Revise your marketing plan 169
Your business image and branding techniques 169
Target your market 174
Your marketing budget 178
Don't let 'em out the door... 181
Where can you improve? 182

CHAPTER 9: Are Your Written Presentations Professional? **185**
Communication is your key to success 186
The art of writing professional letters 187
How to set out a smart letter 187
Sample letters for all occasions 190
How to write a powerful media release 195
How to prepare a professional media kit 199
Pitch yourself to the media 200
How can you improve your written skills? 202

CHAPTER 10: Do Your Verbal Skills Need Enhancing?.................. 205
Business is all about communicating 206
Telephone talk 206
Cold-call with confidence.................................... 209
Make fruitful follow-up calls................................. 210
Speak your way to success 212
The "Five Ts" of terrific talking 213
Networking—breaking the ice 219
Improve your communication skills 222

CHAPTER 11: How Do You Apply Communication Skills to Marketing? .. 225
Use low-cost or no-cost marketing magic....................... 226
Communicate in your community 226
Network, network, network! 229
Communicate through speaking 230
Communicate through the media 233
Communicate, demonstrate, and educate 235
Communicate through writing 239
Build credibility using testimonials 240
Apply your communication skills to marketing 242

CHAPTER 12: What Else Should You Know About Marketing? 245
Develop a marketing mix 246
Build a database—build customer loyalty 246
Out-service the competition 248
Marketing and the Internet 251
Making surfing easy 252
"Hit-or-miss" media advertising 255
Don't waste marketing time and money 259
Now plan your marketing approach 260

CHAPTER 13: How Do You Improve Your Sales Skills?.................. 265
Selling is an everyday experience 266
Dispelling the sales myth 267
Consumers are filling a need 267
Use the six-step sales process 268
The "Five Ws" of selling 268
The "Six Ps" of selling 272
Can you improve your sales skills? 280

CHAPTER 14: How Do You Operate in Crisis? **283**
  Do you still have passion? 284
  "Let's not talk about failure" 285
  Heed the warning signs 286
  Ten steps for operating in crisis 288
  Failure of a sole proprietorship 295
  Failure of an incorporated business 297
  What are directors' liabilities? 297
  Think about your family 298
  What will your decision be? 298

CHAPTER 15: Are You Ready to Succeed? **307**
  What does success mean? 308
  Women move into the boardroom 311
  Why women succeed 311
  The challenges women face 312
  But men hold their ground in the business world 315
  Why men succeed 315
  The challenges men face 316
  What is good business management? 318
  Plan to succeed 319

INDEX **323**

ABOUT THE AUTHOR **333**

FOREWORD

I'm sure you have heard the following comment:

Q. "How do I run a small business?"

A. "Start with a big business."

There's more truth than humor in that statement. As a business owner for the past twenty-five years, I've grown my business from gross sales of $76,000 in 1976 to today's gross sales of $25 million. And then along comes this book *Taking Your Business to the Next Level* by Frances McGuckin. Where were you when I needed you the most?

Her easy-to-read "how to" book on growing your business is a refreshing, insightful step-by-step process for all who seek the elusive success formula. "Aha" ideas bounce off every page of Frances McGuckin's second book.

This very practical book will show you how to identify the "Top Ten" mistakes and avoid them, how to find your customers, how to sell, how to control your finances, how to develop a team, how to achieve extraordinary results, how to develop important communication skills, plus much, much more!

Buy this book, read this book, and improve your performance, productivity, and profitability. You'll be glad you did and you will turn your small business into a successful big business. And it won't take you twenty-five years like it took me.

Peter Legge, MA, CSP, CPAE
President and Publisher
Canada Wide Magazines & Communications Ltd.
Author/Publisher/Professional Speaker

ACKNOWLEDGMENTS

This book is one "big idea" that flourished, grew, and blossomed. However, it wouldn't have blossomed so beautifully nor reached fruition without the help and support of caring colleagues and friends.

One may author a book, but it takes teamwork to complete it. There are many people to thank, so starting from the beginning, a special thank-you to a top-class production team who produced the second Canadian edition of *Business for Beginners*—Heidi LeRossignol, Tita Zierer, Shirley Olson, Naomi Pauls, and Lee Fodi. You gave birth to an international baby.

Part of the team to thank are those special people who contributed information. They include my friend and colleague Lorne Kelton, who contributed sales tips for Chapter 13; Cal Purcell, Vice President of Government Relations and External Affairs for Sprott-Shaw College, who contributed a great deal of information for the same chapter; and Christina Severin-Henriksen, a longtime friend and past employment agency owner, who contributed information on hiring employees for Chapter 7.

To two fine professionals, Donald Starr, CPA, and Christopher Fletcher, Attorney at Law—who both practice in Blaine, Washington—thank you so kindly for your help in giving input into the legal and accounting aspects and for being there to answer my many questions.

To Peter Legge, a truly inspirational, outstanding role model, successful entrepreneur, and internationally acclaimed, award-winning speaker, who kindly wrote the foreword for this book, a big thank-you. Peter's awards include Toastmasters International's Top Speaker in North America.

Of course, it's no use writing a book if no one wants to publish it. Special thanks are extended to Catherine Fowler of Redwood Agency in California, a dynamic literary agent who had total confidence in both books. To Peter Lynch, my editor at Sourcebooks, Inc., I appreciate the wonderful opportunity to become part of your authors' team, and thank you for your faith in me.

A special thank-you to Team Canada for supplying the excellent information on exporting and the questionnaire "Are You Ready for Exporting?" in Chapter 6.

To all those entrepreneurs who appear in the Real Life stories, thank you for being an important part of this book. To my very dear and beautiful teenage daughter, Katrina, what can I say? Thank you for understanding this stubborn writing maniac. I love you too. To my wonderful 96-year-old mom, Emilie, and son, Richard, what would this world be without your love and constant support? You are all my inspiration and reason for keeping on keeping on.

PREFACE TO NEW EDITION

WHY WRITE ABOUT GROWING A BUSINESS?

When *Business for Beginners* was first published in 1997, people constantly said to me, "Fran, you have to write a book about staying in business, because I desperately need it." After having an accounting and consulting practice for nearly twenty years, that was not exactly news to me; in fact, I sold that part of the business in 2000 because the continual business failures were just too depressing. By January 2001, the first edition of *Big Ideas for Growing Your Small Business* (now titled *Taking Your Business to the Nest Level*) was off the press, published by McGraw-Hill Ryerson.

Times and technology quickly change, and as I travel more extensively speaking to entrepreneurs—from San Antonio, Texas, to St. John's, Newfoundland—the more I realized that the new keynote and workshop material that I had developed to reflect these ongoing changes needed to be between these covers, so here it is. I thank everyone I have met over the years; one way or another, many of you are an important part of this book.

HOW WAS THIS BOOK WRITTEN?

No different from anyone else, I spent time dreaming about what I wanted. Perhaps different from some, I spent a lot of time making those dreams become a reality. This book became a reality through my stubborn persistence (inherited from my mom), setting and focusing on a goal, and working relentlessly over summer (ugh) to meet a tight publishing deadline. You see, dreams are only dreams, but they must become goals to make them happen. No one can make your dreams happen except you.

WHY WAS THIS BOOK WRITTEN?

Still on the subject of dreams and goals, my two main goals were to write books and give seminars to help reduce small business failure—and to earn enough income to do what I most enjoy (riding my horse, oil painting, sleeping in, and getting dirt under my fingernails).

Those goals gave birth to my first book, *Business for Beginners: A Simple Step-by-Step Guide to Starting a Small Business.* Its unexpected success has been overwhelming! With over 130,000 copies sold to date, there is now a Russian edition and electronic rights have been sold to a national accounting and tax software company. By 2005, it will be published in six countries, with *Taking Your Business to the Next Level* published in four countries.

WHOM IS THIS BOOK WRITTEN FOR?

If you have just started a business, or are growing too quickly or too slowly, or want to make more profit, or learn more, this book is written for you. My message to you is simple. You have your entrepreneurial dream, and no one can take it from you—except you. If you set your goals, give them time limits, focus, learn, are open to change, and use the information in this book, nothing can stop you from growing your dream into a dynamic and profitable business. You can do it.

I would love to hear your comments or questions. Please visit my website at *www.smallbizpro.com* for more business information, or email me at *contact@smallbizpro.com*.

INTRODUCTION

SMALL BUSINESS IS BIG BUSINESS

With the onslaught of career-changing baby boomers and women outstripping men in business start-ups, self-employment has skyrocketed in the last decade. Coupled with changing technology and seesawing economic conditions, there is a proliferation of small and home-based businesses (HBBs), with HBBs accounting for over 50 percent of North American business start-ups. Women-owned businesses account for nearly 40 percent of North American businesses. Small business is indeed big business.

Millions of self-employed entrepreneurs chase the great entrepreneurial dream of self-sufficiency, being their own boss and making lots of money. Those who follow the formulas for success usually achieve their aspirations, and more. Those who wing it on a whim run the risk of failure. This book was written to help entrepreneurs realize their dream. Let me help you realize yours.

WHAT DOES "GROWING A BUSINESS" MEAN?

Growing a business means learning all aspects of profitably managing, marketing, operating, and administering it. Too many businesses fall through the cracks because owners don't know what steps to take to rectify problems. This book lists the sixty jobs that an entrepreneur is responsible for. How do you cope with all these chores and generate a profitable income? Let me show you.

By learning how to circumvent operational stumbling blocks, your business has a better chance of success. The secret is to make the time to learn how. Most proprietors are "too busy" working *in* their business to work *on* it. This book is designed to teach you how to work smarter, not harder, thereby increasing your profits while decreasing your stress level.

MORE OR BIGGER?

Many people have the misconception that growing means "more." More sales, more employees, more overhead expenses—and more headaches. Not so. Who needs those stresses? However, if you aren't generating the expected profits, then there are reasons why. The answers are in this book.

Then there are those entrepreneurs with aspirations of "bigger." To take your business to the next level, you must stop first to consolidate your ideas. Bigger is only better if you do it right. Do you want a bigger business generating bigger profits, or do you just want to make your business more profitable and less stressful?

WHAT WILL YOU LEARN?

If you read this book thoroughly and use the worksheets, tips, and big ideas, it will guide you through the necessary growth steps. In a nutshell, it:

• helps you assess where you are and where you are going;
• teaches you the Eight Essential Entrepreneurial Skills;
• offers workable and practical solutions to problems;
• teaches you the Seven Tools of Change;
• offers practical time-management techniques;
• helps you get organized and operate efficiently;
• shows you how to increase profits;
• helps you assess whether you are ready for growth;
• guides you through hiring and motivating employees;
• offers practical marketing and selling strategies;
• guides you through operating in crisis; and
• includes many self-assessment worksheets and checklists.

The first chapter addresses how important you and superior customer service are to your business. It explores the most common mistakes that precipitate growth or operational problems. Take the "Where Am I Now?" questionnaire at the end of Chapter 1 to assess both your emotional and physical business health.

If you use the information found in this book and complete all the questionnaires, worksheets, and checklists, you will be well on your way to formulating your success plan. The rest is up to you.

CHAPTER ONE

Are You Taking Care of Business?

You'll make mistakes. Some...will call them failures,
but I have learned that failure is really God's way of saying,
"Excuse me, you're moving in the wrong direction."

OPRAH WINFREY

There is a reason you picked up this book. Something motivated you to make time in your busy day or evening to start this journey. If you currently own a business, perhaps you have been operating only a few weeks or months and are experiencing some doubt and uncertainty. Maybe you have been in business for several years, but your expectations are not being met. Perhaps you are experiencing rapid growth, feel out of control, or are even worrying about failure. You may be lacking creative ideas to grow your business and are looking for some solutions. I think you will find some in this book. ✒

WHERE ARE YOU NOW?

Few people understand just how difficult, challenging, and sometimes lonely being self-employed can be—until they own their own business. There is no one to train you, watch over you, motivate you, mentor you, or tell you what you are doing wrong. The old adage "You learn by experience" is fine in some situations, as in learning to ride a horse. You can take a few falls from a horse and probably survive, but you can't afford to have too many falls in business. More often the general rule is: "Learning by experience will cost you nothing but money." A small business—in fact, any business—can't afford to lose money.

Many people dream of owning their own business sometime during their lives. Perhaps opening a business was not a dream, but the only solution to a financial nightmare. Perhaps you were laid off, downsized, capsized, retrenched, cut back, computer-replaced, too young, too old, too expensive, too good—or not good enough. Whatever the reason, you are here now, on your own in a highly competitive, business-eat-business marketplace.

TAKE FOUR STEPS TO SUCCESS

By reading this book, you have taken the first step toward making your business work for you. The second step is to work on the necessary skills to make you a confident, competent, successful business person. The third step is to put some of these ideas and information into practice. The fourth step is to constantly monitor your progress and never become complacent.

Your dream or harsh reality?

For many, the dream turns into cold reality all too soon. What you thought would be an exciting experience has become a daily grind of managing dozens of chores at once and tackling mountains of paperwork with not enough time to do it all. Your loved ones are complaining that you are always working and grumpy. For some strange reason, the dollars you expected to make so easily just aren't materializing. "Why is it happening like this?" you ask yourself. "What am I doing wrong?"

Don't feel alone with these thoughts. Most entrepreneurs have experienced these same feelings, although some are reluctant to admit that "my business is a giant headache." Who honestly wants to admit that it is nothing like they dreamed of or that they are afraid of failure and need help? No one. We all have our pride. Although being your own boss has many tangible benefits, each day is hard work and a challenge. Hard work aside, the rewards in building a successful small business are countless. Those who do it right realize these rewards and would never go back to a nine-to-five job.

Grow with your business

Some of the information in this book doesn't apply just to business. As you work on improving your skills, you will gain confidence and be pleasantly surprised at how the rest of your life becomes more fulfilling. Every time you learn a new skill, you gain more self-esteem. When you gain more self-esteem, you gain more confidence. More confidence enables you to overcome the fear of tackling something new.

The learning process is exciting and self-rewarding. When you are no longer held back by doubts and fears and are armed with new knowledge and confidence, your goals are within reach. It's a wonderful feeling to reach those goals because *you* made it happen. What could be better?

YOU ARE YOUR BUSINESS

No matter how fancy your office or building, how fantastic your products or services, how professional and snazzy your marketing materials, or how competitive your prices, there is only one person who will be responsible for the business's success. That person is *you*. Before customers use your business, they ideally prefer to build a relationship of trust with *you*—the expert in your field who offers brilliant customer service.

Never forget these four important words:

> # You are your business.

You may have the best product since the invention of the Internet, but if you can't efficiently and effectively market and manage your business, it will just sputter along. Many small businesses are operated by less than five people, but most are only one person—the sole proprietor—you. What's the use of having a beautiful store or wonderful technical talents if you can't relate to people or you have few business skills? It doesn't usually work.

Are you in top entrepreneurial shape?

To start, take a good look at yourself to ensure that you are in top entrepreneurial shape. You must be multifaceted, like a polished diamond, with all-round business skills. As you grow through formal learning and experience, you should gradually transform into a smooth business machine with well-oiled cogs, all synchronized together. You are a combination of sixty different employees, as you'll see in Chapter 2. That chapter will also help you build your inner entrepreneurial skills.

Seven Tips
for Entrepreneurial Success

There are seven key areas of your business that work intrinsically together to make it successful. If you fall down in one of these, it can directly affect the others and your overall progress. Check this list to see how you are progressing.

                                                              Yes

1. **Be administratively astute:** Your paper flow, accounting,   ☐
   inventory and computer systems are incredibly efficient. Your
   employees are happy, motivated company ambassadors.

2. **Be constantly creative:** You are always looking for new and   ☐
   exciting ideas and methods to grow your business. You don't fear
   change and change with the times.

3. **Be customer conscious:** Every customer is important to you.   ☐
   They refer you, are loyal, and you give them the red carpet
   treatment before, during, and after the sale.

4. **Be fiscally fit:** You monitor the financial figures regularly,   ☐
   work to a business plan and have a monthly budget. You plan for
   taxes and future growth, and confer regularly with your accountant.

5. **Be positively positioned:** You have a good sense of humor, keep educated, and stay up with competitors. You have built a positive work environment and can be flexible. ☐

6. **Be technologically terrific:** You have harnessed technology to your advantage and streamlined systems. You have a website and use your database for marketing. ☐

7. **Be a trend-tracker:** You attend industry conferences and trade shows and read industry magazines, e-zines and reports. You keep up with global, consumer, local, and national news and trends, and adapt accordingly. ☐

BUSINESS IS ALL ABOUT SERVICE

As you will no doubt read in more detail in future chapters, service is a key ingredient in the successful recipe. Because *you* are your business, you are responsible for finding and keeping customers. People expect service, and if you don't give it, your competitors will. Most small businesses cannot compete price- or selection-wise with larger competitors. The one important area where you can compete is with outstanding customer service.

We all have those "sloppy service" stories which we relate with great relish to our friends and family. Of course, this is the worst type of word-of-mouth advertising; it quickly wreaks deadly havoc on your reputation.

Make each customer a VSP

Your best cost-free advertising is good word-of-mouth referral. Customers make you money, build your business, and pay the bills. This makes them VSPs—Very Special People. They deserve your undivided attention. Not only will you keep them, they will refer others to you. The

> ## COMPLAIN ABOUT POOR SERVICE
> *You are doing a business a favor by telling the management that you have been treated badly. Otherwise, they will lose your business and won't be afforded the opportunity to apologize. We always remember what it's like to be at the receiving end of poor service, so vow to treat your customers the way you expect to be treated.*

bonus? You will make some wonderful friends and experience the satisfaction of making people happy.

Yet it's amazing how many well-established business owners—some who have been in business for decades—don't practice basic customer service. Their reasons? "Oh, I'm just too busy!" or "I don't have enough staff to do that." What lousy excuses! If big business can practice great customer service, as in the Real Life example "Small Airline—Big Service," then a small business should do even better.

Real Life) **Small Airline—Big Service**

Traveling to Edmonton, Canada, in winter, I booked a WestJet flight from our local airport. After several futile attempts to land in the fog, the inward-bound flight was rerouted. As a guest on a live TV show, I had to catch a flight—and soon. The ticketing agent kindly held up rescheduling all the other passengers to rebook me out of another airport on the last flight that would make my time deadline. I had to hightail it an hour's drive in thick fog to the airport.

Arriving at the checkout desk totally breathless (after probably breaking a few land speed records, getting lost in the fog, parking in the wrong lot, and running to the next terminal in heels dragging two suitcases), I was the perfect picture of the stressed-out traveler. After relating my tale of woe to the patient ticketing agent, I then realized that on my return, my car would be at one airport and me at another—quite a logistical problem.

"Not a problem," said the friendly booking agent. "I'll rebook you back to this airport. It'll cost you another $215."

"What?" was my astounded reply. "It wasn't my fault you couldn't land the plane!"

"We would cover the cost for mechanical failure," she informed me, "but not for inclement weather."

With a little convincing, she finally agreed to change the booking at no charge. Now that is big service for a small airline. Of course, I tell everyone about their great service, and being a busy speaker, that's a lot of people. No wonder WestJet won a national Entrepreneur of the Year award.

THE TOP TEN MISTAKES IN GROWING A BUSINESS

On the subject of taking care of business, there are many facets to running a smooth and successful operation. Even seasoned entrepreneurs make mistakes, although the wise ones quickly learn and take steps to correct them. Here are the ten most common mistakes made by both new and not-so-new entrepreneurs. Making any of these can cause serious operational problems or hinder growth. Can you identify with any of them?

1. No growth plan

Just as you wouldn't build a house without blueprints, a business cannot survive and grow without a practical, well-researched plan. Successful businesses use and revisit their plan regularly before making any growth decisions. If you don't have one, this book will guide you through the process.

2. Wrong business, wrong location

You may have opened a retail store, only to find that long hours and hard work don't necessarily equate to a profit, let alone an acceptable wage. Perhaps you chose a service business, only to find that you are technically good at your work but not so good at the administrative "stuff." The competition may have become too tough or the demand for your service may not be what you had envisioned. You now have to decide whether to continue with a concentrated effort or try your hand at something else.

Location, location, location makes or breaks a retail store. "But the rent was cheap!" you say. "Why is the rent so cheap?" I ask. Retail stores need a prime location with good visibility, walk-by traffic, and ample, accessible parking. Otherwise, you will spend a fortune in costly advertising or lose money by holding regular, low-profit sales to draw in new customers.

Too small a location could mean a costly move within a couple of years. Usually, you leave expensive renovations and fittings behind. Some people move to a location far

---

RULES TO KEEP YOUR CUSTOMERS HAPPY

1. The customer is **always** right.

2. The **customer** is always right.

3. The customer is always **right**.

too big and expensive for their needs, where the only things that increase are square footage and debts. Two local businesses had to declare bankruptcy because they both moved to larger locations. With more square footage and larger debts, they both became bankrupt within a year of the move. Careful planning would have avoided this fate.

3. Lack of technical skills

Without the necessary technical expertise, what can you offer your customers? They look to you as the expert. Learning management and industry skills can take years. If you have chosen a business that dictates learning new technical skills, your frustration level must be high. Consider taking evening courses if you need to accelerate your learning.

4. Lack of sales and marketing skills

Selling is not everyone's strongest point. For many, the thought is quite scary. A competent salesperson works hard for years to develop the necessary skills. But selling can be learned, especially as you develop more confidence in yourself and knowledge in your field. Chapter 13 explains how to improve sales skills.

Marketing is a weak area for most small businesses, so don't feel alone. If you have a business plan, your market research would have revealed where and who your market is. It's amazing just how narrow your true market is when you start to research. Chapter 8 will help you to grow your customer base. Chapters 9 through 13 will help you to better market your business.

5. Lack of financial skills

You are the CEO of your business, so you must learn about accounting, financial figures and cash flow—not everyone's favorite subjects. If you don't have financial knowledge, you probably won't succeed. Never hand the financial reins to someone else. The good news is you can learn these skills as well. Read Chapter 4 and increase your financial knowledge.

6. Undefined financial resources

Staying solvent and profitable requires a planned, stable cash flow. In most cases, sustained profit and growth is a slow process taking years. Work with a cash flow forecast and monitor it closely. It will indicate where and when you may experience cash shortages so that you can plan ahead and research where you may find funding for future growth. You then need to research how to obtain this funding; banks are particular about approving loans—are you creditworthy? See page 124 for lending criteria.

7. Lack of market research

Some people don't spend enough time learning or updating the demographics of their market—that is, where and who their market is, if there is a market for their business, and whether the market is changing. Keeping one step ahead of the competition requires regular research on their pricing, customer service policies, and marketing strategies. To you, your widget is the best invention since Eve, but it isn't if no one wants it, needs it or can afford it.

8. Investment in trendy businesses

There are those who jump on the bandwagon of trendy businesses without researching their potential longevity. A business should have a projected life of at least ten years. By the time some trends are established, they are already on their way out. Study future trends to ensure that you continue to fill a long-term niche.

9. Over-projection of sales, under-projection of marketing costs

Optimistic figures may look good on paper, but who are you fooling? Whether you are new or firmly entrenched in your business, work with a business plan that projects realistic sales. Losses are common on start-up, so be practical and budget for them. You also need to know your break-even point—that is, the sales required to meet all monthly overhead expenses. This subject is explained in Chapter 4.

> **CATER TO LONG-TERM TRENDS**
> ....
> *One key to growth is diversification. As an example, what could you do to service all the home-based businesses springing up in abundance—a long-term and growing trend. Most self-employed people don't have much time to shop, wash and maintain vehicles, fix computers or go to the hairdresser. Be creative. Diversify and cater to a huge growing trend that is being fueled by baby boomers.*

Shoestring budgets leave little over for effective marketing. Plan to spend a minimum of 10 to 15 percent of projected sales in the first two years. Some businesses spend even more. Don't blow your marketing budget. Research the techniques that work best for your type of business and then utilize the many suggestions in the marketing chapters.

10. Professionals are not consulted

Once their business is operational, few people budget to regularly meet with an accountant, business consultant, or lawyer, so unless you are all of these, you need help. Accountants are trained to recognize financial problems, and lawyers are necessary to review leases, employment contracts, loan agreements, and franchise, partnership and buy-sell agreements. If you are experiencing problems, please turn to a professional for help.

TAKE THE TEST: THE "WHERE AM I NOW?" QUESTIONNAIRE

So are you taking care of your business? Now is a good time to address where you stand. Writing it down makes you face reality and brings to your attention situations that you may have previously overlooked—or have ignored. Admitting that there may be a few problems is a giant step in the right direction. Read Figure 1.1, the "Where Am I Now?" questionnaire at the end of this chapter, think carefully about your answers, and answer honestly.

How will you rate?

This questionnaire is designed to draw your attention to the areas that are causing operational problems. It will indicate where you went off track and assess your current enthusiasm. Don't be too discouraged if you obtain a low score, as addressing these problems now will allow you to develop a sensible plan of action. If you identify critical operational problems, your score could be extremely low, if not a minus.

For example, if you started because you were laid off and couldn't find work, you probably started the business feeling pressure to

> ## CHART YOUR PROGRESS
> ●
> *In six months to a year, take the "Where Am I Now?" questionnaire again and compare the two results. If you have worked hard to grow your business, you should be pleasantly surprised at the results.*

bring in an income—and fast. In this state of mind, most people start out tired and depressed. Poor decision-making and bad judgments often occur. You may have seen your friends succeed and been tempted to emulate their successes. You could have started the wrong business or not had the necessary skills to make it work smoothly. You may have even lost your passion and stopped attending to small but important details. If you consulted professionals with your plan and researched the market, you started out right. Give yourself a big pat on the back.

Commit to overcoming obstacles

Education overcomes many problems. You won't succeed without learning how to organize and administer both your business and yourself. Growth creates problems for most businesses, but the good news is most problems can be overcome. You will find many solutions to your problems between these covers.

Most important, you must have the right attitude toward your business. Keep motivated and positive; start each day feeling charged, because if you operate in negative mode, the business will suffer. Remember—*you* are your business. Goal-setting enables you to measure your progress, and attainable goals are what will keep you motivated when the going gets rough. (See Chapter 6 for more information on setting goals.) Now that you have identified some areas that need work, continue on to the next chapter.

Chapter 2 focuses on developing the necessary entrepreneurial skills and offers positive solutions to adapting to change. It highlights the many jobs you are responsible for and analyzes your current workload to see where you may need some help. Be sure to complete Figure 2.6, the "Where Am I Going?" questionnaire. Take the time to answer it honestly; it is self-scoring to give you some immediate feedback.

Figure **1.1**

The "Where Am I Now?" Questionnaire

First test   **Second test**

Date completed: _____   **Date completed:** _____

1. I have been in business for:

   a) _____ weeks   b) _____ months   c) _____ years

2. I started because:

   (Circle only the most accurate response.)

   a)   I was laid off and couldn't find work

   b)   I no longer wanted to work for my employer

   c)   I was not getting enough recognition or pay for my work

   d)   I was worried about job security

   e)   My work was boring and posed no challenges

   f)   My goal has always been to own my own business

   g)   I have planned this for years, and now I am ready

   h)   My family owns its own business

   i)   All my friends seem to be self-employed

   j)   Owning my own business seemed like an attractive idea

   k)   Other:_____

3. I chose this business because:

   (Circle only the most accurate response.)

   a)   I have worked in this field for more than five years

   b)   I have excellent technical skills in this area

   c)   It was a challenge that drew on my strengths

   d)   It required start-up capital of less than $10,000

   e)   I could work from home

   f)   I saw an advertisement that really appealed to me

   g)   The business proposal promised an immediate income

   h)   I always wanted to own a business like this one

   i)   I thought I could learn how to operate it quickly

   j)   I have had a business before and this appeared to be a
        profitable concern

4. Before making the decision to start this business, I:
(Circle each applicable response.)

a)   consulted an accountant or consultant with my idea

b)   researched the current and future market

c)   researched the competition

d)   researched the product or service

e)   prepared a business plan

f)   prepared projections and cash flow sheets for two years

g)   had an accountant review my business plan

h)   had a lawyer review contracts and leases

i)   checked local government regulations and licensing agencies

j)   had enough money on hand to operate for a minimum of six months

k)   set short- and long-term goals

5. I financed the business with:
(Circle only one applicable response.)

a)   my own capital

b)   my partner's and my own capital

c)   a small business loan from the bank and one-third of my own capital

d)   money from my family

e)   cash from my retirement savings

f)   a small business loan and a little capital

g)   my own capital plus d) or e)

h)   my own capital plus a line of credit

i)   a line of credit

j)   money obtained mainly through credit cards

k)   an extension on my home mortgage

l)   a higher-interest loan, not from a bank

6. I am experiencing difficulties with my business in:
(Circle each applicable response.)

a)   making enough profitable sales to pay the bills

b)   knowing how to reach my market

c)   finding effective methods of advertising

d)   selling and closing potential deals

e)   understanding the necessary paperwork

f) understanding the bookkeeping and accounting requirements

g) keeping on top of the paperwork

h) motivating myself to work

i) keeping organized

j) not having enough recreation or family time

k) keeping a positive attitude

l) drawing business away from my competitors

m) keeping my prices competitive but profitable

n) getting my customers to pay me on time

o) finding the right employees

p) keeping inventory turning over quickly

q) knowing how to manage my inventory

7. At this time, I know the following about my business:
(Circle each applicable response.)

a) the seasonal sales trends

b) my average gross sales each month

c) my average monthly gross profit

d) my monthly break-even point

e) how much my customers owe me

f) how much I owe to suppliers and tax departments

g) my approximate personal tax situation for year-end

h) the correct balance in my bank account

i) my estimated sales in the next six months

j) how much I can safely draw from my business each month

k) how I am going to market in the next three months

8. My current state of mind in relationship to the business is:
(Circle only the most accurate response.)

a) I am still very excited about the future

b) I am always planning ahead and thinking of innovative ideas

c) I love what I am doing and am very content

d) I can foresee great potential for the future

e) I am uncertain about the future

f) I am not sure if I made the right decision

g) This was not what I expected it to be

h) It's hard work and the glamour has worn off

i) I get tired and have trouble motivating myself

j) I am depressed because I don't earn enough money

k) I don't think I am an entrepreneur after all

l) I think I'd prefer to be an employee again

m) I could close the doors tomorrow and walk away

9. At this time, my future plans for the business are:

(Choose the one item which best describes your future plans.)

a) to learn everything I can and to work on making it succeed

b) to locate my problem areas and try to resolve them

c) to be profitable, to diversify, and to grow

d) to build this business to help support my retirement

e) to build the goodwill and sell within the next few years

f) to seriously analyze where I stand before I go much further

g) I don't have any future plans as yet

h) I'm having enough trouble surviving day-to-day, never mind the future

i) to sell it for what I can and get out

Total your score for questions 2 to 9 by using the following formula and writing your points scored (or lost) in the space provided.

Score

Scoring

Question 2: 1 point for a-e; 5 points for f-g; 2 points for h-k _____

Question 3: 5 points for a-c; 3 points for d-e; 2 points for f-j _____

Question 4: 15 points for all items circled; 7 points for 7-9 circled;
5 points for 4-6 circled; 1 point for 1-3 circled _____

Question 5: 5 points for a-c: 4 points for d-g; 3 points for h-i;
no points for j-l _____

Question 6: Deduct 1 point for all items circled in this question _____
Bonus: add 10 points if no items are circled

Question 7: Add one point for each item circled _____
Bonus: add 5 points if all items circled

Question 8: Add 5 points for a-d; deduct 1 point for e-f; _____
deduct 3 points for g-j; deduct 5 points for k-m

Question 9:10 points for a-e; 3 points for f; no points for g-i   _____

Total Score   _____

Score analysis

71 points: You are obviously an excellent entrepreneur who is doing everything right. Congratulations! Keep on doing what you are doing.

60-70 points: Well done and bravo! You have made a successful start and have pinpointed a few areas where you know you need to improve. Work on these areas with proper guidance, and you will definitely build or improve on a fine business.

30-59 points: There are some important areas you should address. For the most part, you have made a valiant effort to "do it right." Don't ignore problems or shortcomings as they likely can be overcome.

10-29 points: The warning bells are sounding. You have to evaluate what you are doing wrong or not doing at all. It's not too late to work on the areas of concern, but it will require your dedicated commitment.

(–) to 9 points: Perhaps you should consider letting the business go before you get deeper in debt and more depressed. Entrepreneurship is not for everyone. Some of the most successful people have quit or failed multiple times before eventually succeeding. If you are willing to accept professional guidance, you could get your business back on track. If it is the wrong business or you have lost interest, let it go.

CHAPTER TWO

Do Your Entrepreneurial Skills Need Fine-Tuning?

*With ordinary talents and extraordinary
perseverance all things are attainable.*

THOMAS BUXTON

A **true entrepreneur has the ability to learn and develop a multitude of abilities and talents.** Entrepreneurs are risk-takers, dream-makers, visionaries, and decision-makers. They are often creative and impulsive, driven and tireless in working toward their goals. Many people are self-employed, but only a few are true entrepreneurs. If you better understand what makes an exceptional entrepreneur, you can improve on the areas that are holding you back from truly realizing your dreams.

YOU'RE THE BOSS

Being your own boss is not as glamorous as it first seems. Who do you blame when things go wrong? Who looks after the business when you are ill? Who makes decisions? Who has to fire employees? Who is responsible for paying the bills? You—that's who. Were these distasteful tasks a part of your dream? Do you have the human resources skills to handle delicate situations? Learn-as-you-earn, hands-on experience is not necessarily the best way to operate a business.

THE EIGHT ESSENTIAL ENTREPRENEURIAL SKILLS

To cope with the many daily challenges, you need a positive attitude. Although technical skills are necessary, a true entrepreneur develops the Eight Essential Entrepreneurial Skills and uses them daily. You have to be *SCCOPPED*—an all-round people person with the following skills and qualities. When you have read this section, ask yourself: Am I *SCCOPPED*? Then check off the boxes below to see how *SCCOPPED* you are and where you need to focus your attention.

Figure **2.1**

Am I SCCOPPED?

A SCCOPPED PERSON HAS:

Self-motivation and discipline ☐

Confidence ☐

Communication skills ☐

Organization ☐

Passion and a positive attitude ☐

Persistence and perseverance ☐

Expertise ☐

Dreams and goals ☐

1. Self-motivation and discipline

If business looks a little grim and there are no foreseeable solutions, it's difficult to face the day—let alone feel motivated. If there are orders to fill and work to complete, motivation is usually not a problem. So how do you become motivated? Working positively and seeing results is motivating. Developing confidence, organizational skills, and a positive attitude will help. In other words, self-discipline will evolve from developing the other entrepreneurial skills.

2. Confidence

By becoming an expert in your field, maintaining a positive attitude, and keeping organized, you gain confidence just knowing how you are going to tackle each day. If you are passionate about your business, you automatically radiate confidence. Excellent technical skills will feed your confidence. In business, knowledge and confidence are what convince customers to buy from you. To gain and maintain confidence, you have to work hard at your business. For most, it evolves over time and with experience. If you do it right, confidence is one of the lasting rewards.

3. Communication skills

Communication is the ability to convey your message clearly, concisely, competently and confidently. In business as in life, communication skills are a must. You must sell yourself before you can ever sell your business. You will need to compose a variety of professional correspondence, so effective writing skills are essential. In many instances, they are your only foot in the door. These skills can all be practiced and learned. Chapter 10 is devoted entirely to the art of verbal communication.

4. Organization

What is organization? It is the ability to plan and execute a series of tasks in an orderly

MONITOR YOUR CONFIDENCE BUILDERS

Confidence comes from trying something new and succeeding. When you close a sale or customers refer you to others or send a thank-you card, confidence builds. When you draw a hard-earned paycheck or succeed through a new advertising strategy, your confidence is strengthened. When these events happen to you, stop and note how good you feel. That's your confidence kicking in.

fashion, to find any piece of paper within twenty seconds, or to arrange a cupboard so that you aren't buried in junk upon opening the door. It's the ability to arrive at appointments, to complete work on time despite emergencies, and to allocate your priorities, working through them in sequential order. It is the ability to complete all of the above—and more—without losing your cool.

How can an unorganized person learn to be organized? Through discipline and practice. First, you must want to be organized. By being more disciplined and motivated, your desire to be more organized will increase. The busier you get, the more organized you need to be. Chapter 3 offers many practical tips on time management and organization. They are simple strategies that are not difficult to implement, and are proven to work.

5. Passion and a positive attitude

Passion! Defined in the dictionary as appetite, desire, ardor, and hunger, these words aptly describe the very essence of what drives an exceptional entrepreneur. You need to have a love affair with your business. Passion inspires your creativity and motivates you to reach for your goals. It builds confidence and gives you the determination to persevere. Passion helps to close a sale. It creates a hunger to improve your skills. Enthusiasm will allow you to play the game well, but passion will score you the goals.

Without passion for your business, what will positively motivate you? Money, desperation or the competition will only motivate you for the short term. There are no books written about "How to get passionate about your business." If you ain't got it, you can't learn it—you are probably in the wrong business.

Positive attitude

I'm sure you have asked friends: "How are you today?" only to be regaled with stories of deaths, debts, disaster, divorce, and despair. If you wanted macabre entertainment, you could watch a soap opera. Do you feel inclined to approach or associate with depressing people? Of course not.

> **PRACTICE POSITIVITY**
>
> ●
>
> *Project a positive attitude in your business. People will not remember you favorably for your negative attitude, but they will remember you for your positive, upbeat approach to life, and will refer you to others. If you possess a sense of humor, all the better. Start practicing and be amazed by the results.*

We can all be depressed without help from our friends. In business, the principle is no different.

No one can teach you how to have a positive attitude. As you develop confidence in your abilities, your positive attitude will develop. If you are the eternal pessimist, you shouldn't be in business. To feel more positive, work on the other skills and read some books on positive thinking.

6. Persistence and perseverance

Highly successful people don't use the words "I can't" or "I quit." They have learned that you learn by your mistakes, and that setbacks are only challenges. It is not a crime to fail, but it is a crime not to learn from failure.

Persistence and perseverance take over where passion leaves off, keeping you going through the long and sometimes tedious process of reaching your goals. Some call it stubbornness or "stick-to-it-ness." Whatever term you use, perseverance ensures the task is completed properly and that your goals are attained.

7. Expertise

Quite frankly, if you are not an expert in your chosen field, you should not be in business, as you are sometimes responsible for people's lives and safety. Learn all there is to know about your industry or profession so you are an expert before you hang out your shingle. When you are sure of your advice to others, your confidence builds. The more you know, the more your customers will have confidence in you and refer you to others.

> ## LEARN THE PERSISTENCE PRINCIPLE
> ·····················
> *This gem from an old Toastmasters magazine has guided me through many difficult times. "The persistence principle says: 'It's too soon to quit.' Highly successful people pursue their goals relentlessly. They know that perseverance is a key ingredient for success. Patience and diligence, like faith, can remove mountains. Successful people overcome mountains of rejection, dismissal, and repudiation by operating on the persistence principle."*

8. Dreams and goals

Operating a business without having dreams and goals is rather like sailing without a rudder and compass. Without goals, you will flounder, so never lose sight of them. Because long-term goals take time to achieve, reward yourself by setting short-term goals, or baby steps. These should be achievable weekly and monthly goals. After a few months, you will be surprised at just how far those baby steps have taken you.

Once you have set goals, your passion, confidence, and positive attitude will drive you to achieve them. When you are an organized, motivated, and disciplined expert with excellent communication skills, your persistence and perseverance will ensure your success.

HOW TO SURVIVE AND SUCCEED IN A CHANGING WORLD

An important part of developing good entrepreneurial skills is learning to address change positively. We live in a rapidly changing world. To survive, you have to be nimble. To thrive, to succeed to your expectations, you have to understand change and how to embrace the challenges and the opportunities that it presents.

BIG IDEA: DREAM

Ask yourself: Why did I start this business? Do I want it to grow? How big? How many people will it employ? Do I want to expand into other branches? When? When do I plan to buy a fancy company car? When do I plan to retire, where and with how much money? How much will my business be worth in ten years if I work hard at making it a success? Indulge yourself in the luxury of a little dreaming, then write down your goals. See Chapter 6, Figure 6.3 for a goal-setting list.

Many disasters have happened globally that we cannot change or control. They bring home the strong message that it takes many skills to succeed in business in our changing world. Both Canada and the U.S. have had their fill of natural and economic disasters. Each catastrophe immediately changes the way that business is transacted, just as you must be open to changing the way you do business to survive and succeed. When disasters happen, the tough get to work but the weak rarely survive.

For example, after 9/11, the economic downturn in the U.S. took years to start turning around. Businesses that had survived for decades suffered because they *were* not and *are* not willing to change. The statistics in Figure 2.2, taken from the *Small Business Advocacy* May 2003 newsletter, clearly show the increases in the numbers of businesses that have failed.

Figure 2.2

U.S. Business Start-Up and Closure Statistics

U.S.	1990	1995	2000	2001	2002
New firms	584,892	594,369	574,300	545,400	550,100
Closures	531,892	497,246	542,831	**568,300**	**584,500**

Reprogram your negative thinking tape

You don't want your business to become one of these sad statistics, so you may have to change the way you think and operate. Now, it's not news that the world is constantly changing. It's not news that many people can't keep up with change. It's not even news that many people don't enjoy change. What *may* be news is that by taking a positive approach, you may learn to enjoy change and even look forward to it. And as business owners, we more than anyone should be receptive to change, because the way we do business is always changing.

YOUR GOLDEN BOX OF OPPORTUNITY

Imagine your business as a golden box of opportunities. What you do with it is up to you. By looking at change in a positive way, you will

DON'T FEAR CHANGE

According to various reports, over 80 percent of what we hear is negative; and when faced with an ambiguous situation, most people will predict a negative outcome. For each positive comment that a child hears each day, he or she hears twenty-three negative responses. So it makes sense that as adults, many of us fear change and automatically take a more negative approach to change, because that's the way we were brought up. Fear of change sets limitations. Don't limit your potential.

have a golden opportunity as bright as that box. Because the world is changing all the time, you can't go through life operating on the same old paradigms. *They just don't work.* To survive and thrive, be a creative thinker. Constantly think outside the box, bringing new and creative ideas into your golden box of opportunity.

Think Outside the Box

BRING NEW IDEAS INTO YOUR BOX

YOUR BUSINESS IS A GOLDEN OPPORTUNITY

Whether you are large or small, you have to always be looking ahead. Ask yourself: If you don't change, what will happen? If you do change, what will happen? In most cases, if you do change, the results will be positive and will help you to succeed.

Use the Seven Tools of Change

Because change is not easy, here are seven golden tools to help you better adapt to change. Put them into your golden box of opportunity and use them every day.

Tool 1: Make planned changes

Yes, you may have to change certain aspects of your business, but first ensure that you plan well ahead and carefully so that you understand the ramifications of that change. Analyze whether each change will have a long-term, positive effect.

Tool 2: Notice small changes

You may not notice your lawn growing every day as it's a small change, but in a week, there's quite a difference. Small yet significant changes can seriously affect the health of your business. Notice the changes happening in your profession, industry and business. Recently, I noticed that my anti-virus program wasn't running. A small yet significant change; I'm glad I noticed it.

Tool 3: Make small changes

Now it's one thing for me to tell you to change the way you do business, but most people find change quite difficult. The good news is, you don't need to make drastic changes. Start by making small positive changes—baby steps. See the Real Life story "Put on a Smiley Face" for a perfect example.

Tool 4: Take positive and creative action

Don't *react* to change, as this usually results in a negative outcome. Try positively *acting* with change. When a problem arises, be creative in your thinking and solutions. Turn adversity into opportunity. This is what sets a true entrepreneur apart from the rest.

Tool 5: Practice change

Change takes time and practice. As creatures of habit, we like things just the way they are.

> ## FIND CREATIVE SOLUTIONS
> ....
> *Using the same old solutions usually doesn't positively solve a problem. What is the first thing an employer does when a business is losing money? They lay off the staff—in whom they have invested large amounts of time and money—and cut expenses, instead of finding creative ways around the problem and more creative ways to grow their business. It could be a simple solution—an aggressive customer follow-up program or offering employees flex-time and performance incentives, all examples of positive, creative changes. You need a positive, motivated staff to help you survive the tough times.*

But in this ever-changing world, we must find ways to become comfortable with change. If you start with the little things, the bigger challenges don't appear as insurmountable when they happen. Start practicing by making some simple changes in your life. Sit in a different chair in the living room, praise your child when you are tempted to chastise her, or call a customer instead of emailing.

Tool 6: Research industry trends

The way business is transacted within your industry is always changing. Are you making time to keep abreast of those changes? Attend industry conferences and seminars, subscribe to e-newsletters and industry magazines, and read the business section of the newspaper, not just the sports or your horoscope.

(Real Life)   Put on a Smile

When I deliver my keynote on positive change, I always put up a large smiley-face poster with the words "Smile—Make Your Day" in large letters. A week after talking to a group of private college owners, I received a call from Suzanna, the owner of a computer skills college.

"Fran," she said, "I'm no artist, but after you talked about making small positive changes, I went back to the college and drew your smiley poster on a sheet of paper and put it on the computer lab door. There had been a lot of recent changes, and the students were fearful of what lay ahead. It's amazing how that one sheet of paper changed the way they reacted when they walked through that lab door. They smiled, and their whole attitude changed. It was such a small, simple thing to do. It really encouraged me to think about making more positive changes."

Remember Tool 3: Make small changes. Then engage Tool 3 and practice those small, positive changes.

Tool 7: Make time for change

Yes, I know, you are "too busy," but too busy doing what? Schedule some focused planning time. Make a list and plan what is important to you and your business and where you feel you need to make some changes. Start with a small positive change and monitor the results. They will spur you on to making bolder changes.

Which tools of change does your golden box need?

You don't have to be a rocket scientist to figure out some small, simple and positive changes that will move your business forward. Following is a list of the Seven Tools of Change in Figure 2.3. Check off the ones that need your attention and commit to using one or more of these tools daily.

Figure 2.3

Tools of Change Needed For My Golden Box

Tool 1: Make planned positive changes ☐

Tool 2: Notice small changes ☐

Tool 3: Make small positive changes ☐

Tool 4: Take positive and creative action ☐

Tool 5: Practice change ☐

Tool 6: Research industry trends ☐

Tool 7: Make time for change ☐

THE A TO Z ENTREPRENEUR

Your entrepreneurial wardrobe is crammed with a variety of hats which you regularly change each day. Not only do you need to develop the Eight Essential Entrepreneurial Skills outlined earlier, you also have a multitude of tasks, some not particularly to your liking. Figure 2.4 lists some of the hats you'll wear during your business day.

There are sixty jobs or "hats" listed, and you may be able to add more. A sole operator has a mammoth task in organizing each day. If you have employees, it can be even more difficult, because now you also have to schedule, train, supervise, and pay them. Which priority comes first? It's not easy—success requires careful organization.

Figure **2.4**

Your Entrepreneurial Wardrobe

Advertising manager, administrator, accounts payable clerk, accountant

Banker, bookkeeper, budget planner

Computer technician, credit manager, controller, customer service agent, CEO

Debt collector

Expert, educator

Finance manager, fixer

Gofer, goal setter

Human resources officer

Investor, insurance planner, invoice clerk

Jack-of-all-trades, janitor, job coster, journalist, juggler of jobs

Keyboard operator, keynote speaker

Legal advisor

Manager, marketing strategist, motivator, mail clerk, media relations manager

Networker

Office clerk

Payroll clerk, personnel manager, president, promoter, problem solver, purchasing agent

Quality control officer

Receptionist, receiver

Secretary, salesperson, shipper

Technician, trainer

Umpire

Vendor, visionary

Writer, warehouse manager

Xmas party planner

Yellow Pages advertiser

Zookeeper (organizer of all the above)

TAKE THE TASK TEST

Solutions to many operational problems are addressed in this book, however, there is no solution if you are not motivated enough to work on solving your problems. When your daily responsibilities are arranged into more defined categories, they represent all the tasks listed in Figure 2.5.

Instructions

Examine the list of jobs numbered one to ten, highlighting the ones you enjoy and do well. Then with another color, highlight the ones that you really hate. Now change colors again to highlight the ones that you don't have time for. Finally, to complete the exercise, change colors to highlight the ones that you need to develop more expertise in.

Figure **2.5**

Your Daily Task List

1. **Accounting:** budgeting, paying bills, financial planning, credit management, debt collection
2. **Administration:** purchasing, mail, filing, correspondence, reception, invoicing
3. **Computer:** data entry, word processing, contact management, learning software, maintenance, upgrades, email, website
4. **Correspondence:** advertising copy, letters, press releases, articles
5. **Employees:** hiring and firing, training, motivation, payroll, arbitration
6. **Maintenance:** office and other equipment, tools, vehicles, building
7. **Problem-Solving:** troubleshooting, quality control, customer service
8. **Sales:** marketing, promotion, advertising, delivery, follow-up
9. **Warehousing:** inventory control, shipping, receiving, storage
10. **Your Job:** completing all the above in addition to generating income

You will probably find that many of the jobs you hate are the ones you don't make time for. Most of these are critical to the success of your business. At the end of this chapter is Figure 2.6, the "Where Am I Going?" self-evaluation questionnaire. Transfer your highlighted information to questions 8, 9, 10 and 11.

ENTREPRENEUR OR OPERATOR?

If you want your business to flourish, you can't afford to be bogged down with time-wasting chores. Many talented individuals prefer to work *in* their business, not *on* it. You have to make your business happen, but it won't if you are just an operator. A typical operator is someone who is happiest doing his or her chosen job, such as designing websites, landscaping gardens, or repairing vehicles. Their day consists mainly of scheduling the income-generating workload and doing it.

Real Life   The Resurrected Entrepreneur

Ron worked solidly for three years developing a business magazine. The business was starting to break even and make a small profit—but at what cost?

He was working days, nights, and weekends, with constant deadlines to meet and advertising space to sell, sell, sell. The pressure was terrible, and he began to hate it. His wife dreaded talking to him. Although suffering from entrepreneurial burnout, Ron was determined to make it work. Something had to give—which it did. He called me one day in a state of excitement.

"Fran, I just have to tell you the news!" he blurted. "I've just spent three days mulling this whole thing over, and I've decided I can't handle the pressure anymore and to wind the whole business down and shut up shop. I feel like a ton of weight has been lifted off my shoulders!"

"Ron, you can't do that!" I replied, somewhat stunned. "You've spent three years working hard on your business, and it's doing so well!"

"My wife hasn't seen me for three years, and I've been hard to live with. This feels like the right decision," he replied.

"Well, first, when was the last time you bought her some flowers?" I asked.

"I can't remember."

"Then buy her a dozen red roses and a thank-you card for still being your wife," I suggested. "Now to this other matter. You've created a very saleable business. You've developed a fine product and are starting to make some profit. Why wouldn't you at least consider selling the business—you know—for money?"

"Hey, I never thought of that!" Ron laughed. "Guess I just couldn't see the forest for the trees." We talked about the value of the work he had put into the magazine, and Ron finally hung up, promising he would think carefully about selling the business and would buy his wife some flowers.

A few weeks later, he called again.

"Fran, I just had to tell you that I have two offers on the business. I'm so glad we talked. I must have been in bad shape not to realize the value of all that work."

"Ron, I'm thrilled! Tell me how you did it."

"Well, Fran, I was heading for failure with a capital F. After talking to you, I focused on a business plan for eight or nine days. I turned off the phones and worked on it until I got the numbers working sensibly. I took time to address all the serious problems and how to overcome them. There is so much strength in a written proposal—it doesn't fly until it goes down on paper and you work on tightening it up. It's an incredible experience," he continued excitedly. "I have the bounce back in my step now—I know it's going to work!"

Ron chatted on with great enthusiasm about his plans, and I breathed a sigh of relief. It would have been a shame for the magazine to fold because he burnt himself out. Oh, by the way, Ron did buy his wife an armful of flowers.

Ron had lost his passion because he pushed himself too far. He was one of the lucky ones, able to regenerate his passion by addressing the problems and getting help. Later, he told me that he had found a partner who brought a sales staff with him, and there were now seven people working on the magazine. Not only was the magazine resurrected, it now has a chance to grow. One person alone couldn't do it all, but many hands made the magazine successful.

Somewhere along the line, this same person still has to make time to complete the other tasks. Michael Gerber said it best in *The E Myth Revisited*. "The typical small business owner is only 10 percent Entrepreneur, 20 percent Manager, and 70 percent Technician."

GETTING BY WITH A LITTLE HELP FROM YOUR FRIENDS

Ron's Real Life story is no different from that of many others in small business. I'm sure you know of at least one of your friends who has faced a similar situation. Not all businesses fail due to lack of cash flow or management skills. Many fizzle out because the owner does. This fate can be avoided. Put a value on your time, realize your strengths, and acknowledge your weaknesses.

For example, you stare at the mountain of paperwork, wondering what to do. It's year-end and time to prepare your books for the accountant. They haven't been touched for a year. My, how time flies... You feel depressed. Besides, you never really understood what you were doing anyway. What is the wisest move you can make now? To get help, of course.

WORK SMARTER

If you are too busy doing your work and not working on what is needed to make your business grow, you will eventually suffer from entrepreneurial burnout. Many owners burn out after a couple of years. They lose their passion and become overwhelmed by all the "stuff" they have to manage, willingly letting go of their business when it becomes too much. This sad ending can be avoided by learning to work smarter, planning for growth and planning for help.

Should you hire friends?

In one simple word—no. I have heard only disaster stories from people who hired friends or a friend of a friend. You immediately place a responsibility upon yourself that you don't need. Friendships can be lost, so if you value a friendship, tell your friend thanks, but no thanks. Read more on this subject and use the employment guidelines as set out in Chapter 7.

Some friendly advice

On the subject of friends, be careful of heeding their advice. How many times have you asked a friend for advice, only to realize later that it wasn't such good advice after all? We all ask friends for advice, or for a referral to a "good hairdresser" or a "good lawyer" or a "good mechanic."

If you need professional help, find it yourself by researching and asking questions, or by being referred by a professional association. Friends are wonderful people, and we all need them; but when it comes to business, you should be the one who makes the important decisions, not them.

WHAT DO YOU REALLY WANT TO DO?

Reread the questionnaires in these last two chapters and ask yourself these three questions:

1. Where do I want to focus my efforts?

2. Do I want to learn how to work smarter?

3. Do I want to learn how to grow bigger?

> ## BUDGET FOR HELP
> *Picture yourself as a huge circus tent. You cannot stay supported without the aid of guy ropes and poles. Your associates and other professionals are those poles and guy ropes. We all reach out to others during our lives, and your business needs that help also, or the tent will collapse. You cannot afford not to enlist help. Budget for a few hours of help a week for the time-wasting chores or in the areas in which you lack expertise, and consult professionals for advice.*

Don't make this decision yet; just keep it in the back of your mind as you read on. Whatever you finally decide, you must first ensure that your business is stable enough and operating at peak efficiency. The next three chapters will show you how to work smarter and help you to increase your profits and efficiency. We shall start with everyone's favorite subject—getting organized and time management.

The "Where Am I Going?" questionnaire

The information in these first two chapters is designed to make you take a good look at yourself and your business at this moment. By completing the following self-evaluation questionnaire in Figure 2.6, you can target the key areas that need work.

Put the plan into action

Now that you have taken the time to write down your goals and concerns, you are already on the road to building a more profitable business. Make a commitment to work enthusiastically on these areas.

Don't expect miracles right away. Problems take time to resolve and new skills take time to learn and put into practice. With a plan of action and a concentrated effort, you will overcome many of these problems, gaining more confidence as you gain more knowledge, skills and control of your business.

Figure **2.6**

The "Where Am I Going?" Questionnaire

1. I think I have made the following mistakes as listed in "The Top Ten Mistakes in Growing a Business" (Chapter 1, page 7):

_____

_____

_____

_____

_____

2. Of these mistakes, the following ones give me serious concern:

_____

_____

_____

_____

_____

3. From question 6 in Figure 1.1, the "Where Am I Now?" questionnaire (page 13), I am experiencing difficulties in these areas:

_____

_____

_____

_____

4. From question 7 in Figure 1.1, the "Where Am I Now?" questionnaire (page 14), I need to improve my financial knowledge in these areas:

_____

_____

_____

_____

_____

5. My score for the "Where Am I Now?" questionnaire was: _____

6. Of the Eight Essential Entrepreneurial Skills, I need to improve my:

_____

_____

_____

_____

_____

7. My current goals for this business are:

_____

_____

_____

_____

_____

8. Of the sixty A–Z entrepreneur's jobs (page 28) I can competently handle _____ of them.

9. The jobs I don't like doing are:

_____

_____

_____

_____

10. The jobs that I need to develop more expertise in are:

_____

_____

_____

_____

_____

11. The jobs I could delegate to someone else are:

_____

_____

_____

_____

_____

12. My customer service could be improved in these areas:

_____

_____

_____

_____

_____

CHAPTER THREE

Are You Organized —Or Out of Control?

<o>

Chaos often breeds life, where order breeds habits.
HENRY BROOKS ADAMS

<o>

It appears that the more technologically streamlined we become with time-saving gadgets (like email—hah!), the more we feel overwhelmed and overworked.** How on earth did the Stone Age people manage? I mean, hunting, dragging, skinning, cutting up, cooking, and eating those dinosaurs was a mammoth job (no pun intended). What do we have to complain about?

GET ORGANIZED

With all today's time-saving devices, still no one has enough time. "I'm too busy!" is the universal cry of entrepreneurs and employees alike. For entrepreneurs, attending to sixty different jobs is sometimes impossible, so of course, hiring help is the most practical solution. But for many fledgling businesses, this isn't yet an option as the money just isn't available. What to do?

Simply stated, you have to become organized. "Oh, that's easy for you to say," you think, "but how?" One young woman who started a retail fish store with her partner complained one day, "No one told me it would be like this! I have to be up at the crack of dawn to go to the fish market, I'm open six days a week, there's so much to do in the store that I never have a moment to even think of writing up my books, let alone do anything for myself. It's a twelve-hour day or more just in the store!"

The Cycle of Business

Reread the section in Chapter 2 about the sixty different integral functions involved in operating a successful business. All business functions can be organized into a monthly cycle, which in turn can be broken down into weekly, and then daily cycles.

The most necessary functions that cannot be ignored on a daily and monthly basis include:

SET GOALS AND PRIORITIZE

Many challenges can be overcome by learning to be more focused and methodical in your daily routine. If goals and priorities are set and the small jobs are attended to in an orderly fashion, they cease to become overwhelming mountains.

- attending to telephone calls, faxes, email, and correspondence
- follow-up, networking, job quotations, marketing, purchasing
- billing customers, banking, paying the bills, reviewing finances
- calculating and paying state, federal, and personal taxes
- updating accounting records, collections, planning cash flow
- keeping abreast of news, industry information, and changes

Let one of these areas become unorganized or neglected, and the business will suffer. As a business grows, systems must change and become more sophisticated. This means getting rid of the shoebox system. Successful businesses rarely operate from shoeboxes. To accomplish all that you set out to do, you and your office may need some reorganization. Let's start with you.

Multitasking is mind-cluttering

According to Thomas Davenport and John Beck of the Accenture Institute for Strategic Change, most businesses today suffer from some degree of organizational ADD—Attention Deficit Disorder, brought about by too much multitasking and a lack of focus. A report published by the American Psychology Association states, "Not being able to concentrate for, say, tens of minutes at a time, may mean it's costing a company as much as 20 to 40 percent in terms of potential efficiency and productivity due to multitasking." Imagine what you could do with an extra eight to sixteen hours a week!

Which time zones are you operating in?

Rand Stagen, of the Stagen Leadership Institute *(www.stagen.com)*, clearly demonstrates in his Time Zones Model™ how easy it is for us to waste time and, in doing so, not accomplish our goals. He divides time into four time zones:
- **Proactive zone:** strategic thinking and planning, preparation, building reserves, maintenance, renewal
- **Distraction zone:** unnecessary interruptions, distracting calls and email
- **Waste zone:** inefficiencies, trivial activities, excessive entertainment
- **Reactive zone:** urgent demands, crisis, stress

He advises that productivity can be significantly increased and stress decreased by:
1. Increasing your awareness of which time zone you are in at any given moment
2. Avoiding distractions and minimizing waste by asserting boundaries and raising standards
3. Reinvesting the time you've saved into being more proactive and strategic.

Get Your RPM Going: Review, Plan, Then Map Your Time

Realizing that I was becoming a victim of the "time crunch n' munch," with what appeared to be an overwhelming workload in an impossibly narrow time frame, I sat down and decided to see if what was ahead could be accomplished. Developing a weekly time map was the end result—a system along with some helpful tips that I have been able to share with many entrepreneurs. Keep on track with a time map. See Figure 3.1 for an example.

Figure 3.1

How to Use a Weekly Time Planner

Weekly Time Planner: Week of February 10 to February 17

Time	Monday	Tuesday	Wednesday	Thursday	Friday	Saturday	Sunday
8:00	Breakfast and Treadmill				Airport to Calgary	Pickup at Hotel ◊	Sleep In
9:00	Practice Keynote	Practice Keynote	Practice Keynote	Phone, Email	◊	Deliver Workshop	◊
10:00	Prepare Handouts ◊	Follow Up: Phone, Email	Follow Up: Phone, Email	Follow Up: Phone, Email	◊	◊	◊
11:00	◊	Workshop Material	Handouts M/Planner	Practice Keynote	◊	Eat ◊	Fitness
12:00 Noon	Lunch CBA	Lunch Hair	Lunch Rewrite	Lunch Pack	◊	Flight	Clean Stalls
1:00	Material	◊	Keynote	for Calgary	1:30 Coach	◊	Grocery Shop
2:00	Dentist	◊		Prepare Home	Speaking	◊	◊
3:00	Time with	Prepare Materials	Overheads	for Away	◊	◊	◊
4:00	Katrina	◊	◊	Chiropractor	◊	◊	◊
5:00	Dinner Chores	Dinner Chores	Dinner Chores	Dinner Chores	Make Up Boxes	◊	◊
6:00		◊ Meeting	Board	◊	Dinner	Dinner Caps	Dinner Chores
7:00	◊	◊	Handouts	Library Seminar	Practice Review	◊	◊
8:00	Board Meeting	◊	Material	◊	Gym	Airport	Weights
9:00	Weights	◊	Weights	Pack	Practice	◊	Office
10:00	Lock Up	Lock Up	Lock Up	Check	Bed	◊	Lock Up

Step 1: Review

Each weekend, plan the following week's activities by first referring to the appointments in your planner. Transfer the time blocks onto your weekly time planner, noting in each block what you will be doing. Then color over these sections with a pink highlighter. These are committed time blocks.

Step 2: Plan

Using a priority list, write each job on a column pad. Head the columns Job and Deadline Date, then determine each one to be an A+, A, B, or C in priority. List everything you need to accomplish that week, including important work, growth planning, phone calls, follow-up, and administrative work. You often find that "C" priorities don't really need doing. Cleaning filing cabinets is usually a "C" priority that I tend to neglect, until I eventually set aside a morning, or I try to clean them as I use each one.

Step 3: Map

Next, review each day of the week, then block out all your personal time, from the moment you get up to when you officially "switch off." Include meal breaks, family commitments, traveling, shopping, fitness, volunteer work, and entertainment. Color these sections with a blue highlighter.

Step 4: Manage focused time

What you now have left on your time map are the spare "golden" time blocks to complete your "A+" and "A" priorities. You may be surprised at how little time you have left. Use the remaining time blocks to map in what must be accomplished by the end of the week. Estimate the time that each job will take, allocating smaller jobs—such as administrative functions—into grouped time blocks (e.g., one hour for follow-up and paying accounts). Color these blocks in a bright yellow highlighter so that they stand out. Ensure that some of this golden time encompasses some growth planning.

> ## YOUR MAP IS YOUR MASTER
> ....
> *Keep the time map in front of you on your desk or workbench. Refer to it regularly throughout the day. It becomes your "boss" and will help you stay on track. As you accomplish each task that is on your priority list and time map, cross it off and give yourself a pat on the back.*

Real Life) **No Time for Business**

Jeremy had worked in the family appliance business for many years and knew it inside-out. It became too easy to get involved in the day-to-day minor calamities, so he often returned home feeling that he hadn't accomplished anything.

After attending my workshop on time management, he got excited about the idea of time mapping, and sat down during lunch to start mapping out his time to make room for follow-up.

"I'm so excited!" he told me after the break. "I realize now that I was wasting my days, and now I have organized them to incorporate follow-up and some projects that have been put off for a long time."

Returning home from the conference, he reorganized the parts inventory, which was a real mess, and got on the phone to customers and prospects, easily drumming up new business. It felt good. But after a couple of weeks, he allowed the small stuff to get in the way again, so he let go of the time-mapping. I called him to check up, suggesting that he get back on track, delegate more responsibility and decision-making to his employees, and try allocating just a half-hour a day to follow-up and special projects.

"It did feel good getting all that done," said Jeremy. "I realize now that I have to keep doing this to break the bad habits. The business is there waiting for me—I just have to make the time to pick up the phone and go after it."

Map your own time

Figure 3.1 represents one of my "weeks from hell." However, by time-mapping two weeks ahead, I accomplished everything, with time to spare. The time blocks in ordinary type represent the "blue" or personal time. Those in italics represent "pink time," appointments and traveling, and the bold blocks represent the "golden" planning and focused time. Try your hand at preplanning your next week.

ORGANIZE FOR THE "FIVE Fs"

"We work to live, not live to work" is a popular saying. However, for some, the reverse is often the norm. What good is success, money, or fame if you don't have a happy family life, inner peace, and happiness? An unbalanced life creates damaging physical and mental stress. You become less productive and less motivated.

SCHEDULE IN EVERYTHING

To ensure that you allow for every contingency, block out time for traveling to appointments, parking, and networking. Schedule in some planning, "thinking," and closed door time when you can be completely focused. Allow a couple of hours of catch-up time for emergencies or distractions. Block time each day for follow-up and marketing.

As you plan each week, make time for life's important "Five Fs":

1. **Fitness:** Exercise aids positive, creative, and clear thinking—and your health. It's amazing the benefits one feels from just a half-hour walk or work-out. Your weight will decrease and productivity increase.

2. **Food:** Learn to make healthy choices and eat regularly. Ditch the junk food. Keep the machine fueled with good premium "gas." Don't skip meals and include a balance of food groups.

3. **Family:** They are the most important people in your life yet often the ones to suffer. Plan to spend chunks of time with them and ensure that it is quality time.

4. **Friends:** People who work long hours often complain of spending little time with friends. Make a point of scheduling in some much-needed time with them. Never be "too busy" and neglect your friends—you need them more than you think.

5. **Fun:** Think positive and be positive. Let yourself go and have a little fun. It's one of life's most important yet often forgotten ingredients.

INVOLVE THE FAMILY IN FITNESS

If your teenager (or dog) is suffering from lack of exercise, why not share your fitness time with them? Dogs and children can go for a short walk with you. For mothers with teenage daughters, why not join a gym together? Personal trainers can come into your home and set up programs, so there's really no excuse, is there?

But twenty-four hours is not enough—right? Wrong!

No one can argue that there are only twenty-four hours in a day. Yet these days, many people feel they have no time for themselves, and certainly little time for the "Five Fs," particularly fitness. So here is the solution. Take the twenty-four hours and divide them into forty-eight half-hours. If you can't find one-fiftieth of a day for fitness and another fiftieth for your family, then you seriously need to review your lifestyle and make some radical changes.

ORGANIZE THE OFFICE: MANAGE TIME

If you are currently sitting in an office piled high with junk and papers, you will need some basic organizational equipment, so be prepared to go out and spend some money on these valuable tools. There is a huge assortment of organizational products available to suit both your budget and personal taste.

Once you have purchased the right tools, you can get down to organizing your office. Filing cabinets are usually the office's hidden disaster zone. Using the following system, you should theoretically be able to find any piece of paper within twenty seconds. Remember, a cluttered desk and office equals a cluttered mind, so here are some tips to de-clutter all three:

- When bills are received, check them for accuracy and attend to any anomalies. Then file them alphabetically in an "accounts to be paid" file. If you have a large volume of monthly accounts, you can use either an expanding file or a separate folder for each regular supplier.
- Keep a graduated file holder on your desk to hold files you will be working with that week.

- Keep a weekly follow-up file and review it daily during your planning time.
- You'll probably never clean out your whole filing cabinet at once, so each time you pick up a messy file, quickly clean it out before you put it away. Put a small colored dot on the file so you know it is cleaned out. Use a different colored dot each year.
- File paid accounts alphabetically and then chronologically. Use a separate folder for the suppliers you use the most and a "miscellaneous" file for occasional suppliers. File the last-paid invoice at the front in case you need to refer to an invoice.

ORGANIZE YOUR FILES

There are some files that you should always keep in your cabinet, such as asset purchases, contracts, and correspondence from government and tax agencies. So that you can easily locate important documents, make separate files for the following information:

1. Business and tax files

State and local taxes; workers' compensation; payroll; payroll guides; incorporation documents; asset register; insurance policies; shareholder's loan; telephone and equipment leases; IRS employer number; licensing agencies.

2. Banking and financial files

Bank statements, canceled checks, and posted check stubs; credit card contracts and information; bank and loan agreements; financial statements for three years; cash expenses, petty cash, and expense reports belong here. Many of these are important files that should not be cleaned out and put into storage. Your asset register should contain all business asset purchase invoices. You will need this information for your accountant and for when you sell your business.

> ### COLOR-CODE FILES
> *To easily locate files in your cabinet, use the color-coding system. Use different colored suspension files and matching file folders to house the various categories of paperwork (e.g., projects, marketing information, customer files, etc.) with matching color tabs to index them. To keep individual files organized, use a two-hole punch at the top of each folder. Fasten the papers in chronological order with metal fasteners. This prevents papers from getting lost or out of order.*

KEEP CUSTOMER FILES

It may be helpful for reference, purchasing, marketing, and statistical purposes to keep customer information files with copies of quotations, correspondence, and invoices. Because you need to keep a numerical copy of each invoice, you may have to print invoices with an extra copy to use in this file.

3. Sales invoices

If you bill just a few invoices a month, staple them together after posting to your accounting records and file them numerically. For a large volume of invoices, use binders. Save time by having the printer drill the invoices to suit your filing needs.

Voided invoices must be filed, or the tax department may think you are laundering money, so don't throw them away. All invoices should be numbered to provide an audit trail for both you and the tax audit department. Stamp all invoices "posted" when they are entered to your books. Keep unpaid posted invoices in a file for collection purposes.

4. Marketing files

Follow-up files (keeping follow-up files handy allows you to keep in contact with "work in progress"); media; corporate and personal profiles; testimonials; advertising copy; contact lists; correspondence.

UTILIZE YOUR FILING SYSTEM

Make your filing cabinet work for you. Use the top drawers for files that you use regularly, and store less-used documents in the bottom drawers. Follow-up and current customer files can be stored either on your desk or close to your regular work area by using the graduated file holder. This enables files to be at arm's length and the tabs to be easily read.

If you use this filing system, making additions or deletions where necessary, you should be able to find any piece of paper within twenty seconds. When a customer calls and you need to refer to your files, they will be impressed that you don't waste their time by shuffling through drawers. Efficiency in these situations can only be a positive in your customer's perception of how you operate your business.

ORGANIZE YOUR COMPUTER

Computers are the lifeline of most businesses. With the number of viruses circulating in cyberspace and the unpredictability of software, back-up and regular computer maintenance is essential, because in most cases, no computer equals no office and often, no work. Here are some tips to help keep your computer information in order:

> ## CLEAN OUT YEAR-END FILES
> *At year-end, you can empty the fiscal year's files into storage boxes. Clearly identify the contents on the box before storing them. Store accounting records for seven years as the IRS could spring a surprise audit.*

- **Back-up:** Use either CD-ROMs or a zip drive (approximate cost $140) to back up files daily. Store disks safely, and keep another copy out of the office in case of fire or theft.
- **Word processing files:** Word processing programs are often unstable and can shut down. The written word is often lost forever—it's difficult to recapture original thoughts. Set your back-up timer to your desired time; every two minutes is ideal. You can change your back-up time using Help under the Windows menu.
- **Defragment the hard drive:** Once every few months, go to Help and type in "defragment hard drive" or install Norton Utilities. This process will re-organize your hard drive to optimize space and efficiency. A large hard drive will take two hours to defragment.
- **Virus protection:** Don't switch on your computer without a good virus protection program running. Use the live update and scan function weekly or schedule the program to do it.
- **Contact management:** Use a contact management system to dispose of that drawer full of business cards you can never find. It may be as simple as using your Address Book in Microsoft Works, or a more refined software system such as Maximizer, Act, or Goldmine.

CLEAN OUT EMAIL
....

It's too easy to let emails collect until there are a thousand messages in your in-box and sent files. Once a week, sort by From, and your emails will be listed alphabetically. It's much easier to delete unwanted mail when it is grouped together by name, not date. It's amazing just how quickly you'll delete unwanted mail.

ORGANIZE YOUR EMAIL

Email is the blessing—and the curse—of business. It has encouraged us to become a disconnected society, hiding behind the keyboard instead of verbally communicating with people. It comes unwanted, unexpected, and unplanned for. It saves and wastes copious time. Try these suggestions to better manage it:

- Turn off the email notification sign and sound during focused time.
- Set up in-box folders for different departments. Either have the mail directed straight to that folder or move important emails to those folders after printing out a hard copy.
- Block in time on your planner for checking and answering email.
- Set up filters in your browser and contact your server to see if they can pre-filter mail. My website host and high-speed Internet provider now filters spam, and it has astoundingly cut it down by 75 to 80 percent.
- Although spam is illegal, some will filter through. Anti-spam software is effective, but watch for personal mail that can sometimes slip through.
- Set up email so that it doesn't open automatically. Delete anything that is junk mail.

If you make a point of performing these simple functions, your computer and you will operate more efficiently, and downtime will be kept to a minimum. Now you have to find the time to do all this, so the next thing to organize is your time commitments.

ORGANIZE AND MASTER TIME

Because time is so valuable and in such great demand, you need to put a value on yours and spend it wisely. Remember those four time zones? How much time do you spend in the distraction and waste zones? Here are some tips to help you better master time in three areas that eat up countless wasted hours.

Tame telephone calls

Because many businesses are so reliant on email, the personal touch is often sadly lacking. However, the telephone can also become a time-munching enemy. Try these strategies for handling those calls:

- During "focused" time, put the telephone onto voice mail and screen calls, or instruct employees to handle any phone inquiries. It's surprising what you will achieve without interruptions.
- If someone calls to chat, explain you are on a deadline and politely ask if you could return the call later.
- Leave a message on your voice mail saying that you will return calls within two hours.
- Don't give customers your cell number unless it is an emergency. Use driving time to think, plan, or listen to an educational tape or CD.

> ### BE PREPARED FOR "DOING COFFEE"
>
> *"We must do coffee next week" can be an expensive time-waster. If someone wants to meet you for coffee (unless it's to your benefit), ask them to email their questions. Then, when you meet, instead of going through the whole introduction and explanation routine, you can get right down to business. Let them know how much time you have and stick to that time frame.*

Limit lunches and "doing coffee"

When you are invited out for lunch—which, of course, can be important for networking purposes—thoroughly examine the benefits of and reasons for going. Many experts find that people want to take them to lunch just to pick their brains and get free information. If you are feeling time-crunched, guard against coffee or lunches for frivolous reasons. Be selfish and ask yourself:

- WIIFM? (What's in it for me?)
- If there's NIIFY (nothing in it for you), graciously decline until you do have the time.
- Carefully choose the people you want to mentor and give free advice to. Set the parameters for the time you spend with them.
- Although time is of the essence, don't forgo an opportunity to meet an important contact face-to-face. More business can be transacted in one short meeting than by copious phone calls or emails.

CAPTURE THAT BIG IDEA

....

Many great ideas are lost because there is no pen and paper available to write them down. Purchase a mini-recorder with a headset. Then, when you are driving, or even out walking, and you think of something you need to remember, record it on tape for when you return to the office.

Manage meetings

Countless conferences and meetings have been rushed, ruined, or have gone overtime because the agendas were not carefully planned. When you plan a meeting, take these factors into consideration:

- **Budget for contingencies:** Schedule in a few extra minutes to allow for latecomers or problems with equipment or seating.
- **Carefully plan agendas:** Allow time for clapping, introductions, thank-you's, and handshakes, and for presenters to enter and leave the stage.
- **Inform all presenters:** Let presenters know that their time allotment is precise and no overruns are permitted.
- **Confirm all presenters:** Call all presenters on the agenda the previous day to confirm their attendance and the address of and directions to the venue.
- **Adhere to agenda:** If you chair a meeting, state at the beginning that you will be strictly adhering to the agenda times. If a speaker becomes long-winded, interrupt and firmly state that there is a set agenda. Suggest that the discussion continue after the meeting or be tabled.
- **Plan for breaks:** At conferences, allow plenty of time for room changes, restroom breaks, coffee line-ups, stragglers and networking.
- **Preselect an audience member** to signal presenters for the last five minutes, two minutes, and one minute. Using the green, amber, and red card system works for some.

ORGANIZE A MONTHLY ROUTINE

Business is cyclical so certain monthly tasks have to be completed. The more you work to a routine, the easier time management becomes. Once new habits are established, you will feel more in control and able to focus on growing your business. Figure 3.2 outlines some of the necessary monthly administrative functions, along with a suggested time frame.

Real Life) Terrible Timing

Janice was thrilled to be asked by her association to plan a morning business conference. Eager to get as much content into the few hours as possible, she planned three speakers during the breakfast, a short break, and then two workshops before lunch. She had never planned an event before and didn't get any advice on how to go about it.

The first speaker started late and ran over time by twenty minutes. The next keynote speaker realized the problem and offered to cut her keynote short to catch up some time. The third speaker also went overtime. The participants then needed to go to the restroom and change rooms, so the next round of workshops, which were in four different rooms, started late.

The presenters had to cut their one-hour workshops down to forty minutes, which annoyed both the presenters and the participants. Some of the presenters didn't finish on time, so by the time the participants changed rooms and the second round of workshops started, they too had to be shortened to finish by noon.

The terrible timing created many negative comments and feelings. Workshop presenters were upset at the shortened presentation time and participants expressed their resentment at being rushed and not getting the content they wanted. The overall evaluations for the morning were not good.

The negative outcome could have been eliminated by careful timing of the agenda and by Janice speaking to all the presenters beforehand to stress the importance of keeping to their allotted time. Having a prearranged signal to complete presentations would have helped too. The morning dampened the participants' enthusiasm to such a degree that when asked on the event evaluations whether they wanted this event next year, many answered no.

Many meetings and conferences suffer the same fate by being poorly planned. Astute time planning is crucial to a successful venture.

Figure 3.2

Monthly Administrative Functions

Function	Suggested time frame	Benefit
Ordering supplies	Beginning of the month	Extends credit period by nearly 30 days
Billing customers	Beginning of new month	Increases cash flow
Collections	Once a week	Keeps cash flowing
Payroll reconciliation	By end of first week	Avoid overdue penalties, plan cash flow
Paying accounts	Twice a month	Avoid interest, plan cash flow
State taxes	Beginning of new month	Plan cash flow
Payroll taxes	Beginning of new month	Plan cash flow
Accounting	When bank statements arrive	Monitor progress immediately
Review financial situation	When accounting completed	Tax and future planning, catch errors
Marketing and follow-up	Each morning	Generate income
Staff meetings	Once a week, Mondays	Start week positively as a team

ORGANIZE THE HOME OFFICE

No doubt the thought of operating from a home office initially sounded like the best idea since cyberspace, but as many have experienced, it's not really that glamorous. Once again the Eight Essential Entrepreneurial Skills from Chapter 1 must be harnessed to make a home office a practical place to do business.

Countless problems that you hadn't thought of surface, often presenting very irritating situations. Let's look at some of the common problems that home operators experience, along with some suggestions to keep you better organized and motivated.

Family frustrations

Train your family to leave you alone during working hours. This takes time and patience, so you must take your business seriously or your family won't. Explain that it is a great benefit to have you at home, however, you are unavailable—excluding emergencies—during working hours when the door is closed and the "do not disturb" sign is showing.

Children usually adapt to these rules and understand them quite well after they are aged seven. Make time in the afternoon when they come home from school to have a "coffee break" with them. A little quality time is important to both you and your children to maintain a balance.

Stress to your partner or spouse the importance of having uninterrupted quality work time. If you say you'll finish at 5:00, avoid making exceptions so that the family doesn't resent the business. There is always the evening to complete any urgent work.

Grappling with growth

Many businesses start in a small office, only to find that they need more room. Look in furniture catalogs to see how you can utilize floor-to-ceiling storage shelves, computer and desk organizers, bookshelves, and filing cabinets. Throw away "stuff" and keep the office basic and efficient. If the situation becomes unbearable, prepare some projections of the sales volume required in order to profitably move to commercial premises, and make this your goal. Along with the sales projections, recrunch some financial numbers and don't make a move before preparing a well-researched, practical plan.

> # DON'T OVER-VOLUNTEER
> ....
> *Volunteers are part of what make our society such a wonderful place to live and work; however, over-committing to volunteering causes unnecessary stress. If you are asked to sit on a board of directors or to volunteer for an organization, tell them you will get back to them with an answer in a couple of days. Think about WIIFY. Review your available time and commitments. If you have the time, can clearly see the personal or business benefits, and know you will do a good job, only then should you say yes.*

Dealing with other diversions

If a neighbor calls, comment that you would love to chat and will return their call after five. Stress that you have work to finish. Don't fall into the trap of "taking a break" with your neighbor. You wouldn't do it if you were working for someone else, so don't do it now.

It's difficult to work during fine weather. You can hear the neighbor's lawn mower or chainsaw and would dearly like to be out there with them. Make it a goal to achieve certain priorities, and when that work is completed, turn on the voice mail and go out to play. You will achieve far more when you return feeling

SEEK ALTERNATIVE SPACE

It's a common dilemma for your business to be too small to move to commercial premises, yet too large for your residence. If local regulations permit, you may be able to utilize accessory buildings or build an addition. Another option is to rent a mini-storage warehouse or a small workshop. My son exchanges shop rent for use of his tools, paying only for a portion of electricity and hence keeping the overhead to a minimum.

refreshed and energized. There have to be some benefits to being home-based, but don't play at the expense of letting your customers down. A well-organized entrepreneur will schedule in some playtime each week and reap the benefits of feeling more positive.

Sharing with shift workers

There couldn't be a worse combination than trying to operate a home-based business and living with a shift worker. The two are not compatible if you entertain clients or work with noise-generating devices, particularly telephones. You and your spouse will have to work together to meet each other's needs. You shouldn't have to downsize your business operation because of this, but finding workable solutions takes time (earplugs work). Telephone and fax ringers have to be turned down, and you may have to visit clients instead of them coming to you.

PLAY A LITTLE

Considering that the fine weather season is relatively short in some parts of the northern United States, it's not such a bad idea to play a little. You need your rewards, and often, home-based self-employed people don't take enough relaxation time, so plan to play a little.

Overcoming geographic isolation

On my speaking tours to remote locations, I have been impressed by many entrepreneurs who manage under adverse circumstances. One couple living in a remote country area operates two craft businesses. They face the challenges of generator-powered electricity, a radiophone, and no direct Internet access. Their property is a two-hour drive from the nearest town on a route of potholes surrounded by road.

Yet they have overcome these challenges by utilizing a local answering service, checking messages daily, and by having a local company host their website. They keep in touch with the business world by subscribing to trade magazines and regularly attending seminars, conferences, and trade shows to maintain their presence and networking contacts. There is always a way if you are determined to succeed.

Ten Tips ## *to* Keep Your Day Organized

1. For home office operators, start each day at a regular time as though you were preparing to leave for work. Dress neatly and forget working in your robe or pajamas—you cannot function in work mode sporting slippers, stubble, and sloppy clothes.

2. Quickly tidy the house first thing in the morning or in the evening. If your home is untidy, you won't work efficiently. Don't even think about performing household chores during a working day. They are not a priority.

3. At the end of each day, clean off your desk and make a list of things to do tomorrow in order of priority. If you start the day with messy desk syndrome, you will not function at peak performance. As you work, keep your desk organized.

4. Return emails requiring an answer within twenty-four hours, or you'll forget. You can do this in your pajamas in the evening or when you are preparing your list of things to do.

5. Review your follow-up file daily and make any phone calls after 9:30 a.m. Allow people time to settle in at work. Avoid follow-up after 3:00 p.m. when sugar and concentration levels are low. Forget follow-up on voice mail on Friday—most people are in TGIF mode and are not receptive or not there.

continued

---

6. Keep your priority list close to you on your desk, or use sticky notes, transferring the information to your list once or twice a day.

7. Open mail and attend to it immediately to stop a pile-up of papers. Note important account payment dates, check accounts, and file them to be paid. File or attend to other correspondence. If you can't attend to something immediately, note it on your priority list and place it in your in-box. Review your in-box once a day.

8. Write up the bank deposit and attend to payment discrepancies. Review your planner and accounts to be paid file.

9. Work to a structured routine. Stop for lunch, catch up on the news, and finish at the same designated time each day. Take a short walk to recharge the batteries. Spend quality time with your family and return to the office in the evening if necessary.

10. Refer to Chapter 4 under "What Are Source Documents?" to learn how to organize your accounting information.

PLAN TO STAY ORGANIZED: A CHECKLIST

This chapter has discussed many areas of your business requiring astute organization. You may already be a well-organized person in control of all facets of the operation. If you are, then feel proud of yourself and keep up the good work. If you need some organizational help, complete Figure 3.3, a checklist that will guide you through the process. If you can already check off over twenty "completed" boxes, treat yourself to lunch.

Now you're in control

Once you are physically and mentally organized, you will feel better able to control both your business and your personal life. The next step is to gain control of the financial aspect of your business. You can't do one without the other, so Chapter 4 will show you how.

Figure 3.3

Operation "Get Organized" Checklist

Area to organize	Needs work	Already organized	Completed
1. Use a weekly time map to plan time	☐	☐	☐
2. Plan time for the "Five Fs"	☐	☐	☐
3. Plan regular, specific fitness time	☐	☐	☐
4. Start a priority list system	☐	☐	☐
5. Purchase equipment for filing system	☐	☐	☐
6. Clean out old files	☐	☐	☐
7. Organize all business files	☐	☐	☐
8. Install a back-up system	☐	☐	☐
9. Change back-up timer to two minutes	☐	☐	☐
10. Know how to defragment hard drive	☐	☐	☐
11. Install anti-virus program	☐	☐	☐
12. Update virus protection weekly	☐	☐	☐
13. Install contact management program	☐	☐	☐
14. Organize email and folders	☐	☐	☐
15. Organize a telephone call system	☐	☐	☐
16. Review availability for volunteering	☐	☐	☐
17. Qualify lunch and coffee appointments	☐	☐	☐
18. Clean desk each morning or evening	☐	☐	☐
19. Attend to banking and mail daily	☐	☐	☐
20. Develop a structured daily routine	☐	☐	☐
21. Use a daily planner	☐	☐	☐
22. Use a monthly administrative routine	☐	☐	☐
23. Delegate time-consuming chores	☐	☐	☐
24. Do follow-up calls each day	☐	☐	☐
25. Monitor business monthly	☐	☐	☐

CHAPTER FOUR

Are You in Control of the Financial Reins?

—◄◦►—

Money is better than poverty, if only for financial reasons.
WOODY ALLEN

—◄◦►—

Just as historians record the evolution of the world in writing, so must you record the evolution of your business from conception. Using a universal, age-old system devised many centuries ago called double-entry bookkeeping, the progress of your business is recorded in figures. ❧

WHAT DOES ACCOUNTING TELL YOU?

Mention the words "accounting, bookkeeping, and taxes," and the average entrepreneur shudders. Oh! To be left alone to run their business without this time-wasting, hateful chore. Those who are not diligent in monitoring their business's financial records often experience an untimely financial demise. See Chapter 14 for an intimate discussion of this subject. The astute entrepreneurs who utilize their financial information to monitor progress and make decisions are usually successful.

Accounting records act as a financial barometer for your business. An accurate set of accounting records transferred into financial statement format and carefully analyzed can tell you the following:

- whether projected gross profit margins are being met
- where expenses are contributing to losses
- whether actual results are meeting projected results
- what percentage each overhead expense is costing in relation to sales
- which products or services are selling the most
- which products or services are profitable or losing money
- how much is collectively owing in accounts receivable and payable
- how much each customer owes and how much you owe each supplier
- the dollar cost of asset purchases from start-up
- the accumulated depreciation of assets and their book value
- how much the business owns in assets
- how much the business owes in liabilities
- the accumulated profits or losses
- the working capital situation
- your current tax situation, personal and corporate
- whether you are financially ready for growth
- whether wages and management salaries are too high (or too low)
- how to make future projections based on past history

How does accounting work?

If you understand how the accounting puzzle fits together and the logical reasoning behind it, organization of your records becomes easier. Accounting dictates that you maintain careful records. These records are compiled from all those everyday pieces of paper you deal with: invoices, bank deposits, cash receipts, paid accounts, credit card statements, and check stubs. If the information is transcribed incorrectly from these documents, then your accounting records will be wrong. Although accountants make big bucks correcting errors in clients' books, it is depressing and expensive work.

SHOEBOX OR COMMON SENSE?

Even if you prefer to operate in the dark, the sad fact is, the government requires that you maintain accurate accounting records and prepare financial statements at year-end to assess both the business's and your personal tax situation. You can throw everything into a box, present it to your distraught accountant and cross your fingers as the year-end results are crunched. Or you can be sensible and realize that accounting is an important and integral part of growing a successful business.

THE SIX-STEP ACCOUNTING CYCLE

Accounting records start from the first day you spend money on your business, so hopefully, you kept all the receipts and entered them into your records. Information from these papers is entered into accounting journals, which have both a control and descriptive entry. One is a debit and one a credit.

Debits and credits follow a formula which is more easily understood once you learn a few basic principles. If you use accounting software, enroll in a course on manual bookkeeping to ensure you understand how to make correct entries. Otherwise your records will be wrong, and often, mistakes are never found.

The accounting cycle follows six steps, which are shown in Figure 4.1.

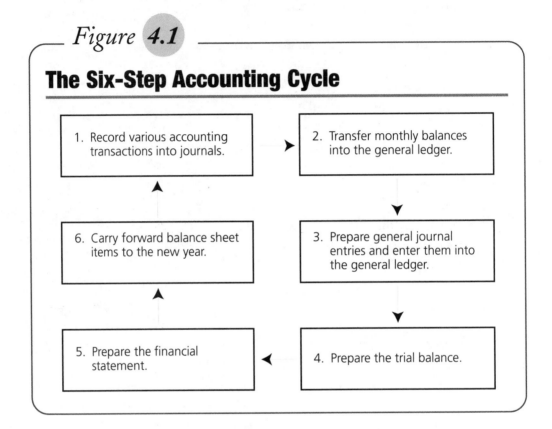

Figure **4.1**

The Six-Step Accounting Cycle

1. Record various accounting transactions into journals.

2. Transfer monthly balances into the general ledger.

6. Carry forward balance sheet items to the new year.

3. Prepare general journal entries and enter them into the general ledger.

5. Prepare the financial statement.

4. Prepare the trial balance.

Step 1

Each transaction is recorded into the appropriate columns in the correct journal monthly. The columns are totaled both down and across, with debits equaling credits.

Step 2

The monthly balances are transferred into a general ledger, which is organized by account name in financial statement format. When the monthly totals from all the ledgers are entered and the new ending balances in the general ledger added, the debit entries should equal the credit entries.

Step 3

Any entries that cannot be recorded through the normal journals are prepared in a general journal, then entered to the general ledger, usually by your accountant at year-end. Many businesses use monthly journal entries to keep their reporting precise. These entries consist of depreciation, prepayments, bad debts, and expenses that have not been billed but belong to that fiscal year (for example, an accountant's year-end fees are included as an "accrued expense" to the fiscal year).

Step 4

A trial balance is prepared from the general ledger in account order, listing all debits and credits with both totals agreeing. If prepared manually, a worksheet is used to calculate the final financial statement entries.

Step 5

Financial statements are prepared from the trial balance. The difference between the income and expenses represents either a profit or loss, which is transferred to the "retained earnings" account on the balance sheet. The financial statement is then prepared in a standard format.

Step 6

The income and expense accounts are reversed out to zero balances. The balance sheet items are carried forward to the next year. If interim financial statements are prepared, the income and expense accounts are not closed off until year-end. If you use an accounting software program and keep your books up-to-date, a financial statement can be quickly printed at the touch of a keyboard button when you need it.

WHAT ARE SOURCE DOCUMENTS?

Accounting records are a compilation of the following source documents—those papers that seem to breed on your desk into large piles. To organize your accounting, here are the documents you will need, their purpose, and the journal they are entered into:

- **Sales invoices, cash register tapes:** Used to record monthly sales plus taxes. These are recorded into a **sales journal**, which can give you useful sales information. Invoices are entered numerically, with canceled invoices entered as "void" to ensure an accurate audit trail.

- **Bank deposits:** Monies deposited into business bank accounts are recorded into a **cash receipt journal**. These deposits itemize the customer, invoice number paid, the amount, and discount taken. It also provides for an itemized accounting of cash deposits, loans, or other income. This journal is reconciled monthly to the bank statement.

- **Checks:** Checks are recorded into a **check disbursements journal**, which is used to itemize costs by expense category, and for reconciling to the bank statements monthly. Each check stub should detail what the expense is for.

- **Credit card expenses:** Keep all credit card receipts attached to the original purchase invoices. When the statement arrives, highlight the business expenses and break them down into the different expense categories. They are recorded in either the cash disbursements or accounts payable journal, depending on how your accounting is set up.

- **Cash expenses:** To keep a record of the money you put into the business, expenses that you pay for on behalf of the company are entered into a **cash expense journal** with a description of the expense. The check disbursements journal records the money you draw from the business.

KEEP ORGANIZED AND INFORMED

By keeping source documents well organized and detailed, putting your accounting together to prepare financial information becomes easier. A financial statement or a trial balance can be produced quickly when you need it. With the source documents correctly entered to the journals, ready for entry to the general ledger, or correctly coded and ready for entry into your accounting program, the worst job is over.

- **Accounts to be paid:** Referred to as accounts payable, if you prepare regular financial statements, you use an **accounts payable journal** to record unpaid trade accounts. These are listed in the month of purchase with an expense description. When the account is paid, the payment is recorded in the "Accounts Payable" column in the check disbursements journal.
- **Other information:** Transactions that cannot be recorded in any of the above journals are recorded in the **general journal**. An example is trading services or products with a supplier. If you have limited accounting experience, keep details of these transactions for your accountant.

THE GENERAL LEDGER—YOUR BUSINESS "BIBLE"

The financial statements are prepared from the general ledger, which is a record of all your business' financial transactions since its inception. It is your most valuable asset, as it can be used to give you financial information at any period in time. A number and a name is assigned to each account.

The monthly balances of all the columns in your accounting journals are transferred into the general ledger, which is organized into individual asset, liability, equity, income, and expense accounts, based on the format of your chart of accounts (see a detailed explanation on page 68). Often with accounting software, source documents are posted to an accounting journal then automatically posted to the general ledger. Ah, the wonders of technology.

By using a chart of accounts designed specifically for your business, you can break your accounting information into general ledger accounts that allow you to closely monitor individual expenses, rather than grouping expenses together. This way, when you need to review an expense, all the entries in the general ledger account can be easily identified and analyzed.

Ten Tips
for Tidy Accounting

The key to organizing the accounting process and making it run more smoothly is to practice good daily habits. Here are some tips for keeping your records organized:

1. For retail stores, if you use a manual accounting system, record cash till tapes daily into the sales journal—it's a five-minute job that becomes a chore if you only do it once a month.

2. Detail bank deposits carefully. If other income is not correctly recorded, it can be mistaken for sales income, and you'll pay tax when you shouldn't.

3. Never leave a check stub blank. Record checks in numerical order, including void ones.

4. Reconcile your bank account monthly and correct the balance in your checkbook.

5. Use a ring binder (available at banks) for checks. It's easier to enter data and to reconcile the bank account.

6. Don't use debit cards or make cash withdrawals through bank machines unless you keep fastidious accounting records. It makes for complex, time-consuming accounting, and increases the chance of errors. Write checks where possible.

7. Keep credit card receipts and invoices in the plastic wallet found in most check binders. This keeps them safe and easy to find when the statement arrives. Empty your wallet regularly, and keep an envelope in your vehicle marked "cash expenses" where you can store receipts so you don't lose them.

8. If there is room on your credit card statement, detail the account code for the expenses. This makes entering credit card charges an easier task. If there is no room, attach a sheet to each statement page.

9. When bills arrive, check them for accuracy. Mark important payments—such as government taxes—in your planner.

10. Keep accounts payable in a "current payables" folder, in alphabetical order for easy access.

FINANCIAL STATEMENTS—YOUR BUSINESS HEALTH BAROMETER

To plan for growth, use your financial statements regularly as a management tool in decision-making. Accounting programs make data preparation and monitoring results simple in comparison to the days of handwritten ledgers. Entries that once took days to complete are finished in a matter of hours, and financial statements are printed easily and efficiently. So there is no excuse not to take control of the financial reins and listen to what your figures are telling you.

Financial statements are broken down into two sections—a balance sheet and a statement of income and expenses. Countless business owners have no concept of what these documents mean, only that they do or don't have to pay income tax at year-end. Not paying taxes means no profit, so don't jump for joy when your accountant tells you there is no tax to pay. Rather, be extremely concerned that there is a real problem. Financial statements will indicate where problems lie, so spend time with your

REVAMP YOUR CHART OF ACCOUNTS

How your chart of accounts is designed can make the difference between basic or more detailed reporting. More information allows you to closely monitor expenses and profit margins. Information can be incorporated into updating your business plan, enabling you to make more accurate decisions and projections. As you experience growth, you will need to refer regularly to your business plan and financial statements. Review your current chart of accounts to see where you can break it down into more informative groupings so that it will better highlight areas of concern.

accountant until you understand how to interpret them. If you prepare in-house financial statements during the year, make time to carefully review them.

DESIGN AN INFORMATIVE CHART OF ACCOUNTS

Accounting follows a standard format using a chart of accounts that can be specifically designed for your business. It is set out in financial statement format and allocates a number to each general ledger account. For ease of comprehension and correct statement preparation, set up your general ledger in the order shown in Figure 4.2. Familiarize yourself with the account numbers and ensure that data is entered to the right account. Your accountant will help you to design an informative chart of accounts for your business.

Figure 4.2 outlines the income and expense accounts for a small business that repairs lawn mower equipment and sells new and used equipment and parts.

Figure **4.2**

Snappy Lawn Equipment Services Inc.
Chart of Accounts

Revenue:		Cost of sales:	
4000	Sales, new equipment	4400	Opening inventory
4010	Sales, used equipment	4500	Purchases, new equipment
4020	Sales, new parts	4510	Purchases, used equipment
4030	Sales, used parts	4520	Purchases, new parts
4040	Sales, shop labor	4540	Purchases, used parts
4050	Other income	4550	Purchases, oil and gas
		4560	Labor, shop
		4580	Equipment repairs
		4590	Shop supplies
		4600	Closing inventory

Overhead expenses:

5000	Accounting fees		5280	Rent
5010	Advertising		5290	Repairs & maintenance, store
5020	Bad debts		5300	Seminars & trade shows
5040	Bank charges		5400	Telephone, fax, & Internet
5050	Casual labor		5410	Travel & accommodation
5060	Depreciation		5420	Utilities
5070	Employee benefits		5430	Vehicle gas
5080	Fees, licenses, & taxes		5440	Vehicle repairs, insurance
5090	Insurance		5450	Wages, sales
5100	Loan interest		5460	Workers' compensation
5110	Legal and professional fees		5500	Corporate taxes
5200	Management fees		5999	Suspense account*
5210	Marketing and promotion			
5220	Office supplies			
5230	Office wages			
5270	Promotion, meals			

*Items that need explanation at the time of entry; once resolved, this account will be zero.

How to use costing information

By designing a detailed chart of accounts, the owner can monitor individual sales categories, along with their associated costs. By breaking down the opening and closing inventory for each sales category, the gross profit can be calculated and compared to projected returns.

If this exercise is completed quarterly, seasonal fluctuations can be monitored. This information helps in ordering inventory, comparing actual profit margins to projected ones, and planning future cash flow. Figure 4.3 on page 70 gives a sales analysis using Snappy Lawn Equipment Services Inc.

HOW TO ANALYZE AN INCOME STATEMENT

By breaking down each section of the financial figures and comparing the performance in each area, you will better understand your business and pinpoint its strengths and weaknesses. From here, you can make informed management decisions based on past and recent history. You will need to analyze these areas:

1. **Sales:** the product lines that are producing the most (and least) profit; where you experience seasonal highs and lows and how to diversify during these quiet periods

2. **Cost of sales:** material, labor, freight and production expenses; whether they are increasing, why they are increasing, and how costs can be trimmed

3. **Gross profit margins:** actual margins against projected or expected margins, what is causing any noticeable profit erosion, or conversely, what has contributed to an increase in profits

4. **Overhead expenses:** where overhead has significantly increased and why, how it can be reduced without reducing efficiency and profitability.

Analyzing Snappy's first six months

Following is an analysis of Snappy Lawn Equipment's first six months. Snappy's owner tended to get caught up in the day-to-day operations rather than monitor the progress of the business. Decisions were made without first consulting the financial information, and now the business is suffering.

Figure 4.3

Snappy Lawn Equipment Services Inc.
Sales Analysis

SALES AND COST ANALYSIS   SIX MONTHS JANUARY TO JUNE 20__

	Jan.–March	%	April–June	%	Total	%
Sales:						
New equipment	$ 3,250	14.5	15,720	18.2	18,970	17.5
Used equipment	1,110	5.0	3,790	4.4	4,900	4.5
New parts	4,030	18.0	14,160	16.4	18,190	16.7
Used parts	1,760	8.0	4,640	5.4	6,400	5.9
Shop labor	12,320	54.5	47,950	55.6	60,270	55.4
Total sales:	$22,470	100.0	86,260	100.0	108,730	100.0
Cost of sales:						
New equipment	$ 1,950	8.7	8,640	10.0	10,590	9.7
Used equipment	390	1.7	1,140	1.3	1,530	1.4
New parts	2,420	10.8	7,790	9.0	10,210	9.4
Used parts	620	2.8	1,620	1.9	2,240	2.0
Shop labor	5,890	26.2	28,090	32.6	33,980	31.3
Total costs:	$11,270	50.2	47,280	54.8	58,550	53.8
Gross profit:	$11,200	49.8	38,980	45.2	50,180	46.2

1. Sales

By analyzing the sales for a six-month period, we can see that the first quarter reflects the winter drop in sales. New and used equipment account for 19.5 percent of sales and parts 26 percent. Shop labor at 54.5 percent of sales reflects the largest source of income. In the following quarter, sales increase by nearly 400 percent as spring is traditionally the season when customers have their equipment repaired or replaced.

New and used equipment sales have increased proportionately during the second quarter and now constitute 49 percent of gross profits. It is evident that repairing equipment should remain the focus of this business. The owner should compare the sales percentages to projected figures. Perhaps he envisioned more new or used equipment sales. If so, the figures should be studied and the reasons for lower sales established.

Is it a lack of target marketing, or competition from chain stores? How could the business increase sales? Should money be spent on diversification? Should the owner focus on growing the repair division? This detailed sales analysis provides enough information to help make informed decisions.

2. Cost of sales

Because shop labor constitutes a large percentage of sales, labor costs should be scrutinized. The labor income of $12,320 in the first quarter was generated by one employee working full-time for February and March at a cost of $20 per hour, with a shop charge-out rate of $45 per hour. The shop billed 274 hours in two months although the employee was paid for 346 hours, or 79 percent of actual paid time. Therefore, 21 percent of his paid time was not billable.

In the second quarter, two full-time employees were paid $20 an hour and one part-time employee was paid $16 an hour. In addition, one part-time shop worker was hired at $12 an hour. The shop billed $47,950, or 1,065 hours at $45 an hour, and paid wages for 1,560 hours. Therefore, using the financial information found in this exercise, it reflects that the employees were 68 percent productive. The owner should monitor labor productivity to ensure it meets projections, planning for a 32 percent nonproductive factor. If more billable hours were projected, now is the time to find out why productivity has decreased.

The purchase price of new parts and equipment normally fluctuates as suppliers offer specials during the busy selling seasons. Although more product is sold, the gross profit margins are significantly lower. Better discounts are offered on larger orders. Therefore, the cost of new equipment and parts will vary, and this is reflected in the cost of sales percentages. These costs should be watched to ensure they remain consistent with projections.

3. Gross profit

Gross profit is calculated by deducting direct costs from sales before overhead. Cost of sales is key to a profitable operation as gross profits pay for all other expenses. The gross profit of $50,180 for six months reflects an average of $8,363 per month. In the first three months, the gross profit totals only $11,200, hardly enough to pay the rent and owner's salary. This is common with seasonal businesses, so an astute owner will have an off-season contingency plan.

In the second quarter, gross profit has dropped from 49.8 percent to 45.2 percent, a decrease of nearly $4,000. The six-month average reflects a 46.2 percent gross profit. In this case, the owner was assuming a gross profit of 50 percent, so he should study the messages the figures are telling him to evaluate why gross profits have dropped four percent.

CATCH COSTLY ERRORS QUICKLY

Use your financial figures not only to review past performance, but to plot future profits. The more accounting figures are reviewed, particularly the cost of sales, the sooner the reasons for unprofitability can be pinpointed, before valuable profits are frittered away.

4. Overhead

On reviewing the overhead expenses for Snappy Lawn Equipment Inc. in Figure 4.4 on page 74, you will find that with operating a retail location and being both a service and retail business, overhead costs are high. Snappy's owner is running a fairly tight ship and understands the need to spend money on advertising and promotion. While overhead expenses can be marginally lowered, the most viable solution is to work on increasing sales, productivity, and profitability.

In Snappy's case, higher wages because of inefficient administrative systems contributed to lower productivity. Because the business deals in thousands of parts, copious time was spent searching for suppliers in the various catalogs and microfiche records. The solution was to find an efficient inventory program and supplier database. Once in place, employee productivity increased dramatically, with unproductive paid hours reduced by ten percent. In six months, this increased gross profits by over $5,000.

KNOW YOUR BREAK-EVEN POINT

Most businesses experience seasonal peaks and lows that affect cash flow. There are times when you need more capital to purchase inventory and times when business is either too slow or too busy. To operate efficiently, you need to know how much it costs to open your doors. Even a small home-based business incurs monthly costs that have to be paid for from gross profits.

How do you use this information?

If you don't know what your monthly overhead expenses are, you could be spending money that you shouldn't. Documenting your break-even point is essential for comparing actual expenses to projected ones and for upgrading your business plan. Even if you don't use a business plan—although we shall assume that you do—knowing your break-even point allows you to monitor daily, weekly, and monthly sales.

Reviewing overhead costs will reveal the months when cash flow will be tight. Astute financial planning is necessary to survive these difficult months. Figure 4.4 shows an example of how Snappy Lawn Equipment Services Inc. calculated its break-even point.

MONITOR CHANGING COSTS

If any of your operating costs significantly change—either increasing or decreasing—recalculate your break-even point to reflect those changes. There may be some months when your break-even point is higher—or lower—due to seasonal changes, such as more or fewer employees to align with seasonal demands. You may have to calculate two or three break-even points if you are subject to seasonal peaks and ebbs.

Figure **4.4**

Snappy Lawn Equipment Services Inc.
Break-Even Point Calculation

	Six months actual		One-month average		First quarter actual	
Sales:	$108,730		18,121		22,470	
Less cost of sales:	58,550		9,758		11,270	
Gross profit:	50,180	46%	8,363	46%	11,200	50%
Overhead expenses:						
Accounting fees	900		150		450	
Advertising	3,150		525		1,575	
Bad debt allowance	600		100		100	
Bank charges	510		85		255	
Computer supplies	330		55		165	
Employee benefits	6,000		1,200		2,400	
Freight	390		65		195	
Fees, licenses & taxes	210		35		105	
Insurance	450		75		225	
Loan interest	1,980		330		990	
Management fees	8,000		2,000		2,000	
Marketing & promotion	1,350		225		675	
Office supplies	720		120		360	
Office wages	2,250		450		900	
Promotion – meals	450		75		225	
Rent	6,600		1,100		3,300	
Repairs – equipment	600		50		150	
Repairs – store	600		50		150	
Security system	210		35		105	
Seminars, trade shows	600		50		150	
Sign rental	390		65		195	
Small tools	600		100		300	
Shop supplies & gas	600		100		300	
Telephone, fax, cell	1,500		250		750	
Utilities	1,050		175		525	
Vehicle – gas	1,380		230		660	
Vehicle – insurance	600		100		300	
Vehicle – repairs	600		100		300	
Vehicle – lease	2,100		350		1,050	
Workers' compensation	850		170		340	
Total overhead:	45,570		8,415		19,195	
Average gross profit:	50,180		8,363		11,200	
Shortage/surplus:	$ 4,610		(52)		(7,995)	

Break-even point analysis

Snappy needs to generate sales of $18,300 a month to pay all expenses. The business is currently operating at a break-even point. The first three months reflect sales of $22,470, with monthly overhead costs of $8,415. The overhead factor alone costs $25,245 for three months, plus $11,270 for the cost of sales. This means a shortfall of $14,045 in cash flow. This shortage is remedied within the next three months but a contingency should be in place to finance the quieter months

The six-month figures show net profits of $4,610, but only because employees were laid off during the quieter months and management reduced their salaries by $4,000. Without this salary reduction, the business would not have made a profit as many costs, such as rent, cannot be reduced.

Possible solutions

If this business operates at break-even point for the first six months of the year—which traditionally are the busiest—it is quite feasible that the next six months will reflect a loss. The owner needs to seriously consider ways to remedy this situation, including these tactics:

- review marketing strategies to see if current methods are generating the expected sales
- review the staffing structure to ensure each employee is working to maximum efficiency
- review overhead costs and trim unnecessary expenses
- research ways to diversify the business or to increase sales
- continue to reduce the owner's salary during quieter months
- review administrative and shop systems to pinpoint inefficient or time-wasting tasks.

Could Snappy diversify?

Creative marketing strategies can increase sales. Perhaps a pickup and delivery service could be offered, or used mowers offered as replacements during the repair period. These service-oriented incentives could help to increase business.

A customer database should be established and customers reminded by phone to bring in their equipment for service. Snappy could submit bids to landscaping companies offering to repair their equipment. Perhaps an investment in some snow- or debris-removal equipment would pay off. Services could then be contracted out to businesses with customer car parks or people needing clean-up work. Of course, all ideas first require some market research.

USE CONSERVATIVE CALCULATIONS

••••••••••••••••••••••••••••••••

As a general rule, a service business should calculate to bill an average of four to five hours a day. It doesn't sound like much, but if you remember the long list of other jobs you have to do, the hours quickly disappear. It is better to be conservative in your calculations than to over-project your income and not be able to meet commitments.

Your Business's Break-Even Point

The highest percentage of small businesses are service-oriented, followed by retail, manufacturing, and distribution. No matter which type of business you own, you must know your break-even point. Following are some simple calculations to help you establish and monitor yours.

Service businesses

Service businesses usually generate most of their income through billable hours. The misconception with these businesses is that you can bill eight hours a day—which you can't, unless you work long days and eventually become a burnout candidate.

To calculate the break-even point of your service business, list the monthly operating overhead costs. Once these figures are established, make the following calculation, which allows for twenty working days a month. This exercise demonstrates that two hours a day must be billed to cover overhead costs, and four hours a day to make a profit of $2,900. Any hours billed over this amount are a bonus, as shown in Figure 4.5.

Figure 4.5

Example of Break-Even Point Calculation: Service Businesses

Monthly overhead costs:	$2,730 divided by
Hourly billing rate:	$65
Equals hours to pay overhead:	42 per month
Minimum hours a day to bill:	2.1 (20 working days)

$65 per hour x 4 hours a day x 5 days a week x 4.33 weeks =

Gross sales:	$5,630
Monthly overhead:	2,730
Net profit and owner's wage:	$2,900

Retail, manufacturing, or distribution

Businesses that rely on fixed gross profit margins can easily establish their break-even point. For example, bookstores work on an average of a 40 percent gross profit margin. Snappy, as both a service and a retail business, would make the calculation as shown in Figure 4.6.

Figure 4.6

Break-Even Point: Snappy Lawn Equipment Services Inc.

Projected gross profit margin	46%
Projected overhead costs per month:	$ 8,415
Divide $8,415 by 46% =	$18,293

To check:

Gross sales to break-even = $18,293 x 46% = $8,415

Knowledge is motivational

Knowing your break-even point is not only essential, it is motivational. By dividing the required monthly sales by 4.33 weeks, you now have a weekly sales target. You can break the figure down even further into a daily goal. If you are experiencing regular days when the break-even point is not being met, ask yourself: "Why am I opening the doors? To pay the landlord? How can I increase sales on these slow days?" A retail store should at least cover overhead costs and management salaries each day.

Now is the time to calculate or review the break-even point for your business. Use either the last financial statement or tax return information, ensuring the overhead cost is up-to-date. List the current monthly overhead costs of your business as shown in Snappy's example and complete Figure 4.7.

Figure 4.7

Calculate Your Break-Even Point

Service industries:

Monthly overhead including owner's wage:	$_____	
Hourly billing rate:	$_____	
No. hours monthly to pay overhead:	$_____	A
No. hours weekly: divide A by 4.33	$_____	B
No. hours per day: divide B by 5 or 6 days	$_____	

Retail, manufacturing or distribution:

Gross profit margin percentage:	$_____	
Monthly overhead including owner's wages:	$_____	
Divide overhead by _____ percent	$_____	
Gross sales to break-even:	$_____	A
Weekly sales: divide A by 4.33	$_____	B
Daily sales: divide B by 5 or 6 days	$_____	

HOW TO DECIPHER A BALANCE SHEET

An income statement tells only one side of the story. To get the complete picture, you must understand the components of a balance sheet. This lists the assets, liabilities, and equity of the business at the time the statements were prepared. A business may have many assets, but if the liabilities are high and profits low, then you need to know why.

Snappy's six-month balance sheet as shown in Figure 4.8 tells us valuable information that couldn't be found on the income statement. Banks take particular interest in balance sheets as they reflect the overall management and performance of the business.

It is surprising how few small business owners understand the importance of the messages that a balance sheet sends. Make it a point to get to know yours intimately and compare the results regularly.

Figure 4.8

Snappy Lawn Equipment Services Inc.
Balance Sheet

BALANCE SHEET AS OF JUNE 30, 20__
(Unaudited)

ASSETS

  Current assets:

Cash at bank	$ 4,280	
Accounts receivable	17,900	
Inventories	62,300	
Prepaid expenses	2,100	86,580

continued

Fixed assets:

Computers	6,200	
Vehicle	2,000	
Equipment	18,200	
Furniture & fittings	8,300	
Leasehold improvements	4,900	
	39,600	
Less accumulated depreciation:	(19,300)	20,300

Other assets:

Incorporation fees		750
TOTAL ASSETS:		**$107,630**

LIABILITIES

Current liabilities:

Accounts payable	$ 44,700	
Sales taxes payable	3,800	
Withholdings payable	2,450	
Current portion long-term debt	10,450	61,400

Long-term liabilities:

Bank indebtedness	32,350	
Shareholder's loans	36,470	68,820
		$130,220

SHAREHOLDER'S EQUITY (DEFICIENCY)

Capital stock		$ 100
Retained earnings	(27,300)	
Net profit (loss for period)	4,610	(22,690)
TOTAL LIABILITIES & EQUITY:		**$107,630**

THE BALANCE SHEET SHOWS...

Current assets (items that can be converted to cash within twelve months)

Snappy's **bank account** is not healthy considering the trade suppliers that need to be paid. Fortunately, much of Snappy's business is cash, and the account is replenished daily. If the **accounts receivable** customers were analyzed, it would show that over 60 percent of the money is over forty-five days due and that many accounts are over ninety days due. Attention is not being paid to collections.

Most of Snappy's cash is tied up in **inventory**, which is not moving as fast as was planned. It is important to keep fast-moving items in stock and to closely monitor increasing inventory levels. The **prepaid expenses** *(expenses paid in advance of the current fiscal period)* consist of a lease deposit and insurance. During the next fiscal period, the applicable prepaid expenses are allocated to that period by your accountant using an accounting general journal entry and will not show as an asset but as an expense.

Fixed assets (assets owned by company, not for resale, value per item over $100)

Although the books show a purchase value of $39,600, the assets have depreciated to half their original worth and now have a **net book value** after accumulated depreciation and leasehold amortization of $20,300. The **total assets** of the business are valued at $107,630.

Current liabilities (any debt due and payable within twelve months)

The **accounts payable** represent unpaid trade suppliers. Many of the accounts are slipping into ninety days because of high inventory levels and poor collections. If the suppliers' terms are not met, the business could endanger its credit rating. The **sales taxes** and **employee withholdings** are payable in July, so cash should be made available by then.

The **current portion of the long-term debt** represents the principal portion of the bank loan due to be paid within twelve months. This loan was incurred to purchase equipment and to help finance the inventory.

Long-term liabilities (debts due to be paid over a term longer than one year)

The **bank loan** must be repaid in full in four years, with principal and interest payments amounting to nearly $1,200 a month. The capital injected by the shareholder is recorded in the **shareholder's loan**. Banks would be pleased to see that the shareholder has put a substantial amount into the business.

Shareholder's equity (capital shares, accumulated profits or losses)

The shareholder has issued **capital stock** of 100 shares at a par value of $1 each. The business has been operational for two years, and the **retained earnings** show accumulated losses of $27,300. Some of this is attributed to start-up costs and some to operational losses. The profit for the period reduced the losses by $4,610.

Summary

The **working capital** *(current assets less current liabilities)* seems healthy at $25,180; however, the business is operating in a loss situation and has too much money tied up in accounts receivable and inventory. There are many factors that would concern a bank on reading these statements. At this stage, an allowance has not been made for depreciation, which will reduce profits when the statements are prepared at year-end. Management should be concerned, as it will take some sound business decisions to keep the business viable. Following are some suggestions to keep profits on track.

WATCH YOUR MARGINS

It's easy to let small price increases get away from you—what's a few cents here or there? But if you are dealing in a variety of products and the competition is aggressive, it is surprising how easily small margin decreases become large ones.

INCREASE YOUR GROSS PROFIT MARGINS

Without healthy gross profits, there isn't enough left to cover overhead costs. Many operators make the mistake of not watching their cost of sales or performing some simple and regular job costing. The main factors that slowly erode profits are listed in Figure 4.9; check those that apply to you—these areas need attention.

Figure 4.9

Gross Profit Erosion Factors

Common problem	Review?
1. Starting with low prices to attract customers	☐
2. Not increasing prices when raw material costs increase	☐
3. Wage increases	☐
4. Freight, duty, and brokerage increases	☐
5. Offering too many specials or discounts	☐
6. Too much slow-moving inventory	☐
7. Fear of losing customers if prices increase	☐
8. Not increasing prices because of competition	☐
9. Inefficient production equipment	☐
10. High wastage or spoilage factor	☐

What is the solution?

There is often no easy solution to increasing profit margins. If you started in a highly competitive business or if more competitors moved into the area, you have some work ahead. Using effective marketing techniques to improve sales and exposure is necessary, as is recalculating costs when raw material or other costs increase. Schedule some regular focused time into your planner, as explained in Chapter 3, to review costs and profit margins. That is working on your business, not just in it.

Having a panic attack and spending fruitless dollars on a huge advertising campaign is not the answer. Spending $2,000 on advertising at a 40 percent gross margin means that $5,000 in sales must be generated to cover this cost. Start by looking in-house and take Figure 4.10, the "Twenty-Question Profitability Checklist."

STOP, LOOK, AND OBSERVE

How can you improve your profit margins? Sometimes you just need a gentle reminder to stop and take a long, hard look at your business. Our economy is always changing; it is constantly affected by the international, national, and local economies, consumer trends, and changing technology. Are you keeping up with the times?

REVIEW YOUR CURRENT OVERHEAD

If you don't peruse your financial figures regularly, why don't you start now? Waiting until year-end is too late. Update the figures, sit down with your accountant, and review your current overhead costs carefully, particularly expenses where you do have control—you can't control rent, but you can control marketing and some office costs. See where you are being frivolous and trim those unnecessary expenses. Often, overhead expenses have increased, not because something was needed but because it was wanted. There is a difference.

IS YOUR OVERHEAD OUT OF CONTROL?

As competition increases and technology changes, overhead becomes even more difficult to control. We used to manage with just telephones; now we need faxes, voice mail, extra phone services, email, pagers, cell phones, Internet service providers, and websites, to name a few. Time and money are spent replying to these communications, learning new programs, and upgrading computer equipment.

Marketing efforts have to be stepped up to stay competitive, and production equipment must be upgraded to increase efficiency and keep prices competitive. Often, overhead costs are incurred without the owner first calculating whether the business can sustain the extra cost. Before committing to extra expenses, answer the questions in Figure 4.11, the "Twenty-Question 'Do I Need It?' Checklist" at the end of this chapter.

Figure *4.10*

Twenty-Question Profitability Checklist

	Yes	No
1. Am I purchasing raw materials at competitive prices?	☐	☐
2. Are there suppliers who can offer better prices?	☐	☐
3. Could I streamline production or distribution costs?	☐	☐
4. Is inventory slow-moving and often unprofitable?	☐	☐
5. Could I afford to replace inefficient equipment?	☐	☐
6. Could employee productivity be increased?	☐	☐

	Yes	No
7. Would an employee incentive program help?	☐	☐
8. Could I diversify my products or services?	☐	☐
9. Could I offer better service to my customers?	☐	☐
10. Is my discount structure too high?	☐	☐
11. Could I lower discounts without losing customers?	☐	☐
12. Am I monitoring my marketing efforts carefully?	☐	☐
13. Am I using unproductive marketing techniques?	☐	☐
14. Is it time to change marketing strategies?	☐	☐
15. Is the competition becoming too powerful?	☐	☐
16. Can I afford to offer something that the competition doesn't?	☐	☐
17. Am I effectively networking?	☐	☐
18. Am I keeping up with technological changes?	☐	☐
19. Am I monitoring increasing costs carefully?	☐	☐
20. Are consumer trends adversely affecting my business?	☐	☐

PLAN FOR YOUR FUTURE

Don't just think about the future of your business; think about your own current and future financial stability. By regularly monitoring your progress and keeping accounting records up-to-date, you are better able to plan for growth, taxes, and retirement.

Seven Tips
for Successful Planning

1. As a rough rule of thumb, take 15 percent of net sales each month and put it into a separate bank account toward corporate taxes or future asset purchases.

2. Plan for 10 percent of your paycheck to be deposited into a monthly retirement tax-savings account.

continued

3. Review business assets that need purchasing. If you purchase them before your corporate year-end, you can take advantage of the depreciation.

4. Before year-end, review other expenses that will incur just after year-end. Perhaps a vehicle or equipment needs repairing or you need a new brochure. If you have the cash flow, make those purchases before year-end to reduce your taxes payable.

5. Build a profitable business and build goodwill—a valuable asset. When you are ready to retire or move on and sell the business, the track record of the business and its ability to sustain good management wages and corporate profits determines the goodwill value.

6. Have a succession strategy. Approximately 75 percent of businesses close down when the principal owner becomes ill or dies. All that hard work for nothing! Plan who will take over the business or how it will be disposed of in the event of this situation arising. Have adequate life insurance on both your partner and yourself.

7. Have an exit strategy. If the business doesn't meet your financial expectations and starts to consistently lose money, know how you will dispose of it, how you will pay off the debts, and where you will stand financially if this happens.

Now you are controlling the financial reins

This chapter is designed to increase your financial knowledge and to show you how to put it to work for your business. Once you understand and utilize financial information, you will be in control of the financial reins. Chapter 5 shows you how to apply this knowledge to streamline other areas that may be eroding your profits.

Figure **4.11**

Twenty-Question "Do I Need It?" Checklist

	Yes	No
1. Will this expense help increase efficiency?	☐	☐
2. Will it save the business money?	☐	☐
3. Have I calculated how much money it will save?	☐	☐
4. Do I know how long it will take to produce profitable results?	☐	☐
5. Am I committing to a long-term lease or contract?	☐	☐
6. Can I make the payments if sales do not increase?	☐	☐
7. Am I currently operating above the break-even point?	☐	☐
8. Will this expense help to generate more sales or profit?	☐	☐
9. Will time be needed to educate staff?	☐	☐
10. Will any transition downtime be needed?	☐	☐
11. Can I manage without it and still maintain efficiency?	☐	☐
12. Will I be uncompetitive without it?	☐	☐
13. Is this just a status symbol purchase?	☐	☐
14. Will it need to be upgraded in the next few years?	☐	☐
15. Is the product covered by satisfactory warranties?	☐	☐
16. Am I aware of all the ongoing maintenance costs?	☐	☐
17. Will we incur serious downtime if the equipment breaks down?	☐	☐
18. Can I keep this new employee fully productive?	☐	☐
19. Is everyone working at maximum capacity before hiring new staff?	☐	☐
20. Will this new employee contribute to the bottom-line profits?	☐	☐

Figure **4.12**

Financial Control Checklist

As you work through the information in this chapter, check off each section when you fully understand it with a "yes." If you don't understand the information, check "no." Then make an appointment with your accountant to clarify what you don't understand or to discuss what needs attention.

Figure	Yes	No
4.1 The Six-Step Accounting Cycle	☐	☐
4.2 Chart of Accounts	☐	☐
4.3 Sales Analysis	☐	☐
4.4 Break-Even Point Calculation	☐	☐
4.5 Break-Even Point Calculation—Service Businesses	☐	☐
4.6 Break-Even Point Cross-Check	☐	☐
4.7 Calculate Your Break-Even Point	☐	☐
4.8 Balance Sheet	☐	☐
4.9 Gross Profit Erosion Factors	☐	☐
4.10 Twenty-Question Profitability Checklist	☐	☐
4.11 Twenty-Question "Do I Need It?" Checklist	☐	☐

CHAPTER FIVE

How Else Can You Increase Your Profits?

---◄○►---

The worst crime against working people is
a company which fails to operate at a profit.

SAMUEL GOMPERS

---◄○►---

Have you ever reviewed your year-end financial statements with your accountant, only to be told that the profits were less than you had expected? "How can this be?" you ask. "Sales have been good, and I'm trying to keep my overhead down. What else could be wrong?" An analysis of your accounting records will reveal where many problems lie. ❧

INCREASE PROFITS BY INCREASING EFFICIENCY

Although the expenses shown on the statements may be acceptable, if you investigate all your current administrative and operational systems, you may still find room for improvement. The key to an efficient operation is of course to work smarter, not harder.

Your business needs an informative administrative system that doesn't drown you or your employees in paperwork. Wasted time is wasted profit. Some businesses don't use detailed enough systems, while others overload themselves with time-wasting paper trails. Although computers have improved efficiency, learning new software frustrates many people. Some find change difficult and prefer to use time-consuming manual systems. Find a balance that gives you the necessary information with a minimum of fuss.

TAKE A SYSTEMS INVENTORY

There are some areas where efficiency can be easily achieved. Chapter 3 showed you how to organize your time, computer, and filing system. Figure 6.6, a checklist in Chapter 6, highlights operational areas that may need reevaluating. Consider these simple suggestions for streamlining your administrative system.

Accounting system

Chapter 4 explained how to use your accounting to increase profit margins and financial efficiency. If you use a manual system, consider changing to a computerized one. A well-designed system gives you all the information you need in less time with fewer errors.

Billing and collections

Accounting systems can accommodate either computer-generated or manual invoices. For a service business such as plumbing, writing invoices on the job is practical, but before data can be entered into the system, invoices have to be coded with an account number. To eliminate this time-waster, redesign your invoices to include preprinted account codes. See later in this chapter for more detailed collection information.

Accounts payable

Use an accounting program that produces an aged analysis of accounts payable. Update the payables weekly so that you have a current payables and receivables list. This saves time when sorting through invoices, and you can allocate your bill payments based on the receivables information.

Design a self-inking stamp with space for date received and a few blank expense account codes. When you have checked the invoice, break it down into the various expense categories and code the invoice. When you enter it into the payables ledger, the preparation work is completed.

Checks

For manually written checks, note the various expense amounts on each check stub. Keep a chart of accounts in the front of the checkbook and code the checks as you write them. This saves you from forgetting what the check was for and having to shuffle through the filing cabinet to find the invoice.

Payroll

Using a software payroll program is efficient as it calculates the paychecks, keeps a record of vacation pay, prints monthly payroll summary reports for employer withholding remittances, and prepares year-end payroll requirements.

USE A PAYROLL SERVICE
....

If you have a few full- or part-time employees, research the cost of using a payroll service. They are efficient time-savers, and the investment is minimal. They also prepare and send in employer tax remittances and prepare all year-end employee payroll records. If you use a manual system, reconcile the payroll monthly and maintain accumulative totals. This saves you from having to add pages of figures annually and allows you to catch and rectify any errors made during the month.

Ten Tips
for Saving Time and Money

1. **Accounting:** Keep detailed accounting records and source documents, so that at year-end, your accountant doesn't waste time and your money sorting out problems.

2. **Advertising:** Monitor and then calculate the financial ROI (return on investment) for each type of advertising and marketing that you do. If it isn't returning dividends, stop doing it.

3. **Bad debts:** Beef up collections so you don't have bad debts. Use the credit and collections strategies outlined in this chapter.

4. **Banking:** Hook up to Internet banking to transfer funds, pay certain bills, and get up-to-date statements to help plan cash flow. Use the night deposit safe for deposits so that you can bank at your convenience.

5. **Communications:** Assess how often cellular phones, pagers, and extra phone lines are used. Often, they are a wasted expense, and you may be able to cut back or find a better deal.

6. **Credit card charges:** Join your chamber of commerce or other business associations that offer cheap Visa and MasterCard rates. They often charge half of standard bank charges.

7. **Insurance policies:** Have your insurance agent review all your insurance policies for the correct coverage and for competitive rates. It's amazing how much you can save while still being sufficiently covered. Underinsuring is not worth the risk involved.

8. **Loan interest:** Shop around at other banks for cheaper loans and lines of credit. Banks are ferociously competitive and will often offer to beat their competitors.

9. **Long distance:** Shop around for companies offering cheap long distance phone service. Their rates are often well worth the change. Use their calling cards when traveling so you are billed at their cheap rate.

10. **Meals:** Assess each promotional meal and whether it is worth both your time and money. Sometimes a meeting over coffee or a scheduled phone conversation works just as well.

IS YOUR INVENTORY UNDER CONTROL?

No matter how efficiently you run your operation, if inventory isn't under tight control, then your financial figures won't be accurate. Inventory management is one of the biggest headaches for most businesses. Any business carrying an inventory relies on regular movement of goods sold at a certain gross profit to maintain the overhead expenses and generate a net profit.

Where inventory maintenance should be a top priority, it's often at the bottom of the list. By the time the problem is pinpointed to mismanaged inventory, thousands of dollars of profit can be lost. If inventory is too large or not turning over, cash flow is seriously reduced. Here are the secrets to efficiently managing inventory:

- prudent purchasing
- avoiding overstocking
- efficient stock control systems
- regular inventory turnaround
- minimal damages and wastage
- correct inventory costing at year-end
- close monitoring of theft
- regular checks of actual to theoretical inventory stocks

How does inventory dictate profits?

Quite simply, if your year-end inventory count is incorrect then the financial statements are wrong. Inventory is equivalent to cash in the bank—you wouldn't consciously throw money away, yet when it comes to inventory, this is exactly what happens. If you are not correctly accounting for wastage, damaged goods, or samples, your material purchase costs will appear inflated in comparison to actual sales. This mistake directly reduces gross profits.

By breaking down these costs, you can carefully monitor such expenses. If they are lumped in with your material purchase account, that cost will be inflated. Put systems into place to control these costly factors. Figure 5.1 shows three common scenarios contrasted with the reality. There is quite a difference in gross profit due to inventory errors.

Figure **5.1**

Inventory Error Comparisons

	Scenario 1 Inventory Overvalued	Scenario 2 Inventory Undervalued	Scenario 3 Purchases Inflated	The Reality Correct Figures
Sales	$152,000	152,000	152,000	152,000
Cost of sales:				
Opening inventory	32,000	32,000	32,000	32,000
Plus purchases	102,000	102,000	112,000	102,000
	134,000	134,000	144,000	134,000
Closing inventory	(52,000)	(43,000)	(47,000)	(47,000)
Cost of sales	82,000	91,000	97,000	87,000
Gross profit:	(46%) $ 70,000	(40%) 61,000	(36%) 55,000	(43%) 65,000

What happened?

1. _Inventory overvalued:_ By incorrectly overvaluing inventory at year-end, gross profits are overstated by $5,000.
2. _Inventory undervalued:_ By undervaluing the inventory, gross profits are understated by $4,000.
3. _Purchases inflated:_ By not separately accounting for damages, wastage, theft, personal use goods and samples, the cost of goods in relation to gross sales is $10,000 higher and there is no way to monitor these costs.

Ten Tips

for **Astute Inventory Control**

The worst mistake is to have little control. I have seen stores place goods directly on the shelves without checking packing slips and without pricing or recording the shipment into inventory. Review your system to see where you can improve.

1. Check for damaged goods or shortages upon delivery.

2. Check supplier invoices for correct quantity and pricing.

3. Implement a system to record receiving and shipping.

4. Make accounting allowances for damaged goods, wastage, personal use, and samples.

5. Perform regular spot checks to compare theoretical inventory to actual.

6. Compare your computer-generated theoretical tally to a thorough manual check at year-end.

7. Regularly compare computer records to actual inventory to adjust any minus quantities.

8. Count and cost inventory correctly.

9. Write off obsolete or unsaleable inventory at least annually.

10. Purchase inventory selectively so that it regularly turns over.

Which system will work for you?

Each business has different inventory management requirements, but the principles remain the same. Goods received are recorded into stock, and goods shipped are recorded out of stock. A manufacturer working with raw materials uses a

ALLOW FOR WASTAGE AND DAMAGES

Most businesses carrying inventory suffer damaged or spoiled goods. Specifically damaged product can be valued and written off, but in businesses such as restaurants or those selling plants, review your average monthly spoilage or wastage and calculate this into your cost of goods sold as a separate item. For example, a florist might allow five percent of floral purchases as a monthly spoilage allowance.

more detailed system than a retail store receiving finished goods. Various raw materials are used in manufacturing, so inventory will move from raw materials to partially completed work to finished goods, and your system must accommodate these transitions.

Manual system

A business dealing with small quantities of products may manage well using an index card system. These cards are designed to record the date of inventory movement, whom the product was shipped to, invoice number, whom goods were received from, and the item cost. Perform spot checks by taking the card and comparing its balance to actual stock.

Computer system

There are a variety of industry-specific inventory programs, many of which tie into accounting programs and other administrative functions. Be careful in your program selection as the wrong choice will create more work and frustration.

Whichever system you use, if your data entry is inaccurate, the resulting information is wrong. Imagine the embarrassment if a customer calls for an urgent product, the records show plenty of stock, and there is nothing on the shelves—or the reverse. Your system should include a regular review of inventory reports for errors.

HOW TO COUNT INVENTORY

An inventory software program *theoretically* counts and costs inventory. It is only accurate if the prices and quantities are correctly entered. At least annually, conduct a physical inventory count to evaluate its monetary cost for the financial statements. This job is probably the worst part of owning a business—next to paying taxes. Take these simple steps to ensure that the final figure is as accurate as possible.

Using an inventory program

1. At year-end, ensure that all sales invoices are processed and that invoiced goods awaiting shipment are not counted.

2. Close the premises to count or count at the end of a working day, always at month-end.

3. Always have two people count inventory together.

4. Print a full inventory report, ready to compare theoretical inventory to actual.

5. Design a sheet to record items that do not agree with the theoretical count. These need to be rechecked or recounted before the inventory is completed.

6. As each item is counted, if it agrees with the theoretical tally, check the item off.

7. If there is a problem, highlight the item and enter it on the checking sheet, including the item description, theoretical tally, physical tally, the difference, and a column for the correct amount.

8. When the correct amount has been established, transfer this information to the inventory sheet.

9. Correct your computer inventory records before the next trading day.

Using a manual system

The manual process is similar. Prepare an inventory tally sheet as shown in Figure 5.2, showing product description, theoretical quantity, physical quantity, a discrepancy column, the item price, and total value. When the physical count is complete, go back and adjust your manual records.

Figure 5.2

Glorious Gifts and Candles: December 31, 20__

Department: *Candles*   **Counted by:**   **Checked by:**
                                 John McKenzie   Sue Taylor

	Theoretical	Physical	Discrepancy	Item Price	Total
8" taper candles, blue	48	52	+4	.25	$13.00
8" taper candles, green	46	46	—	.25	11.50
9" rainbow candles	25	32	+7	.40	12.75
9" white candles	66	61	-5	.40	24.40
3" ball candles	15	15	—	.95	14.25
2" ball candles	12	13	+1	.75	9.75
Page total:	**212**	**219**	**+7**	—	**$85.65**

Real Life   What's in a Decimal Point?

While working as an office manager for a food manufacturing company in Australia, part of my job was to complete the inventory sheet calculations and send the accounting information to the accountant. One day he called, sounding most distressed. The gross profit seemed to be understated by nearly $20,000.

The accounting was thoroughly checked. All seemed in order. The last resort was to check the inventory sheets. Two people had counted and checked the inventory, so that was not the problem—however, the legibility of the inventory sheets turned out to be a huge problem. The plant supervisor didn't have the neatest of handwriting, and on closer scrutiny, a glaring error surfaced. Product that cost $25 a kilogram had been counted as 90.0 kilograms. Luckily, the factory manager realized that the stock would never run that low. The correct count was 900 kilograms. The error made a difference of $20,250 to the gross profit.

HOW TO COST INVENTORY

Cost items accurately

As the Real Life example illustrates, attention to detail in both counting and costing inventory is crucial. Record each item at purchase price and check the supplier's latest invoice for price corrections. Additional costs such as freight or duty are accounted for in other expense accounts. Once the sheets are extended, have the calculations checked by another person.

Account for obsolescence

The smart operator will sell slow-moving or obsolete items through clearance sales before the inventory count. There are still bound to be unsaleable items left that are tying up cash flow. Record these on a separate inventory sheet. Then decide whether they should be completely written off as a loss and disposed of, or their cost value reduced and then sold at a discounted rate.

When this decision has been made, total the amounts to be written off in full, the amount to be devalued, and by what percentage. Give this information to your accountant, who will then make the appropriate adjustments or even prepare these calculations for you.

How to record non-sale items

A portion of your inventory may never sell. These items become an overhead expense. It isn't difficult to apply simple systems to record these expenses.

1. *Samples:* Whether you manufacture chocolates or CDs, you probably offer samples to potential customers. These should be recorded as items coming out of inventory at cost and be charged to a "sample" account.

2. *Damaged products:* You can either reduce the price of a damaged item or

> ## USE TWO PEOPLE
> *The rule of counting inventory is to use two people, as one person may become bored or distracted and make errors. With inexpensive items, these errors could be negligible, but with larger or more costly items, one error may represent many dollars. Inventory sheets should be designed to ensure legibility, for illegibility often causes miscalculations, as clearly demonstrated in the Real Life example "What's in a Decimal Point?"*

KEEP A RECORD OF SAMPLES

If you give samples away, keep a monthly sample list, itemizing the product and cost. You now have a monthly dollar total for your accounting records. Promotional giveaways should be taken out of inventory and charged to a "marketing" account. Review these costs to ensure that you are not going wild with the freebies and blowing the budget.

dispose of it. If you reduce the price, start a "discount sales" account to monitor these occurrences. If you are writing off the full product cost, take it out of inventory and charge it to a "damaged product" account.

3. *Personal use items:* Sometimes management takes products for personal use or to give to employees. For personal use, deduct these products from inventory records and charge either your shareholder's loan or capital account. The same principle applies for products given to employees, only the expense is allocated to the promotion account. If products are exchanged for wages, the value is deducted from net wages payable and becomes taxable.

4. *Waste and spoilage:* Recording each spoilt item—such as food or flowers—is time-consuming. You should know the approximate amount of wastage, and in most cases you can use a set percentage of material costs to be calculated when your financial statements are prepared. Tell your accountant this percentage so that an adjustment can be made. Material costs will be reduced by the dollar amount and the spoilage account increased by the same amount.

5. *Theft:* Inventory theft is always a concern, so strict internal control and security monitoring—particularly for retail stores—is necessary. Retail stores also have to cope with shoplifting. It's often difficult to establish a dollar amount for theft. Where possible, estimate the amount, document the information for tax or court purposes, and give this information to your accountant.

Keep the records straight

Figure 5.3 gives some examples of non-sale accounting entries. These journal entries are first manually documented for audit purposes and then entered to the general ledger. You can now monitor these expenses and include them in your budgets and projections. If any areas are of real concern, they will come to your attention as you read your financial statements.

Figure 5.3

Inventory Accounting Journal Entries

Adjustment	Account	Debit	Credit
1. January samples to customers	Purchases		$346.00
Sample product from inventory	Samples	$346.00	
2. January promotional product	Purchases		225.00
Promotional product from inventory	Marketing	225.00	
3. Damaged SnoozeKing 6' queen	Purchases		155.00
January damaged mattress	Damages	155.00	
4. 26" television taken by M. James	Purchases		379.00
Shareholder's loan, M. James	Shareholder	379.00	
5. 1 - Boomcity stereo to employee	Purchases		145.00
Wages, Terry Johnstone	Wages payable	145.00	
6. January 5% spoilage allowance	Purchases		975.00
5% of $19,500 purchases	Spoilage	975.00	
7. January theft allowance	Purchases		400.00
2% of $20,000 gross sales	Theft	400.00	
8. Sharp Shot 35mm camera stolen	Purchases		125.00
Missing from front display, 05/07	Theft	125.00	

ARE YOUR CUSTOMERS PAYING YOU?

The average new entrepreneur pays little attention to setting and enforcing credit policies. It's exciting enough to have new customers; why upset them by discussing money? They may choose to go elsewhere. As time passes, outstanding receivables mount, cash flow doesn't, and you are unable to pay suppliers on time. Never be too busy to focus on collections as businesses can go bankrupt overnight. It happens all the time.

EXTEND CREDIT

·····································

Where retailers have the luxury of collecting cash or credit card payments, most businesses usually have little choice but to extend credit to align themselves with both the competition and industry standards.

SET CREDIT POLICIES

Cash flow is the essential lifeline for a healthy business. If you haven't already set credit policies, now is the time. Customers prefer to know the cost and your payment terms; in fact, they respect you more if these terms are clearly stated.

Don't be hasty in extending credit without carefully reviewing all the factors and consequences. Businesses have gone bankrupt because they trusted one large customer or didn't monitor their accounts closely enough. If you haven't any formal credit policies, answer the questions in Figure 5.4, "The Thirty-Question Credit Questionnaire," to help you decide whether extending credit is a viable proposition for your business.

Figure **5.4**

The Thirty-Question Credit Questionnaire

1. Can you afford to extend credit?
2. What percentage of sales income can you afford to have tied up in accounts receivable?
3. Are you currently experiencing problems with slow-paying customers?
4. Are you currently handling your collections efficiently?
5. Are your methods successful?
6. Is there room for improvement?
7. What is the most credit you can afford to extend to a single customer?
8. Do you have a line of credit or other arrangements with your bank if needed?
9. Will your bank finance accounts receivable if necessary?
10. Have you discussed credit policies with your bank manager?
11. Are you conversant with standard industry credit policies?
12. Will extending credit affect payments to suppliers?
13. Is your current cash flow situation healthy?

14. What credit policy will you set? Thirty days from invoice date or thirty days from the month of purchase?
15. What action will you take when accounts exceed your credit terms?
16. Will you charge interest on overdue accounts?
17. Is your accounting software capable of automatically adding interest to accounts?
18. Will you reverse unpaid interest if a customer pays an account without paying the interest?
19. At what point will you hold shipments?
20. Will you ask for COD payments until an account is up-to-date?
21. Who will handle collection calls?
22. Will you send monthly statements?
23. Do you have the staff available for these extra accounting chores?
24. Do you have a lawyer to handle letters to overdue accounts?
25. Are you willing to go through the small claims process?
26. Do you understand the small claims process?
27. Will you offer a discount for payment in seven, ten, or fourteen days?
28. What discount percentage can you afford to offer?
29. Do you currently offer credit card or debit card facilities?
30. Can you afford to offer a discount percentage to customers who pay promptly?

HOW TO USE CREDIT APPLICATIONS

Few small businesses bother to use credit applications because it involves another "time-consuming" chore. Don't take this attitude—look at it as income protection. You would be amazed at what you will discover when you start talking to trade references. An excellent customer's payments may have suddenly slowed down—always a warning signal—and credit references should tell you this information.

When a new customer requires credit, tell them you would be pleased to extend credit subject to a credit application being completed and approved in no more than two days. Explain your terms and discount structure for timely payments.

A credit application asks for the following information:

- how long a business has been operating
- its corporate structure and owners' names
- three trade references
- customer's banking information
- the names of signing officers
- the credit limit the customer is seeking

Businesses are usually quite happy to supply trade references. When you call, ask for the person responsible for accounts receivable. Politely introduce yourself and your business and ask if it would be convenient to request a credit reference on one of their customers. When you have the information, don't forget to thank them.

Ten Topical Questions for Credit Checks

Ask the following questions to ensure a thorough credit check.

1. How long has the customer been trading with the supplier?

2. How regularly do they purchase from the supplier?

3 On average, what do they spend each month?

4. Do they pay within the stated terms of credit?

5. Are they consistently late or on time?

6. Have purchasing levels noticeably increased or decreased in the last six months?

7. Have payments become noticeably tardy within the last six months?

8. Have any of their checks ever been returned NSF?

9. Has credit ever been refused for any reason?

10. Does the supplier have any particular concerns with this customer?

Set credit limits

You can now set a credit limit—the maximum amount of credit that you are prepared to extend—based on this information. If a higher limit is required and you don't feel comfortable, discuss the matter. Explain that your company sets limits based on current credit information. Assure the customer that you will be happy to review this limit in the near future. You then have time to assess their payment performance.

> ### JOIN A CREDIT REPORTING AGENCY
> ....
> *Because business can be so volatile, a wise investment is to join a credit reporting agency such as Dun and Bradstreet. You then have access to regularly updated customer credit information, history, and reports.*

MONITOR ACCOUNTS RECEIVABLE

The key to successfully monitoring credit limits is in reviewing and updating the receivable aging list and ledger regularly, as last month's list doesn't take into account current purchases. Monitor current orders before they are filled to ensure they don't exceed the limit. If a new order does, call the customer and let them know, as was done in the Real Life example "Cutting Off the Credit" on page 106. Perhaps they could deliver a check to update the account; most customers will respect your wishes and comply.

Develop a daily collections system

The more accounts you carry, the more crucial it is that you use a daily collections system to keep the checks arriving and the cash flowing. The following is an effective example of a daily routine.

1. Write up the bank deposit daily.
2. Note and follow up on any anomalies, such as short payments or discounts.
3. Mark each check off your aged receivable list.
4. Review the aged receivable list for overdue accounts.
5. Phone customers with a gentle reminder.
6. On the aged receivables list, note the date that they promised to send you payment.
7. If the check has not arrived by that date, make another phone call.
8. Note any comments or promised payment dates on the aged receivable list.
9. If there appears to be a payment problem, start a collection file for the account.
10. If you are concerned, notify shipping to put a hold on all orders.
11. Notify the customer that shipments are on hold until the account is brought up-to-date.
12. If it is obvious that the account is not being paid, be prepared to take further action.

Real Life) Cutting Off the Credit

In a past life, when I was office manager for a distribution company with over 500 accounts, one of my main jobs was credit control. The above daily collections system was most effective. On one occasion, I had no choice but to put the largest customer's shipment on hold. They were an important account as they represented 40 percent of the company's sales, but their payments had recently started slipping. Their account was well overdue and the promised check had not arrived. Meanwhile, their truck still arrived to pick up an order and was sent away empty. It returned in the afternoon with the check.

The funny side to this story was that I later became a victim of the recession and applied for a job as a credit manager, which turned out to be at that same company whose order I'd held. The interviewer was the boss to whom I had refused to ship the order. We laughed in retrospect, and he commented that he had respected me for making that decision. No—I didn't get the job, but came a close second. Collections are becoming small businesses's biggest headache, so take care of your cash.

Month-end receivables procedure

1. Close off the month. Complete month-end closing procedures as soon as possible. Regular posting throughout the month will speed up this process. On the first of each month, all debts become a month older. Be sure that all sales invoices, credit notes, bank deposits, and journal entries are posted, then run your month-end reports.

2. Update the aged receivable list and send statements. Prepare the aged receivable list, itemizing each unpaid invoice by customer and amount into current, thirty, sixty, ninety days, and over. Review any bank deposits received since the first of the new month. Cross these payments off both the aged analysis and the customers' statements. Before mailing the statements, check each one for accuracy and account status.

3. Prepare account reminders. If customers need a gentle reminder, use a self-inking stamp with the message "this account is overdue." Personally signed, polite and to the point handwritten messages to customers you know is quite effective. "Dear Steven, I noticed your account is a little overdue. Is there a problem? Please let me know. Thanks, Jeff." Remember the squeaky wheel.

Include a thank-you message on your statements for checks that may cross in the mail. It could read: "If you have sent payment that is not yet credited to your account, please accept our thanks." Monthly statements help both parties keep better records and often alert customers to missing invoices or account problems.

4. Start collections. Once the statements are mailed, review the aged receivable list, starting at the ninety days and over columns. Call each account, discuss the overdue amount and note any promised payments or other information. If customers request invoice copies, fax them immediately and note this on the list. Work your way through to sixty and thirty days overdue until everyone is called.

WHAT IF YOUR CUSTOMERS DON'T PAY?

There will be always be customers with cash flow difficulties. If they are honest with you, discuss an alternative payment plan. If messages are ignored or you are worried about their financial stability, send a first "account overdue" letter as set out in Chapter 9.

USE A THIRD PARTY

If you don't want any more of a customer's business, use a collection agency. They work on a percentage of the debt, which increases with the debt's age. Having a third party deal with slow payers is often all the clout you will need. A lawyer's letter usually has even more impact.

Now you have started a paper trail. If there is no response, send a second letter. You may have to resort to sending a legal letter, using a collection agency, or filing a small claims action.

Some customers may want to pay but don't have the money. Never ship goods until satisfactory arrangements have been made as it's no use risking further debt. If the customer promises to send postdated or regular checks, and honors their commitment, you decide: do you allow further credit or do you keep them on a COD basis? Only you can make that decision.

Legal action—the last resort

Legal action is a tedious, drawn-out, time-consuming, expensive, unrewarding, and frustrating process. Having processed a few small debt claims, I speak from experience. Although each case was resolved, obtaining payment from penniless people wasn't exactly fun.

Even if you win the case, collecting the debt is another matter. People with knowledge of the judicial system can stretch payments out over a period of years. You might as well forget the whole thing and write it off as a bad debt and a learning experience.

HEED THE WARNING SIGNS

The art of collections is to heed the warning signs of financial problems and stop supplying further goods—no matter how long you have dealt with the customer and how much you trust them. Be persistent in contacting customers before their cash stops flowing.

Document all details

Immediately after a problem arises, start a file and document every detail, promise, conversation, and action. Legal cases are won on documented evidence. The more evidence you produce, the better the odds. For lesser amounts, small claims court is often not worth the bother, but for larger amounts, you might as well have your day or two in court.

Bad debts and your accounting records

An account is considered a bad debt when it is deemed uncollectible or if it has been outstanding for over twelve months. Bankruptcies or a business disappearing overnight are examples of cut-and-dried cases. Some debts are dubious because although they are not twelve months old, you know payment is doubtful. Here are three different accounting scenarios for bad debts.

1. Bad debt expense. In the case of a bankruptcy, closure, or debt owing over twelve months, the whole amount of the debt is written off. Accounts receivable are credited to clear the amount owing, and a "bad debt" account is debited. This now becomes an overhead expense and is subtracted from net profits.

2. Recaptured bad debts. If the gods are with you, some bad debts may be repaid in part or full during the following fiscal year. Your accounting entry would then debit "bank" and credit a revenue account called "recaptured bad debts." The expense you deducted last year now becomes taxable income in the year of repayment.

3. Allowance for doubtful accounts. Most businesses carrying accounts receivables make an annual allowance for bad debts. This is usually a percentage of gross sales, ascertained by a historical average. If you gross $100,000 a year, from experience you may estimate that $2,000, or 2 percent, will be uncollectible. At year-end, a general journal entry is prepared, debiting the bad debt account with this amount and crediting the allowance for doubtful accounts account.

IMPROVE YOUR ADMINISTRATIVE EFFICIENCY

This chapter highlights many hidden areas that contribute to profit or efficiency reductions. To help you analyze how efficient your current systems are, complete the checklist in Figure 5.5 on page 110. Where you answer "needs work," make a point of fixing the problems. Then go back and check the "completed" column.

At this stage, if you implement the systems and advice in the last five chapters, your business will operate at peak efficiency. You will be working smarter. Next, you must decide whether you are content to remain your current size or whether you are ready for physical growth. Read Chapter 6 to ascertain whether physical growth is right for you.

Figure **5.5**

Administrative Efficiency Checklist

	Needs work	Under control	Completed
Accounting system:			
1. Producing accurate, efficient monthly reports	☐	☐	☐
2. Sales invoices precoded for data entry	☐	☐	☐
3. Receivables updated at least once a week	☐	☐	☐
4. Accounts payable updated at least once a week	☐	☐	☐
5. Accounts payable coded on receipt	☐	☐	☐
6. Check stubs coded on payment of accounts	☐	☐	☐
7. Payroll cumulatively reconciled each month	☐	☐	☐
8. Paper-flow systems streamlined and efficient	☐	☐	☐
9. Monitoring all marketing ROI	☐	☐	☐
10. Investigated cheaper credit card bank fees	☐	☐	☐
Inventory system:			
1. Supplier packing slips and invoices checked	☐	☐	☐
2. Theoretical inventory system in place	☐	☐	☐
3. All goods received entered to inventory	☐	☐	☐
4. All goods shipped taken from inventory	☐	☐	☐
5. Regular inventory spot checks performed	☐	☐	☐
6. Computer inventory checked for minus tallies	☐	☐	☐
7. Slow-moving stock regularly cleared on sale	☐	☐	☐
8. Accurate year-end counting system in place	☐	☐	☐
9. Computer prices regularly checked	☐	☐	☐
10. Two people count inventory together	☐	☐	☐
11. Sample product is recorded correctly	☐	☐	☐
12. Damages and waste are recorded correctly	☐	☐	☐
13. Personal goods from inventory recorded	☐	☐	☐
14. Anti-theft systems installed	☐	☐	☐
Credit and collections:			
1. Credit policies established	☐	☐	☐
2. Credit application forms used	☐	☐	☐
3. Trade references always checked	☐	☐	☐
4. Thirty-question credit check completed	☐	☐	☐
5. Joined a credit reporting service	☐	☐	☐
6. Receivables aging list updated daily	☐	☐	☐
7. Collection calls made at least once a week	☐	☐	☐
8. Contacted a lawyer for collection purposes	☐	☐	☐
9. Contacted a reputable collections agency	☐	☐	☐
10. Aware of small claims court procedures	☐	☐	☐
11. Initiated efficient daily collection system	☐	☐	☐
12. Use monthly statements	☐	☐	☐
13. Established an annual bad debt percentage	☐	☐	☐

CHAPTER SIX

Are You Ready for Growth?

---◄○►---

The future comes one day at a time.
DEAN ACHESON

---◄○►---

After speaking to thousands of entrepreneurs, many who had prepared a formal business plan, I have found that most of them have one comment in common: "The business turned out nothing like my business plan projected—I had to keep changing it." Funny how life does that to us, always getting in the way of our best-laid plans.

DID YOUR PLAN GO TO PLAN?

The smart entrepreneurs are those who use a plan and are willing to revisit it often. No matter how long you have been in business, planning should be an integral and important part of your management strategy. When it's done correctly, growing a small business is an exciting experience. You know you are taking positive steps toward success while feeling a sense of accomplishment, increased confidence, and greater self-esteem. You have worked hard to come this far and deserve the rewards. Planned growth is exhilarating—uncontrolled growth is chaotic.

For some, growth suddenly sneaks up on them when they are least prepared. Some people prefer to stay at a certain level of operation, while others plan growth that doesn't happen. Too often, a small business is started without a business plan, or the plan is not revisited before growth decisions are made. A good plan incorporates provisions for sudden or unexpected growth. Do you have the resources to expand, finance a larger inventory, or hire more employees? What about the cost of relocating to larger premises?

Many owners don't even think about growth when they start, suddenly finding themselves trying to handle those sixty different jobs. This leads to poor decision-making, and often the failure of a potentially viable business.

Heed the signs of uncontrolled growth

It's easy to bury yourself in the day-to-day operation without really noticing what is happening. Review the checklist in Figure 6.1 and see how many of the warning signs that your business is growing in a disorderly fashion apply to you.

Figure **6.1**

Is My Business Growth Out of Control?

1. Your desk is a mess, piled with unopened bills and correspondence. ☐
2. Suppliers are calling for payment of overdue accounts. ☐
3. The money seems to go out faster than it comes in. ☐
4. You constantly feel under pressure, tired, and worried. ☐
5. You can't keep up with all the tedious administrative duties. ☐

6. You mutter when the phone rings and don't return calls promptly. ☐
7. Taxes and other government payments are falling behind. ☐
8. Your books are months behind. ☐
9. You don't know how much is owing by customers or to suppliers. ☐
10. Your family complains that you are difficult to live with. ☐
11. You often find yourself working evenings and weekends. ☐
12. You don't take regular vacations. ☐
13. You are not enjoying your work. ☐
14. You make silly mistakes. ☐
15. You wake up feeling tired and depressed and lose sleep worrying. ☐

Checking off any of these scenarios should warn you that it's time to address some important issues. Your business cannot grow if you are uninformed, overworked, out of control, and depressed. You have to change both your attitude and the way you are operating—now.

USE THE SIX-STEP GROWTH ANALYSIS PLAN

Even if you didn't plan how to grow your business, it's never too late to start—but where to begin? Spend time seriously evaluating where you are, where you want to go, whether you can afford it, and how you are going to do it.

The six steps to planning for growth are:

1. evaluating where you are now
2. deciding whether you want to and are ready to grow
3. setting goals
4. planning how you will grow
5. planning how to finance your growth
6. comparing progress to projections

SIT DOWN AND SET GOALS

You can't plan for growth until you have set goals. Have you really thought about what you want from your business? How practical are your goals? How and when can they be attained? As you work through this analysis process, you may discover areas in both your business and personal life that need some fine-tuning.

STEP 1: EVALUATE WHERE YOU ARE NOW

The worksheets and checklists in this book are designed to help you assess and pinpoint your strengths and weaknesses so that you can improve. Your business can't grow without your willingness to do something about it.

Review previous worksheets

The first step is to review and complete previous checklists and questionnaires and to decide on a course of action using Figure 6.2 on page 115.

Chapter 1

The "Where Am I Now?" questionnaire (Figure 1.1) should indicate whether you are feeling positive about your business. It should have identified areas requiring improvement or affirmed that you are heading in the right direction. How did you feel when you answered the questions? Do you still feel that way? Are you mentally ready to objectively tackle growing your business?

Chapter 2

Successful growth needs nurturing with a positive attitude and a determination to overcome all obstacles. Revisit Figure 2.6, the "Where Am I Going?" questionnaire, where you noted areas of concern. You should have also noted the jobs you don't like doing, where you need to develop more expertise, and work that could be delegated. Are you willing to take action in these areas?

Chapter 3

Growing requires that you develop refined organizational skills. There will be more of everything to cope with, so organization is critical to save serious errors and confusion. How did you fare on Figure 3.3, "Operation 'Get Organized' Checklist"? Are you prepared to reorganize yourself, your systems, and your business so that all operate at peak efficiency?

Chapter 4

The "Twenty-Question Profitability Checklist" (Figure 4.10) notes key areas that contribute to the profitability of a business. Of those you have answered "no" to, are you prepared to investigate some viable solutions? Have you calculated your break-even point yet?

Chapter 5

You need optimum administrative efficiency to utilize every dollar of revenue generated. For those areas in Figure 5.5, the "Administrative Efficiency Checklist," that you checked "needs work," will you complete the task of streamlining your administrative operations?

Chapter 6

When you have read this chapter and completed Figure 6.6, the "Going for Growth" action plan, add your answer to the checklist in Figure 6.2. Are you ready for all that is entailed in growing your business?

There are other important checklists throughout this book. They will give you further insight as you work toward growing both your skills and your business. Make time to complete those applicable to your needs.

Figure **6.2**

"Are You Ready for Growth?" Checklist

	Improvement needed		Willing to improve	
	Yes	No	Yes	No
1. Where am I now?	☐	☐	☐	☐
2. Where am I going?	☐	☐	☐	☐
3. Operation "Get Organized"	☐	☐	☐	☐
4. Profitability checklist	☐	☐	☐	☐
5. Administrative efficiency	☐	☐	☐	☐
6. "Going for Growth"	☐	☐	☐	☐

What is your commitment?

If you checked "no" under "improvement needed" to all six items in Figure 6.2, then you don't need to read this book. Congratulations! You are on your way to becoming another Bill Gates. If you checked "yes" to most of the six worksheets under "willing to improve," I congratulate you also. You are truly ready and willing to work positively on growing your business and are obviously

HIRE HELP

If you are suffering from any of the warning signs discussed on page 110, you are definitely tackling too much by yourself and need help. Many people say, "But I can't afford to hire someone, I'm not making enough money." Often it is a catch-22 situation—if you don't get help to grow, you won't.

aware that it will take time, commitment, and hard work. With this attitude and determination, you *will* succeed.

If you have answered "no" more than three times under "willing to improve" and "yes" more than three times under "improvement needed," then perhaps growing your business is not the right decision for you at this time. For those willing and wanting to grow their business, read on to the next step.

STEP 2: DECIDE WHETHER YOU ARE READY TO GROW

In most cases, growth doesn't just happen—you have to make your business grow at a pace that you can physically, mentally, and financially manage. If you have completed the Figure 6.2 checklist, then you are aware of the areas that need work. Solutions usually take time and money to implement, but some can be implemented quickly and at little cost.

To grow or stay small?

Some people don't want to grow. They have developed a lifestyle around their business which complements both their family commitments and personal life. This is particularly true of many home-based businesses owned by women that can be operated part-time while raising a family. Unfortunately, there are many women business owners whose home-based businesses could blossom if they had the focused time to devote to growth. For many, although juggling the family works, it doesn't allow the business to reach its full potential.

If you follow this six-step growth analysis plan, you will know better whether you can cope with growth or whether you should just stay small, work smarter, and become more profitable. Let's look at some of the questions you need to ask yourself.

a) Skills

Refer to the sixty different jobs listed in Chapter 2. If you haven't highlighted the ones you hate to do or can't do, go back and complete this exercise. This helps to pinpoint your strengths and weaknesses. You should have solid financial, marketing, sales, communication, technical, and administrative knowledge. If you haven't, you either have to learn these skills or delegate them.

Many of the jobs you highlight will be administrative jobs that encroach upon the time you need to concentrate on growing your business. Which ones could you delegate? How long will it take you to learn the other necessary skills? Can you still grow your business as you learn?

CHECK HOME-BASED REGULATIONS

Some local government regulations prohibit non-resident employees working from your home, so the choice then becomes to operate illegally—which many people do—or to move the business out, which isn't always financially viable. Before you make any home-based growth plans, check that you fall within the parameters of home-based business regulations.

b) Relocation

Would growing your business mean relocating to larger premises? Can you afford to move? Research the cost of relocating, as it can be expensive. Many home-based businesses are not ready to take the plunge to commercial premises without the in-between step of hiring one or more employees. Others are tied into a commercial building lease for a property that is now too small. Explore all your options to determine the best solution for you.

c) Finances

Growth often requires some financial injection. Answer these questions:

- Is your business stable enough that you could apply for a loan?
- How much income is needed to repay the loan?
- How will you generate that income?
- Is your business paying you a satisfactory wage?
- Is it wise to consider growth if your business isn't yet supporting you?
- How will you convince the bank that growth is your ideal solution?

Study your most recent financial statements. Review the working capital situation and the statement of income and expenses. What are your financial statements telling you? Sit down with your accountant and spend some time finding out.

d) Employees

One of the most difficult tasks is finding the right employees. It's even more difficult to fire incompetent ones. Are you ready to take on the responsibility of hiring and training employees? Do you have the cash flow to ensure that wages and deductions are paid on time? Are you ready for the responsibility of directing and working with someone else? Being a boss doesn't come naturally to everyone.

If you own a home-based business, it is difficult to take that gigantic step straight into commercial premises; you usually need to hire at least one employee to work through the growth stage before making such a large financial commitment. If it is legal where you live, having an employee in the home requires careful thought and planning, as in some ways, they become a part of your family life.

e) Time and energy

You need these two most important ingredients in the success recipe, so ask yourself:

- Am I still enthusiastic and energized about this business?
- Am I feeling overworked, depressed, tired, and a little burned out?
- Will growing the business put undue pressures on me?
- Will my family support these decisions?
- Do I have the time to seriously commit to growing my business?
- Will a well-thought-out plan incorporating hiring staff ease some of these pressures?

Think carefully about these five important areas as you continue on to step three. Make notes of those issues which need to be addressed as you set your goals.

STEP 3: SET GOALS

The importance of goal-setting was discussed in Chapter 2, and now it's time to commit those goals to paper. This step is too often missed on start-up. There is no doubt about it—if you set goals, give them deadlines, and stay focused, you will reach them. The only person who puts limits on you is yourself.

A friend of mine refuses to put limits on her goals. Recently widowed and in a wheelchair due to physical problems, she drives herself everywhere, has taken up painting, and is currently running for a political position. The sky is definitely not her limit.

Goals should not be all materialistic, nor should they all be short- or long-term. Your goals should enrich and enhance four distinct areas of your life:

> ## ELIMINATE FEAR AND LIMITS
>
> *I once said to a friend that the sky is the limit. "Oh no, it's not," she replied. "Why should you limit yourself?" I thought carefully about her words and had to agree—why set yourself limits? The most common reason for not forging ahead and making those dreams a reality is fear of failure. What could you achieve if you took away the fear of failure? Think about it.*

- **Personal goals:** increasing self-confidence and self-esteem, feelings of achievement, inner enrichment, peace and happiness, community recognition, retirement
- **Business goals:** short-term goals, one- to ten-year goals, how long you want to own this business, how big you want it to grow, increasing the goodwill value, "perks" the business can provide, diversification
- **Material goals:** increasing personal assets and net worth—do you dream of a bigger house, a better vehicle, a boat, or travel?
- **Family goals:** Family is the most important asset you have; goals could include improving family lifestyle, developing better relationships, spending more time together, providing children with jobs in the business, having family support, and providing better education for the children.

> ## SHARE YOUR GOALS
>
> *Don't rush into setting goals. Talk to successful business people to see how they achieved their goals. Talk to your family to ensure you have their support and that they understand your goals and how you feel. Include them in your plans.*

TAKE BABY STEPS

If you have ever watched the movie What About Bob? *with Bill Murray and Richard Dreyfuss, you will have heard the phrase "baby steps." I use it most days to remind myself to take one step at a time. Try taking baby steps toward your goals—it really works.*

Write your goals down in Figure 6.3, then either photocopy this worksheet or rewrite it. Put it somewhere highly visible, like the refrigerator or your office bulletin board. Read and affirm your goals daily. When you reach each one, fill in the date that you achieved that goal and highlight it on your list. You will experience an extraordinarily satisfying feeling of power and achievement.

STEP 4: PLAN HOW YOU WILL GROW

This part of your growth plan may take time to develop. A service business or retail store has certain physical and geographic boundaries, unless you plan to open other locations. A manufacturing company may only be able to capture a certain portion of the market due to cheaper exports or competitors. The goal for any business is to make healthy profits. Bigger isn't always better.

Part of planning for growth is to know *why* you want to grow, *how* you will grow, and whether it will be beneficial. Answer these vital questions:

- Am I filling a need and niche in the market?
- What will my position in the market be?
- What marketing methods will I use?
- What are my competitive strengths and weaknesses?
- How will the weaknesses be overcome?
- What is my projected time frame?
- Will growth increase the net profits of the business?
- Will I require outside financing?
- Where will I obtain that financing?

Figure **6.3**

My Go-Getter Goal-Setter Plan of Action

	Goals	Deadline
Personal: 1.		
2.		
3.		
4.		
5.		
Business: 1.		
2.		
3.		
4.		
5.		
Material: 1.		
2.		
3.		
4.		
5.		
Family: 1.		
2.		
3.		
4.		
5.		

Ten Tips for **Expanding Your Business**

If you use that creativity for your golden box of opportunity that was mentioned in Chapter 2, you may find some unique ways to grow your business. Consider these suggestions:

1. Expanding your line of products

2. Expanding the services you offer

3. Offering consulting services

4. Exporting your product or service

5. Importing products

6. Franchising your business

7. Partnering with another complementary business

8. Opening a second location

9. Buying an existing business to expand

10. Offering seminars, workshops, or training services.

STEP 5: PLAN YOUR FINANCING NEEDS

When you have completed the "Going for Growth" action plan (Figure 6.6) at the end of this chapter, you should have identified where additional funding is needed to meet your needs. Research these costs and incorporate them into your projections.

Many of these steps are similar to those required in the preparation of a business plan. What you are now preparing is a strategic growth plan that incorporates a research and development component, a marketing plan, and cash flow, income, and expense projections. No lending institution will entertain the thought of a loan without this information.

Research loan programs

The next step is to estimate the amount you require, based on your projections. It may be as little as $5,000 or as much as $100,000. Which financing product best suits your needs? You may be able to secure a government-funded loan for expansion or export. The U.S. Small Business Administration offers loans to suit most businesses' needs, including the Microloan Program. Their Basic 7(A) Loan Program caters to new and growing businesses looking for capital to purchase assets and fund expansion projects, long- and short-term working capital, and capital for refinancing and export production. Another option is the Export Working Capital Program (EWCP), which provides exporters with short-term working capital. Visit *www.sba.gov/financing/sbaloan/snapshot.html*.

What do banks offer?

As comparable and competitive financing products are available, you need to do some homework. Try your own bank or trust company first, as you should have built a relationship with them and they can put a history to your name. Hopefully this is advantageous to you.

Lenders are becoming more small business friendly, with some offering small business loans under $15,000. Finding the financing you need can be frustrating, but there are many options including:

- overdraft protection and small business credit lines
- business credit cards
- business operating lines of credit
- small business loans
- term loans
- export financing and letters of credit
- business leasing products
- secured lines of credit

BE PROFESSIONAL

Be well groomed, positive, and well armed for your loan application appointment. Take your past and most recent financial statements, business plan, a statement of personal net worth (personal assets and liabilities), any promotional material, articles relevant to your industry, or anything else that will help to inform and project a professional image. Carting in your set of accounting books is not acceptable.

How do banks view your business?

Be well prepared for your appointment at the bank with a professional presentation. Review the contents with your accountant and discuss any potentially weak areas. The bank will examine these key application factors:

- the overall viability of the business
- the viability of the business plan
- the business's ability to repay the loan
- what security is offered
- how much the owner(s) have invested in the business
- past and current credit history
- available management expertise

The three crucial questions

Apart from assessing your overall knowledge plus all of the above, the bank wants to be sure they are investing money wisely. They will perform a variety of calculations from your financial statements to find answers to the following:

1. *Is this business currently "liquid"?* If current assets and current liabilities were liquidated, could the assets pay off the liabilities? Are the owners drawing a satisfactory wage?

2. *Is this business currently profitable?* Are profit margins consistent? Can the business absorb growth costs? Does it have the ability to repay the loan?

3. *Do the financial statements reflect a relatively financially stable business?* What is the debt to equity ratio? Can this business cope with growth? How has it performed during previous growth periods? What would be the financial effect of a downward trend?

If you pass these stringent tests and your growth plan reveals a viable investment for the bank, you should obtain the finances you need to put your plan into action. Read about how one enterprising couple financed their new business in the Real Life example "Tailoring the Formula for Success."

(*Real Life*) **Tailoring the Formula for Success**

How does an out-of-work couple become the proud owner of a 100 percent financed failing menswear store? This story is all about miracles. Turning the store around and growing it by 30 percent in one year wasn't a miracle—this couple has all the right ingredients for a successful partnership.

Derek and Lisa Rickwood wanted to purchase a 44-year-old menswear store. Derek had worked in the men's clothing industry for twenty-three years, many of them at this particular store. His talented wife Lisa had seven years' advertising experience, plus a fashion and writing background. Both are highly creative, artistic, and possess many necessary business skills.

They needed $150,000 to purchase and revamp the store. The whole amount was eventually funded by working with the local small business development center, and with a credit union loan, plus funds from friends. Knowing that he was the only one who could sell the concept, Derek insisted that he be present when his business plan was reviewed by the committee that approved the loans for small businesses.

"Had Derek not been there, we wouldn't have got the loan," explained Lisa. "He knew that this wasn't all about facts and figures on paper. He had to sell himself, which he did."

Rickwood's Menswear Inc. became a reality. Catering to men from head to toe, it offers dry cleaning; shoe and leather repairs; tailoring; alterations; personal after-hour appointments and delivery; affordable, quality clothing; and exceptional service—and an in-house art gallery featuring works by Derek.

The couple kept in constant touch with their accountant, who was thrilled when the store reached break-even point and generated profits in under one year. Even through tough economic times, the store grows steadily each year.

continued

Employing only a bookkeeper, one full-time, and one part-time sales staff, Derek and Lisa wear many entrepreneurial hats. Overcoming obstacles that would frighten most people, their combined talents, expertise, passion, and persistence have turned a struggling store into a success story.

STEP 6: COMPARE PROGRESS TO PROJECTIONS

Once you have a viable growth plan in place with the funds to accompany it, review your financial figures and projections each month. If you borrowed money, it's even more important to see if the investment is reaping the expected returns.

Consult your plan then update financial figures and projections before making any financial decisions—that's why you plan in the first place. By regularly monitoring your progress, you can more readily identify concerns and remedy the situation. Perhaps you didn't achieve your sales projections or your marketing isn't producing the expected results. This information will be reflected in your financial reports.

ANALYZE EXPECTATIONS

When you sit down and analyze where expectations were not met and why, you become more focused on those areas in the future.

Compare spreadsheets

The best method for reviewing your progress is to compare actual results to projections. Study each area of your analysis to determine why the figures vary, and then decide how to resolve any problems. Figure 6.4 shows a one-month comparison for a small woodcraft manufacturing business. Reviewing these figures is a step that not enough businesses take.

Figure 6.4

One Month Financial Comparison

CREATIVE WOOD ART INC., AUGUST 31, 20___

	Budget	Actual	Variance
Sales	$13,000	10,500	(3,500)
Cost of sales			
Materials	2,600	2,415	(185)
Packaging	260	230	(30)
Labor	1,950	1,890	(60)
Freight	130	110	(20)
	4,940	4,645	(295)
Gross profit:	(62%) 8,060	(56%) 5,855	(2,205)
Overhead expenses			
Accounting fees	150	175	25
Advertising	260	240	(20)
Bad debts	50	0	(50)
Bank charges	45	50	5
Employee benefits	890	880	(10)
Fees, licenses & taxes	50	0	(50)
Insurance	100	100	0
Loan interest	300	310	10
Management salary	2,000	2,000	0
Marketing & promotion	400	780	380
Office salaries	500	500	0
Office supplies	100	230	130
Promotion – meals	50	75	25
Rent	700	700	0
Repairs & maintenance	100	420	320
Security	50	50	0
Seminars & trade shows	60	90	30
Shop supplies	100	60	(40)
Telephone	150	185	35
Utilities	110	95	(15)
Vehicle – gas	100	120	20
Vehicle – repairs & maintenance	150	120	(30)
Workers' compensation	175	170	(5)
	6,590	7,350	760
Profit/loss for month	1,470	(1,495)	$(2,965)
Actual gross profit deficiency			2,205
Overhead increase/decrease			760
Profit/loss variance			$(2,965)

What happened?

Sales were $3,500 below projections and cost of sales increased by six percent as materials and wages both increased by three percent, a gross profit reduction of $655. Why did both these costs increase? The gross profit for the month was $2,205 less than projected.

An increase in marketing and office costs and an unexpected breakdown of equipment increased projected overhead by $760. The business suffered a net loss of $1,495 instead of a projected net profit of $1,470, a difference of $2,965. If projected sales were met with the 56 percent gross profit margin, the business would have lost only $70 for the month.

This example clearly demonstrates how easy it is for profits to be affected, sometimes by uncontrollable situations. The message is to use your figures to keep growth plans on track and under control.

GROW YOUR BUSINESS BY EXPORTING

Business has gone global. The world marketplace is now open all day, every day, unrestricted by distance, technological barriers, or country of origin. The entire world is within our reach in ways that were not possible before. Like any business venture, entering the global trade arena presents both opportunities and challenges. At first, you may not even be sure how exporting can help your company, or what the drawbacks may be.

What are the benefits of exporting?

Experienced exporters have a pretty good idea of both the benefits and problems of international trade. Let's look at the many benefits.

- *Increased sales:* If domestic sales are good, exporting is a way to expand your market and take advantage of demand around the world. You may also find foreign niche markets where your product is rare or unique.
- *Higher profits:* If you can cover fixed costs through domestic operations or other types of financing, your export profits can grow very quickly.
- *Economies of scale:* When you have a larger market base, you can produce on a scale that makes the most of your resources.

- *Reduced vulnerability:* If you diversify into international markets, you avoid depending on a single marketplace. A domestic downturn will be less damaging if you have other markets where demand remains high.
- *New knowledge and experience:* The global marketplace abounds with new ideas, approaches, and marketing techniques. You may find them very successful locally, too.
- *Global competitiveness:* The experience your company gains internationally will help keep you and your domestic market competitive in the global marketplace.
- *Domestic competitiveness:* If your company succeeds in the global marketplace, it means your product can compete with the best the world can offer. This ensures your resilience when faced with local and foreign competition at home.

What are the challenges of exporting?

Of course, there are also challenges that accompany these benefits. The good news is that you can surmount them with careful preparation.

- *Increased costs:* An exporting venture means you will have to meet many short-term costs, such as extra travel, production of new marketing materials, and perhaps hiring additional sales staff. You may have to modify packaging, or your products or services, to adapt them to markets abroad.
- *Level of commitment:* It takes time, effort, and resources to establish and maintain yourself in foreign markets. While exporting holds great economic promise for most companies, expect months or even several years to pass before you see a significant return on your export investment.
- *Cultural differences:* You will need to familiarize yourself with the differences in language, culture, and business practices in your target market. If you don't, you risk inadvertently offending your potential customers and losing sales.
- *Paperwork:* You will have to get used to it. Most federal governments require a lot of documentation from exporters of products and services.
- *Accessibility:* You have to be easily available to your foreign customers, which can be difficult due to time and language differences.
- *Competition:* You must thoroughly research the competition in your target market.

SMALL CAN BE BIG

To succeed in international markets, you don't have to be a big-name firm with lavish resources and an entire department devoted to exporting. With the amount of government assistance available to small businesses, exporting either your services or products can be a viable option to diversify and grow your business. As an example, the latest statistics available show that by 1998 statistics, small businesses accounted for 95.7 percent of U.S. exporters, contributing 29.5 percent of the value of exported goods.

Exporting goods versus exporting services

Exporting goods and exporting services present quite different challenges. The former must deal with packaging, customs, and physical delivery, for example, while the latter confronts issues such as work permits, communications infrastructure in the target market, and travel to and from the market.

Are you ready?

What makes a business export-ready? Simply put, the business has a marketable product or service as well as the capacity, resources, and management commitment to compete on a global scale. Figure out whether this is true of your company—and if it isn't, how to make it happen.

First, think about the resources and knowledge your business already has. Take a few moments to answer the questions in Figure 6.5.

If you answer "yes" to most questions, exporting may well be a profitable and viable strategy for growing your business.

Figure **6.5**

Are You Ready for Exporting?

	Yes	No
1. Your expectations: Do you have...?		
• clear and achievable export objectives	☐	☐
• a realistic idea of what exporting entails	☐	☐
• an openness to new ways of doing business	☐	☐

- an understanding of what is required to succeed
  internationally ☐ ☐

2. Human resources: Do you have...?

- the capacity to handle the extra demand associated
  with exporting ☐ ☐
- a senior management committed to exporting ☐ ☐
- efficient ways of responding quickly to customer inquiries ☐ ☐
- personnel with culturally sensitive marketing skills ☐ ☐
- ways of dealing with language barriers ☐ ☐

3. Financial and legal resources: Can you...?

- obtain enough capital or lines of credit ☐ ☐
- find ways to reduce the financial risks of
  international trade ☐ ☐
- find people to advise you on the legal and
  tax implications ☐ ☐
- deal effectively with different monetary systems ☐ ☐
- ensure protection of your intellectual property ☐ ☐

4. Competitiveness: Do you have...?

- the resources to do market research on the exportability
  of your product or service ☐ ☐
- proven, sophisticated market-entry methods ☐ ☐
- a product or service that is potentially viable in your
  target market ☐ ☐

Resources, resources, resources

This information only touches the surface of your exporting options. If you need more in-depth information, visit ***www.sba.gov/oit/info/index.html***. The SBA and partners are your best resources for more clarity on exporting. These partners and resources are described in detail in the SBA's publication, *Breaking Into the Trade Game: A Small Business Guide to Exporting,* which can be downloaded from the above Web page. It walks you step-by-step through the export process, and includes an

International Business Plan to help you carefully evaluate your goals, analyze the industry, and determine the pros and cons of market expansion.

Export advice is also offered through the U.S. Export Assistance Centers, located in many major metropolitan areas. Their locations can be found at *www.sba.gov/oit/export/useac.html*. Professionals from the U.S. Department of Commerce, the U.S. Import-Export Bank, and other public and private organizations can help you reach your export goals.

THE BENEFITS OF INCORPORATION

"Should I incorporate?" ask many sole proprietors planning for growth. For well-organized micro-businesses, perhaps incorporation isn't necessary, but in most cases, it is a practical solution to assist in planned growth. Incorporation has considerable benefits, so read this and discuss the various incorporation options with your accountant. You may take on a whole new perspective when you become Coastal Charters Inc.

Incorporation allows you to:

1. **Plan wages and personal finances:** Once incorporated, you can draw a regular salary and make regular income tax, Social Security, Medicare, and unemployment benefit contributions, which greatly helps in planning cash flow. As an employee of the company, your wage is a corporate expense—which it isn't in a sole proprietorship. You can vary the wage that you take from the business according to cash flow and still be paying the appropriate taxes and employee benefits. At year-end, you receive a W-2 for filing personal taxes.

2. **Structure profits, dividends and bonuses:** Sole proprietors can only make certain deductions from their businesses. When you are incorporated, your accountant can suggest various tax alternatives, including paying more wages, bonuses, or dividends—more money into your pocket and less paid in corporate taxes. Banks understand lower corporate profits when they see healthy management salaries. What they don't like is corporate losses created by top-heavy management salaries or "perks."

3. **Project a more stable business image:** Incorporated businesses are viewed more seriously by suppliers, customers, investors, and banks. Incorporation usually indicates that management has thought seriously about growth and profitability. It projects an image of a "real" business as opposed to a "mom and pop" operation. Obtaining financing as a qualified incorporated business is easier than as a proprietorship.

4. **Enjoy the security of limited liability:** Because incorporated businesses are a separate entity from their owners (shareholders), suppliers understand that if an incorporated business goes bankrupt, they may not recover their money. Directors and officers are still personally liable for certain debts, such as personally guaranteed loans, and fiduciary payments such as excise taxes and employee withholdings.

5. **Grow in a more structured environment:** As your business grows, you may want to add partners or shareholders—a board of directors who can give valuable input. To keep a controlling interest, you must maintain at least 51 percent of the shares. If you are considering "going public" on the stock exchange, the basic corporate structure is in place. If this is your long-term vision, talk to your lawyer so that your incorporation structure makes adequate future provisions.

6. **Benefit from additional tax deductions:** Incorporation allows tax deductions and benefits for both you and your employees that are not available to an unincorporated business. These benefits include business trip and entertainment expenses and even recreational facilities. Contributions to approved pension plans are not only tax-deductible, they earn investment income and grow tax-free until retirement or until

COVER ALL BASES

If a business goes bankrupt, shareholders could immediately start another business. If a proprietorship fails, the owner is personally responsible for all debts, with personal bankruptcy sometimes being the only alternative. This not only leaves a black mark on your credit rating, but also makes personal assets, including your home, subject to liens or seizure. Incorporation allows for safer future planning—particularly if the business fails.

they are withdrawn. Even a one-person incorporated business can deduct health insurance, so for a growing business, incorporating may well save you money while providing attractive taxable benefits.

7. **Corporations have authority:** Incorporated businesses have the authority and power to carry on a variety of transactions that sole proprietors often cannot. They continue to operate after the owner(s) die, and grow and succeed more rapidly than unincorporated businesses.

THE DOWNSIDE OF INCORPORATION

Although incorporation is an obvious choice for a growing business, be aware that it involves more detailed accounting and expenses including:

1. **Incorporation fees:** Ranging from $100 for a Web-based incorporation to hundreds or thousands of dollars for incorporation through a lawyer, costs depend on the complexity of the share structure and whether you register in other jurisdictions.

2. **Increased accountant's fees:** A rollover from a proprietorship to an incorporated business is prepared on incorporation, moving the assets to the new entity and including the share structure. At year-end, detailed financial statements and corporate taxes are prepared. Depending on how complete and accurate your books are, once again, the cost will vary from hundreds into thousands of dollars.

3. **Payroll deductions:** As a company employee, you must maintain payroll records, prepare year-end summaries, have a Federal Employer Identification Number, (EIN) and make monthly remittances to the appropriate tax agencies.

4. **Extra reporting:** Most states send you or your registered office an annual corporate report to file. In some cases, you can now file online. Either you or your lawyer should maintain a record of company minutes in the corporate minute book. The share register should be updated with any transactions.

5. **Other costs:** You may have to print new stationery and business cards or change signs and website information to reflect the incorporated name. If you are rolling personally owned vehicles into the incorporated business, a transfer of ownership is necessary.

"GOING FOR GROWTH" ACTION PLAN

Any change in your operation should be carefully analyzed to identify the causes, effects, and benefits of that change. Many questions have to answered; it's not just a matter of generating more dollars. Research the ten areas in Figure 6.6 to determine the causes, effects, and benefits of change on other areas of operation. Check the areas applicable to your business to formulate your guide for growth.

There is a lot of information to digest here, so you may have to read this chapter a few times if you are going for growth. Of course, you will need help to lighten your workload, so read Chapter 7 to learn how to hire the right person, as there are a variety of hiring options. The following chapters will help you with increasing your communication, marketing and sales skills.

Figure **6.6**

"Going for Growth" Action Plan

	Action needed	Completed
1. Research and development: research and know...		
• the time needed to research the complete growth plan	☐	☐
• the time needed to develop new products or services	☐	☐
• the cost and time involved in registering any patents/copyrights	☐	☐
• that you are not infringing on other patents or copyrights	☐	☐
• you have the qualified staff available to complete the research	☐	☐
• how you will market new products or services	☐	☐
• that you have a complete marketing plan in place	☐	☐

	Action needed	Completed
2. Revenue: research and know...		
• how revenue will be generated	☐	☐
• in what time frame revenue will be generated	☐	☐
• if gross profit margins are acceptable and consistent	☐	☐
• if the pricing structure is competitive	☐	☐
• the life of the product(s) or service(s)	☐	☐
3. Direct costs: ensure that...		
• materials are readily available as needed	☐	☐
• you can meet supplier payment terms	☐	☐
• adequate room is available to store raw materials	☐	☐
• there is enough room to manufacture the product	☐	☐
• equipment meets your production needs	☐	☐
4. Labor: you will need...		
• staff in place for increased production	☐	☐
• to hire the right person with the right credentials	☐	☐
• cash flow to meet extra wage requirements	☐	☐
• to allow for training time and costs	☐	☐
• to factor wage benefits into cash flow	☐	☐
• a contingency plan if employees are absent from work	☐	☐
• to design a reporting system to monitor and evaluate staff performance	☐	☐
• to assess productivity level and capabilities of each employee	☐	☐
• to assess each employee's potential for promotion	☐	☐
5. Overhead expense increase: plan for...		
• extra help to cope with more paperwork	☐	☐
• potentially upgrading the accounting system	☐	☐
• equipment requiring regular maintenance	☐	☐
• more space for extra staff	☐	☐
• extra telephone lines, cell phones, pagers	☐	☐
• incidental cost increases, such as stationery	☐	☐
• upgrading facilities to house extra staff	☐	☐

	Action needed	Completed
6. Asset purchases: analyze...		
• the cost and availability of new equipment	☐	☐
• how you will finance asset purchases	☐	☐
• how each asset will contribute to profit centers	☐	☐
• the life span and maintenance cost of each asset	☐	☐
7. Distribution: be sure you...		
• plan how the product will be distributed	☐	☐
• have sufficient warehousing space	☐	☐
• know costs involved with increased distribution channels	☐	☐
• assess necessary staff to service expanded areas	☐	☐
• assess increased costs involved in packaging or shipping	☐	☐
8. Management: you will need to...		
• review the business's current management structure	☐	☐
• identify current areas of weakness	☐	☐
• identify whether extra management staffing is required	☐	☐
• analyze who you need to fill in the gaps	☐	☐
• know where you will look to find the right person	☐	☐
• ensure you can offer a competitive salary	☐	☐
• prepare job descriptions to ensure each person can competently manage the workload	☐	☐
• design a wage increase and incentive bonus system	☐	☐
• list the benefits and perks and their cost to the business	☐	☐
• design employment contracts that clearly outline job responsibilities and ramifications of unsatisfactory work	☐	☐
• have a lawyer review and advise on the contracts	☐	☐
• prepare detailed cost analysis for each area of the business	☐	☐
• prepare cash flow, income, and expenses projections	☐	☐
• develop a system to monitor marketing strategies	☐	☐

	Action needed	Completed

9. Operational structure: you may need to...

- design detailed written company policies and procedures ☐ ☐
- ensure insurance policies are upgraded with adequate coverage ☐ ☐
- ensure your staff has the necessary technical expertise ☐ ☐
- cope with expansion ☐ ☐
- know how to control extra staff and production loads ☐ ☐
- develop quality control systems ☐ ☐
- know how you will deal with equipment breakdowns ☐ ☐
- know the cost of each hour of downtime ☐ ☐

10. Logistics: be sure to...

- assess your location and how it can cope with growth ☐ ☐
- see if your lease allows for modifications to buildings ☐ ☐
- analyze the costs involved in expanding the current facility ☐ ☐
- know when you may have to move to larger premises ☐ ☐
- research alternative affordable premises ☐ ☐
- research the cost of having to move ☐ ☐
- know how you are going to pay for the move ☐ ☐
- assess whether you would lose customers if you moved ☐ ☐

CHAPTER SEVEN

How Do You Find —and Keep— Good Help?

—◆◇◆—

He that can work is a born king of something.
THOMAS CARLYLE

—◆◇◆—

Recognizing the need for help is a big step toward growing your business. Understanding the skills it takes to become a good employer and then finding the right person for the job are two more giant steps. If you completed the exercise in Chapter 2, identifying the various jobs, you should have a list of the tasks that can be delegated or areas where you need increased skills. ❧

ARE YOU READY TO BE A BOSS?

You have probably come to the conclusion by now that you can't do it all and grow your business as well. Getting help can be as simple as paying someone to clean your house or run some errands for a few hours a week. You don't have to become an instant employer—there are a variety of options, which will be discussed in this chapter.

Good management comes from the top

Being "the boss" sounds exciting, but it requires serious thought. There are many benefits—some tangible, others intangible. You will have someone to bounce ideas off and work pressure will ease. You can now accelerate your work output and growth plans. You will also be faced with some unexpected challenges requiring excellent human resources skills.

No matter how capable and devoted your employees are, they look to you for direction. Good business management starts at the top. Not everyone was born to be a boss and many people have infinite difficulty coping with this role. You are your employee's role model, and the success of your business will depend entirely on your ability to administrate, delegate, and appreciate your staff. Don't be like Lester in the Real Life example "No Management, No Motivation, No Money."

Real Life) No Management, No Motivation, No Money

Lester inherited his deceased father's fifty-year-old farm equipment business. In a fast-growing community, the business was well-known and had steadily grown to seven employees. He was an expert at technical details, but wasn't a good manager. As money always seemed to be available, Lester took more wages, went on extended "business trips," and spent less time in the office. After all, he had all these good employees to do the job.

Then Lester's wife suddenly left him and an ugly divorce ensued. He started taking his moods, temper, and problems out on his employees, who in turn lost their motivation. Ultimately, all the systems broke down. Competitors moved into town, the business's reputation suffered, and Lester mentally gave up, finally selling the business. Between his wife's demands and the suffering bottom line, the financial loss was tremendous.

Expect the unexpected

Employees tend to throw employers an array of curveballs. You will be faced with absenteeism, tardiness, illness, family emergencies, maternal leave, false references, theft, weak excuses, irresponsibility, lying, quitting, alcohol or drug abuse, and poor performance and customer service.

As you plan to hire, consider these challenges and ask yourself how you would handle these concerns. What if you have an urgent job to complete and your employee doesn't show up? Be prepared to expect the unexpected, because it will happen. Before you make the decision to hire, ensure you can answer "yes" to the 12 questions in Figure 7.1.

Figure **7.1**

Am I Ready to Be an Employer?

	Yes	No	Maybe
1. Am I comfortable with delegating tasks?	☐	☐	☐
2. Have I clearly defined the new employee's roles and responsibilities?	☐	☐	☐
3. Can the business financially afford an employee?	☐	☐	☐
4. Am I able to reprimand or correct an employee?	☐	☐	☐
5. Have I calculated the full cost of hiring?	☐	☐	☐
6. Could I fire an incompetent employee?	☐	☐	☐
7. Do I understand all my responsibilities as an employer?	☐	☐	☐
8. Can I clearly communicate my needs?	☐	☐	☐
9. Can I keep my personal life separate from the business?	☐	☐	☐
10. Can I stay positive and motivated when the going gets tough?	☐	☐	☐
11. Do I believe in a positive management style as an employer?	☐	☐	☐
12. Can I demonstrate flexibility where situations dictate?	☐	☐	☐

"I CAN'T GET GOOD HELP THESE DAYS!"

In addition to knowing that you can effectively manage and motivate your employees, you also have to find the right employee. If you ask most growing businesses what their biggest headache is, they will usually reply: "It's finding the right employee! I can't get good help these days!" With good jobs often difficult to find, this statement doesn't seem to make sense, so let's look at some of the reasons for this dilemma.

Understand our changing society

Because society changes so rapidly, much of the old work ethic that baby boomers and older people grew up with has disappeared. Disposable income has decreased while inflation, taxes, and the demand for material possessions have increased. Because of seesawing economic conditions, some employees have worked long-term in negative environments. Over time, many have lost their enthusiasm and motivation.

Technology has replaced countless jobs, displacing a myriad of talented people, who are then forced to realign their careers. Employees who have worked at only one job find change and learning new skills extremely difficult.

Since the '80s, children have grown up in a technological and materialistic environment that doesn't educate them by the "old" standards. A strong work ethic along with good spelling, diction, and presentation skills are often lacking in candidates. It's not surprising that employers experience difficulty finding the right person, particularly if they are looking for employee qualities that are based on hiring standards of previous decades.

Know your employment options

Once you start exploring the available hiring options, you may be surprised at your responsibilities as an employer and the costs involved. If you are home-based, there may be regulations

PAY BY CHECK

Do not succumb to requests for "cash under the table." Besides being illegal, the cash cannot be reported as a legitimate business expense. Usually, the payee has no intention of declaring the income. Then your financial figures do not accurately reflect your true operating costs. Always write a check to correspond with the invoice amount. If this doesn't suit the person, then don't hire them. Honesty is always the best policy.

that prevent you from hiring employees (although that doesn't stop some people). A new person requires training and orientation, so you must make this time available. Now you have to learn to delegate, supervise, praise, and reprimand where necessary—skills that do not come naturally to some. Before you make a hiring decision, there are a number of hiring options to consider.

Casual labor

Hiring someone for an occasional few hours is referred to as casual labor. In essence, these people are self-employed, so you agree to an hourly rate in return for services rendered. They should supply you with an invoice for the time worked, and you should never pay "cash under the table."

Contract labor

A person such as a plumber, who owns their own business and works for a variety of customers, is considered an independent contractor. They should meet the legal criteria and conditions to qualify as a contractor as set out by the Internal Revenue Service (IRS). An informative publication on this subject, Publication 533, Self-Employment Tax, is available online at www.irs.gov/publications/p533/index.html.

Self-employed commission agents

If you need sales help, you can hire a self-employed, commissioned salesperson. These people will also be working for other companies and may not devote their full attention to your business. If you are a manufacturer, you could use a distributor or agent to sell your products to a retailer. Distributors work on a percentage of retail price, so there has to be room in your profit margins to absorb this cost.

> ## PAY ONLY FOR HOURS WORKED
> *Subcontractors can be utilized for bookkeeping, seasonal overload, and marketing projects. You are not committed to paying for unproductive labor hours and can use these services on demand. Subcontractors are responsible for their own income tax and pension plan payments.*

Commissioned employees

A passionate and committed commissioned salesperson could be the answer for increasing sales. The salary structure is usually calculated on a percentage of sales generated. A base salary or advance on commission is usually paid mid-month, with the balance due dependent on sales volume. Unless you make your salary package and incentives attractive, some commissioned employees tend to regularly change jobs. If you find a good employee, reward them well.

Part-time employees

The benefit of hiring on a part-time basis is that hours can be increased or decreased as needed. Part-time employees are still subject to payroll deductions. As you become busier, the employee can assume more responsibility and eventually become a full-time, already-trained member of staff, without you having to go through the time-wasting chore of hiring a new person.

Full-time employees

Be sure of the stability of your cash flow before you hire a full-time employee as you are committing to paying them regularly. As you will see in Figures 7.2 and 7.3 on page 150, hiring is an expensive venture.

HOW DO YOU HIRE THE RIGHT PERSON?

Now that you are aware of where you need help and the various options, is it practical for one person to fill these gaps or would two part-time people with different skills be a better option? Next, prioritize the skills you need. For example, if bookkeeping is not your forte, you might prioritize the job description for a bookkeeper this way:

- **Priority #1—necessary skills:** Accurate bookkeeping and strong attention to detail are needed but how extensive is the job? Do you need bookkeeping up to and including trial balance or just accounts receivable and payables experience?

- **Priority #2—salary:** What salary are you prepared to pay? Research the classifieds or ask a personnel agency to see what qualified bookkeepers are paid. Can you afford this salary?

- **Priority #3—other experience:** What other skills should this person have? Perhaps you need a responsible person with all-round small-office experience.

- **Priority #4—public relations:** Do you need someone with excellent telephone and customer service skills? In many cases, this priority may move further up the list.

- **Priority #5—personality, attitude, and motivation:** These inner qualities can't be learned whereas skills can. A motivated and optimistic person is a key asset to both the business and to you.

- **Priority #6—computer skills:** In today's working environment, computer skills are a necessity. Are you willing to train them on specialized programs or upgrade their current skills?

Think carefully as you compose your priority list, as these priorities will be incorporated into both your advertising and interviewing. The clearer they are, the easier it is to narrow down the candidates. It's interesting to note that when you take the time to write down a job description, the end result often differs from your original concept.

HOW TO RECRUIT THE PERFECT CANDIDATE

Although there are plenty of job-seekers, knowing where to look can be an enormous task. Which hiring method you use will no doubt depend on your time and budget. Some suggestions include:

Hire an employment agency

Employment agencies usually charge 10 to 15 percent of the candidate's annual salary. Research the cost and talk to business associates who have used agencies before. Employment counselors are trained to identify skills, strengths, and weaknesses that you may miss. They will discuss your job requirements in detail, so the priority list will be most helpful.

UTILIZE WAGE ASSISTANCE PROGRAMS
....

Some candidates have taken extensive government-sponsored employment courses. Various state, federal, and local programs pay a portion of salary for hiring these people if you offer some on-the-job training. You may find a well-trained employee and help someone to regain their pride and workplace confidence.

If necessary, the agency will place an advertisement on your behalf. Candidates are thoroughly screened by appropriate testing, interviews, and reference checks. You are then presented with two or three suitable candidates for interviewing and will usually be able to make a final selection. You are only charged when you have hired the candidate, and most agencies offer a three-month guarantee to replace unsatisfactory employees at no cost.

Contact government and community employment services

These no-cost agencies are practical as their primary aim is to reduce the number of people on government assistance. They usually house an extensive online applicant base. People who are registered with them have often been out of work for long periods and are eager to return to the workforce. Don't overlook the benefits of hiring older people—they are mature, knowledgeable, and keen to work.

Place a classified advertisement

OFFER BENEFITS
....

Think about what you are offering besides a job. Can you offer benefits including flexible hours, growth potential, steady employment, a pleasant working environment, team spirit, or incentive programs? In a small-office environment, an incentive system will attract a motivated "go-getter."

If you are prepared to be inundated with résumés, place a well-worded classified advertisement in your local newspaper. With priority list in hand, word the advertisement to appeal only to qualified candidates. Put yourself in the candidates' place as you compose the script. What would make you respond to this advertisement?

If you don't want to be inundated with phone calls, you could ask candidates to email their résumés. This saves time and allows you to review the information in your own time.

Bold, creative headings will make your classified stand out. For example, instead of using

"Bookkeeper Wanted," you could try "Enjoy Figure Work?" This subtle change makes the classified ad immediately sound more personable and will pique the reader's curiosity.

As an example, Sandra needed some staff to expand her small cleaning business. Several advertisements had not attracted the right candidates, so she sought help from an experienced personnel consultant. The following advertisement attracted many responses and Sandra found the perfect person for the job.

Pride In Your Work?

Small, independently owned cleaning service is seeking a person who enjoys cleaning and takes pride in a job well done. Flexible hours, good wages, opportunity for job security. Call Sandra at 123-456-7890.

Surf the Net

Both job applicants and employers find the Internet a tremendous time-saving aid. Many different online employment agencies and services exist, so ensure you understand the billing practices and are dealing with a reputable company.

Examples of two job search sites for both employees and employers are ***www.uscareers.com*** and ***www.career.net.com***. You can post jobs for reasonable fees, with the added benefit of not trying to write a job description in a few words, as with a classified advertisement. Candidates can search by keywords, thus narrowing down their search. Most candidates who use the Internet for job-hunting are quite computer-literate.

> ## LINK TO YOUR WEB PAGE
> *Most newspapers have a classified service which incorporates both the print-based classified ads and an online advertisement. Many job-seekers use this service as benefits include an online, detailed job description and a link to the company's website or email. Candidates can research your business before applying, eliminating many unsuitable applicants.*

Remember—don't hire friends

Chapter 2 suggests that you not hire friends or relatives, so this is another gentle reminder. ***Don't***. Ask yourself: "Would firing a friend ruin our relationship?"

Could I feel at ease reprimanding, supervising or correcting a friend?" If you don't keep your friendships outside of the workplace, you may regret it, as did Marilyn in the Real Life example "Friend or Foe?"

Real Life **Friend or Foe?**

Marilyn hired a trusted friend to supervise her business during Marilyn's extended absence. All appeared to be going well until another employee called her, asking to speak in confidence. It appeared that the trusted friend was indulging in afternoon-long luncheons and taking her family out on company funds—while delegating her duties to other employees.

Marilyn had no choice but to fire her friend. Not only was a close friendship lost, but Marilyn's "friend" sued her for wrongful dismissal. Although Marilyn finally won the case, the stress played havoc on her health. It was a heart-wrenching, costly experience.

WADING THROUGH THE RÉSUMÉ PILE

If you advertise for a candidate, wading through piles of résumés is an unavoidable and tedious chore. Shorten the process by using colored highlighters to follow these basic steps:

1. Quickly read each résumé, highlighting each candidate's qualifications that fit your parameters.

2. Change colors and highlight the negative aspects.

3. Mark each résumé with an A+, A, B, or C grading.

4. Reread the A+ and A résumés thoroughly.

After grading people with the most positive qualifications as "A+," you should now have some suitable candidates to start the interviewing process.

THE ART OF SUCCESSFUL INTERVIEWING

To ensure that you cover all the pertinent interview questions, make a list by rereading your job description and the candidate's résumé. Highlight areas in the résumé that you wish to question and make notes during the interview.

1. Fulfilling your job description

Start by outlining the position to the candidate in order of job priorities. Then ask: "Can you handle this job? Does it appeal to you?" Listen carefully to the answer. Did the candidate appear to answer yes honestly without too much hesitation? If there is hesitation, ask about the concerns.

At the same time, assess the candidate's attitude and eagerness to fill your position. Do they offer some innovative or positive ideas? Did they do any research on your company? Do they show a real passion for the type of work you are offering? How well do they communicate their answers to you? A motivated, positive employee is a real asset.

2. Thoroughly review the résumé

Discuss the résumé in detail with the candidate, particularly the reasons for leaving other jobs. You will learn a lot by listening carefully to answers. Does the candidate blame others for lost jobs? This could be a warning sign. Review qualifications and any certifications. A keen candidate will bring their certificates with them.

3. Personal information

Although it would be helpful to know the candidate's marital and family status, health, age, and other factors that may affect work performance, human rights legislation prohibit these questions from being asked. If you use an employment agency, they can ask these questions as an option on their application form, but they cannot be asked in an interview. You will only find out this information if

ASSESS COMMUNICATION SKILLS
······························

If you require excellent customer service skills, assess the candidate's personality and communication skills. How the person interacts with you will be indicative of his or her communication skills in business. If you sense any negativity in your discussion, the candidate may have an attitude problem. The last thing you need is an employee with an attitude when they deal front-line with customers.

it is volunteered, and you must not let it affect your hiring decision.

4. Ask about expectations

Find out about the candidate's future career goals and how long this position would meet their needs. Ask what they expect of you as an employer. Then tell them what you expect of an employee. Discuss salary expectations, benefits, and how you see the candidate fitting in long-term.

REFERENCE CHECKS

The golden rule for checking references is: *Never hire a candidate without a thorough reference check.* Where possible, insist on business-related references. If someone refuses to give a reference, consider this a red flag. Try talking to someone in a position of authority at the same business, or do not hire the candidate. If an employee was entirely satisfactory, employers are usually more than willing to give a good reference. Don't trust personal references, as it is common practice to have friends and relatives lie, exaggerate, or not know the whole story, as shown in the Real Life example "No Check—No Money."

Real Life **No Check—No Money**

A busy hairdressing salon owner desperately needed an employee when a stylist quit without notice. A friend recommended someone she had known for years, who was hired instantly without a reference check. It was later discovered that the employee had been liberally helping herself to the till and pocketing business income paid to her by customers.

On investigating the employee's background, a belated reference check found one business that refused to give the employee a reference, while the other had fired her for the same behavior.

Ten Key Questions
for Checking References

When you call to check on a candidate's reference, get answers to the following questions:

1. **Employment:** Confirm the dates, position held, and job responsibilities.

2. **Work habits:** Was the candidate punctual and reliable?

3. **Motivation:** Was the candidate motivated and without undue absenteeism?

4. **Relationships:** How did the candidate relate to other employees?

5. **Supervision:** How did he or she cope with being supervised? If the job involved a supervisory role, was it performed successfully?

6. **Personality traits:** Was the candidate honest, trustworthy, cheerful, and positive?

7. **Negatives:** Were there any negative aspects you should know about?

8. **Positives:** Were there any positive aspects that made this candidate special?

9. **Rehire:** Given the right circumstances, would you rehire the candidate?

10. **Other information:** Is there anything else you think I should know before hiring this candidate?

DESIGN A BASIC TEST

....

If the position requires preparing correspondence or using software, ask the candidate to compose and type a business letter or enter some data into the accounting program. Technicians could be asked to answer some specific questions and tradespeople to demonstrate their abilities. Some employment agencies offer applicant testing, usually for a fee. This might save time or prove useful if you are not comfortable doing it yourself.

YOUR RESPONSIBILITIES AS AN EMPLOYER

Understand all the other responsibilities involved in becoming a boss, including determining your hiring structure, knowing the extra costs, and tackling any problems you encounter. Some business owners make the mistake of employing someone before looking at all the costs involved. Then, when cash gets tight, they have to lay them off, which wastes their time, money, and effort, and ultimately, doesn't solve the growth problem of needing help.

Hiring the self-employed

The term "self-employed" applies to casual labor, subcontractors, and self-employed commissioned salespeople. If they do not have workers' compensation coverage, then it is usually your responsibility to provide it, so check the labor codes and workers' compensation regulations in your state. You do not pay any employee benefits and can use their services as required. Self-employed people should bill you at least monthly.

Some chintzy employers hire people on a subcontract instead of an employee basis—an illegal practice. Clients have come to me at year-end to report their subcontract earnings, only to discover that they have to pay large tax and pension sums as they have worked full time for one employer. If these contractors report you to the state Department of Labor, you may be liable for unpaid employee benefits, overtime, and vacation pay. Over a period of time, this can amount to a substantial sum of money.

Commissioned salespeople

Whether you hire on a self-employed or salaried commission structure, decide which expenses (such as auto costs) will be paid by the business. Some employers pay a monthly vehicle allowance, so clearly define your expense limits as they quickly mount up.

A regular expense report should be completed, including a mileage log of all business-related trips. Normal commissioned expenses can include an automobile, telephone, clients' lunches, travel expenses, and a home office. Create a policy dictating whether the employee can claim non-reimbursed employment expenses on their personal taxes. To claim these, the employee usually completes a Form 2106 to file with their taxes.

Part- and full-time employees

Become conversant with federal or state employment standards and payroll requirements. Understand your obligations, including overtime, statutory holidays, vacation pay, benefits, and termination procedures. There is a lot to learn and many forms to complete. Employment standards and other employer information is available to download at ***www.sba.gov/starting_business/employees/law.html***.

You must maintain detailed payroll records for all employees and payroll remittances must be made on time to avoid heavy penalties. At year-end, the whole payroll must be reconciled. It's wise to prepare a full job description outlining the employee's responsibilities, followed up by a meeting with the employee to discuss and clarify issues. An employment contract safeguards against future disputes, so consult with a lawyer.

In all cases, keep a detailed file on each employee. Document all discussions, terms, grievances, and evaluations. Memories are short but paper lasts. This file is invaluable for reviewing work performance or for when an employee has to be terminated.

HOW MUCH DOES AN EMPLOYEE COST?

For a full-time employee, the hourly rate is just the start of your expenses. Add approximately 25 percent to the salary to cover all mandatory costs. Figure 7.2 breaks down a monthly salary calculation.

Figure **7.2**

Example of a Monthly Salary Calculation

40 hours a week x 4.33 weeks per month	173.20 hours
173.2 hours x $15	$2,598.00
4 percent vacation pay	103.92
Federal employer deductions	198.74
State employer deductions	116.91
One statutory vacation	120.00
Workers' compensation (average rate of $3.50/$100)	90.94
Total monthly employee cost:	$3,228.51

This employee costs an extra $3.64 an hour or $630 a month, with an average of two-and-one-half days a month being non-productive due to statutory holidays and vacation pay, so be sure to incorporate the full cost of hiring into your planning. None of these costs—excluding workers' compensation—apply to subcontractors, so be fair when you negotiate their rate.

Other costly factors

The cost of hiring doesn't stop at wages. To help plan your monthly cash flow, review the list of additional employee expenses in Figure 7.3.

Figure **7.3**

Additional Employer Expenses

	Amount
☐ coffee, bottled water, snacks	_____
☐ new lunchroom equipment	_____
☐ office equipment and furniture	_____
☐ computer and accessories	_____
☐ expense account items (auto, travel, etc.)	_____
☐ cell phone or pager	_____

☐ bonuses or incentives	_____
☐ corporate clothing	_____
☐ stationery and business cards	_____
☐ telephone line	_____
☐ parking space rental	_____
☐ medical benefits	_____
☐ staff lunches	_____
☐ training programs	_____
☐ sick leave	_____
☐ vehicle allowance	_____
Total additional costs:	$_____

MAKE YOUR EMPLOYEES "LIFERS"

The secret to being a good boss is striking a balance between being a positive, motivational leader who is respected—along with the company rules—and not being a pushover or a negative influence. Employees need more than money to keep them working at peak performance levels. The more incentive they have, the more your business flourishes. Use the "LIFER" strategy to achieve these goals:

- **Learning:** Most employees want to learn and progress up the ladder; it fulfills the human need for accomplishment. Overworked employers have told me that they have no time to teach employees—yet jobs won't be completed properly and the business suffers if staff are not trained. Schedule training into your agenda or send promising employees to appropriate courses.

- **Incentive:** A paycheck isn't the ultimate incentive. What else can you offer to keep your employees motivated? There are many simple programs you can incorporate, from employee of the month rewards, sales and productivity bonuses, extra time off, or a weekend away for a job well done to the opportunity of promotion based on performance.

> *Learning*
> *Incentive*
> *Fun*
> *Encouragement*
> *Responsibility*

SHOW THE TEAM YOUR APPRECIATION

The secret to a successful employee-employer relationship is team-building. Make all employees feel like an important part of the business—which they are. Show appreciation while still maintaining rules and boundaries. Recognize their efforts and achievements by sharing them with both employees and customers. Have an employee "wall of fame."

- **Fun:** This simple three-letter word is sadly lacking from many businesses. Make work a fun place. Have theme days, red-nose days, a joke of the month competition, smiley faces or happy posters in the lunchroom, and special fun events where employees get to know each other and relax. Become known as a fun business—experience shows that business will increase, as in the Real Life example "Having Fun...and Letting Go."

- **Encouragement:** Every employee needs recognition for a job well done. Never assume that a paycheck is enough. Recognize employees' efforts to make good suggestions, reach targets, or handle delicate or difficult situations well.

- **Responsibility:** Give your employees some responsibility. By making them accountable, you are saying that you trust them to do a good job, which gives them a confidence boost, which in turn encourages them to strive harder.

Real Life **Having Fun...and Letting Go**

Teresa operated a small deli, offering soups, sandwiches, and homemade baked goods. She implemented theme days every few months and found that employees' attitudes changed. They got excited planning for the days, working as a team, and having some real fun. It was infectious. The customers loved it.

By decorating the deli, wearing costumes, and having novelty prizes for customers—coupled with astute business management—business steadily increased. Customers enjoyed the fun and wanted to be involved. Of course, they told a friend who told a friend...

On the other hand, Billie-Ray was a tense, highly strung boss who mothered her employees to death. During one seminar I was holding at an annual conference, she crept out to answer her cell phone. She told me later that her employees were calling from hundreds of miles away to have her solve their problems.

I suggested that she let them know the phone would be turned off and that she trusted their judgment and problem-solving because they were capable people. The next day, Billie-Ray was ecstatic.

"Fran!" she exclaimed. "You'll never guess what! I called the store, did what you suggested, and my employees solved not one but five problems! They said it made them feel so good to have that responsibility. You don't know what this means to me and to them. Thank you."

It was a simple yet effective solution. Show confidence and trust in your employees, let go, and watch your business blossom.

Are you a good boss—or a bad boss?

Take the "Good Boss, Bad Boss" quiz in Figure 7.4 and see how you score. Of course, the more answers you check under "Good Boss," the better the relationship you will build with your employees and the more productive they will be. Now you are team-building.

Figure 7.4

The Dos and Don'ts of Team-Building— Good Boss, Bad Boss Quiz

Positive: Good Boss
- ☐ Always says thank you for a job well done
- ☐ Praises and rewards extra efforts from employees

continued

Negative: Bad Boss
- ☐ Takes the "that's what they are paid for" attitude
- ☐ Expects employees to continually give without recognition

Positive: Good Boss

- ☐ Meets regularly to discuss problems and listens to employees' concerns
- ☐ Starts an incentive system
- ☐ Is understanding of family crises and allows time off for urgent matters
- ☐ Takes employees to lunch occasionally
- ☐ Sends sick employees home
- ☐ Asks how the family is
- ☐ Discusses situations that could threaten employee's job, such as a work shortage
- ☐ Reviews performance and salaries regularly and discusses any job-related concerns
- ☐ Throws a Christmas party or summer barbeque
- ☐ Clearly defines job responsibilities
- ☐ Shares business successes and keeps employees informed of business progress
- ☐ Allows adequate learning and training time
- ☐ Gives adequate warnings of potential layoffs
- ☐ Asks employees to work overtime
- ☐ Pays overtime at the correct scale
- ☐ Doesn't penalize an employee for arriving late due to an emergency situation
- ☐ Keeps mind and door open

Negative: Bad Boss

- ☐ Ignores concerns because it must be done his or her way
- ☐ Complains about rising wage costs
- ☐ Threatens employee with loss of job if too much time off is taken
- ☐ Does nothing extra for employees
- ☐ Makes sick employees stay at work
- ☐ Shows no caring or concern
- ☐ Tells employees that their job could be on the line if they don't perform
- ☐ Gives only mandatory raises and threatens layoff if work performance doesn't improve
- ☐ Does nothing to mark seasonal or special events
- ☐ Expects employees to do anything he or she asks
- ☐ Takes all the credit and tells employees nothing about the business
- ☐ Expects employees to learn immediately, with little or no training
- ☐ Fires or lays off employees on the spot
- ☐ Demands that employees work overtime
- ☐ Pays overtime at normal hourly rate
- ☐ Deducts pay for every minute not worked no matter what the situation
- ☐ Keeps mind and door closed

EMPLOYEE THEFT—AN EMPLOYER'S NIGHTMARE

Unfortunately, countless employees take advantage of their employers by building a relationship of trust and then stealing from the company. The innovative methods used could fill a book. Don't create tempting situations, and do incorporate systems to curtail theft or keep it to a minimum. Here are six of the more common techniques used by employees who steal:

1. Merchandise theft

Employees often take things that don't belong to them. It could be as small as a stapler or as large as a sofa. Theft can be difficult to detect, such as a nibble from the deli section. Make your policies and consequences clear. Ensure you have a foolproof inventory and administrative system.

2. Cash theft

With an efficient accounting system, most cash thefts can be discovered. Monitor the petty cash, and make sure there are legitimate receipts for expenses. Balance retail tills daily, and make employees accountable for losses. Cash used from the till must have a supporting invoice.

3. Time theft

Employees can steal copious time from you: those few extra minutes at breaks, lengthy personal phone calls, playing computer games, sending personal emails, Internet-surfing, arriving late and leaving early, not using equipment correctly and causing breakdowns, taking days off for personal reasons but calling in sick, being hung over and working more slowly, making stupid errors, taking personal detours on company business, and using company vehicles for personal matters. Where will you draw the line?

4. Computer theft

Files can be easily copied onto disks and CD-ROMs in seconds and slipped into a purse or briefcase. The information can be sold to others, or if an employee moves to another job, they could take your customer information with them. Installing the appropriate computer security system may be necessary.

Checking computer-generated checks is of particular importance. One enterprising young woman working in a large payroll department created two fictitious employees, prepared computerized checks, opened false

> ### BE OBSERVANT
> *Watch for any change in an employee's behavior—guilt, overexuberance to help, a sudden aggressive approach, or unusual withdrawal—as it could be a red flag. Watch for repetitive cash shortages during one person's shift as was the pattern in the Real Life example "Stealing with a Smile." If you don't write the checks, know all the suppliers that you write checks to and review the disbursements monthly.*

bank accounts, and regularly cashed the checks. She also gave herself a few hundred dollars a month raise. Because of the large volume of checks, the employer signed them quickly and didn't get suspicious for quite a few months. The total documented theft amounted to over $10,000.

Real Life | **Stealing with a Smile**

In one situation I encountered, a sales assistant insisted on taking the lunch shift, sending her boss out to "make sure she ate well and had a break." When merchandise was sold during this period, she would ring up the sale, then ask the customer if they needed a receipt. If not, she later voided the sale, pocketing the cash.

Finally becoming suspicious, the owner monitored the till tapes closely, discovering the consistent lunchtime voids. The employee was fired, but the estimated loss amounted to thousands of dollars.

5. Reputation theft

A disgruntled employee can do significant damage to your reputation by maliciously gossiping to other employees or by "bad-mouthing" you to friends, customers, and business associates. Your hard work is being destroyed by one malcontent. Watch for subtle warning signs of a troublemaker and keep an open line of communication with your employees. Where appropriate, you may want to instigate an employee suggestion box and an anonymous complaint box. It's amazing what you will learn.

6. White-collar crime

The Real Life example "Stealing with a Smile" is an example of white-collar crime. In many such cases, theft from an employer seems not to be taken as seriously as crimes involving violence or shoplifting. It is difficult to prove unless accurate accounting records are maintained and evidence carefully documented. All you can do is install theft-proofing systems and monitor your employees' actions closely.

YOUR HIRING CHECKLIST

If you are ready to become an employer, use Figure 7.5 to ensure that you follow all the right steps and remember to use the Lifer principles. Good luck with choosing your new employees.

With these hiring guidelines, your new team will soon be in place and you'll be ready to take a giant step forward—nearly. You now need to increase revenues to justify your hiring. Before you can effectively market and sell, you need to know to whom you are marketing. Chapter 8 shows you how to define your customers and polish your marketing plan.

Figure **7.5**

Your Hiring Checklist

	Yes	No
1. I have answered "yes" to all the questions in Figure 7.1.	☐	☐
2. I have defined a need for an employee.	☐	☐
3. I have prepared a detailed job description.	☐	☐
4. I know under what terms I will hire.	☐	☐
5 I have prepared my job priority list.	☐	☐
6. I know which methods are best to locate an employee.	☐	☐
7. I know the benefits I will offer.	☐	☐
8. I have read and graded the résumés.	☐	☐
9. I have made a list of questions for the interviews.	☐	☐
10. I have written out my expectations of an employee.	☐	☐
11. I have checked at least three of the candidate's business references.	☐	☐
12. I have administered a basic test of employee skills.	☐	☐
13. I understand my responsibilities as an employer.	☐	☐
14. I have calculated the additional payroll costs.	☐	☐
15. I have calculated the additional associated costs.	☐	☐
16. I understand what constitutes a "good boss."	☐	☐
17. I will incorporate the "Lifer" strategies into my policies.	☐	☐
18. I have defined how to handle difficult situations.	☐	☐
19. I am aware of theft and have taken steps to prevent it.	☐	☐
20. I can afford to pay an employee.	☐	☐
21. I have read and understand the relevant labor laws.	☐	☐
22. I understand the workers' compensation requirements.	☐	☐

CHAPTER EIGHT

How Do You Grow and Maintain Your Customer Base?

—◦—

The public must and will be served.
WILLIAM PENN

—◦—

Whether a business has been operating four months or forty years, finding and keeping customers remains the biggest challenge. "I can't seem to find new customers," or "My advertising isn't working for me!" are common complaints heard from the majority of small business owners. ๑

ARE YOU MISSING YOUR MARKET?

The key to growing and keeping customers is to plan a focused, targeted marketing strategy that incorporates superior customer service policies. For the small business, service will set you apart from the competition. From the first phone call to after-sales follow-up, growing your customer base is as easy as looking at your business from the customers' viewpoint and changing what is lacking. There are many effective, low-cost marketing methods you can use. If you target a specific market, the results will be far superior.

You are confronted by a vast selection of marketing tools and techniques, and each day, the choices expand as technology progresses. The Internet is a classic example of how most businesses are being forced to change their marketing strategies. Seems that now if you don't have a website, you are hardly taken seriously. The key to successful marketing is to keep up with these changes and focus your strategies on the direction that consumer trends are taking.

So how do you increase your customer base? Where are your customers? Who are they? You need many of your Eight Essential Entrepreneurial Skills to feel comfortable with the challenges marketing poses. If you use hit or miss techniques, these costly adventures usually have minimal return for a maximum outlay. The basics outlined in this chapter will be expanded on in Chapters 11 and 12 to guarantee your long-term business growth.

> ## TRY NOT MARKETING
>
> *Few customers are going to knock on your door to give you business. You have to make it happen. The minute you stop promoting a new business, business stops. Sourcing potential sales, finding avenues for promotion and follow-up should be part of your daily routine. Try an experiment. Stop calling and sourcing out business for a week or two and see how quiet your phone becomes. Never stop marketing.*

UNDERSTAND THE COMPONENTS OF MARKETING

Misconceptions abound about what marketing really means. Marketing is not selling—selling is selling.

Marketing is...

Marketing is informing potential customers about your products or services. By now, you should have defined who and where your market is. To market, you have to advertise and promote to specific consumers using various methods. "Targeting your market" refers to finding out who needs your business and narrowing your marketing focus toward these people.

Promotion is...

Promotion refers to the techniques that you use to attract customers. You can network, communicate with potential customers, go to a trade show, hold an open house or grand opening, and advertise.

Advertising is...

Advertising is using the media, including radio, television, the Internet, coupons or flyers, to carry your message. Many people mistakenly think that printed advertising is the only way to get their name known. Consumers are overwhelmed with advertising, so before you spend expensive dollars, research the success of these methods for your sector.

REVISIT YOUR MARKETING PLAN

If you are experiencing difficulty increasing sales, it's time to use "the three Rs of marketing." Revisit, reevaluate, and revise your marketing plan. Such a plan is essential in effectively marketing your business—which methods you will use, when you will use them, and what they cost. If you don't have one, start now. Revisit it frequently to guarantee its continuing value to your business.

> ## WEAR THE CONSUMER'S SHOES
>
> *Identify the marketing techniques that you have responded to as a consumer. Note the ones that persuaded you to purchase a product or use a service. Would any of these methods work for your business? How can you apply them?*

REEVALUATE YOUR MARKETING PLAN

If your original marketing plan isn't reaping the desired results, it's time to reevaluate why. Many factors affect how consumers view your business and how and when they will spend their money. You may have found that your products or services need modifying to keep up with changing economic or technological trends.

Unfortunately, because consumers' needs and wants are always changing as age demographics and trends change, so must you change the way you market to them. Study your past methods of reaching out to consumers and answer the questions in Figure 8.1.

Figure **8.1**

Review of Marketing Strategies

	Yes	No
1. Is what you thought would work still working?	☐	☐
2. Do you know how it has changed?	☐	☐
3. Do you monitor which methods are succeeding profitably ?	☐	☐
4. Do you know what isn't working?	☐	☐
5. Has your original market focus changed?	☐	☐
6. Do you know why it has changed?	☐	☐
7. Is this a long-term change?	☐	☐
8. Are you spending enough time and money on marketing?	☐	☐

Reevaluate marketing methods and messages

Marketing magic begins with knowing whom you are marketing to and understanding their needs. Analyze your marketing methods and messages and remember that because times change, so must the methods and messages you use. Complete the quick questionnaire in Figure 8.2 as part of the reevaluation process.

Figure **8.2**

Review of Marketing Methods and Messages

	Yes	No
1. Have you recently changed any marketing strategies?	☐	☐
2. Do your messages imply that you will fill customers' needs?	☐	☐
3. Have you "branded" your business?	☐	☐
4. Does your marketing message cater to solving customers' problems?	☐	☐
5. Have you built an ideal customer profile?	☐	☐
6. Are you niche-marketing?	☐	☐
7. Have you explored secondary markets?	☐	☐
8. Have you defined your Unique Selling Proposition (USP)?	☐	☐

What the heck is a USP?

Before you look for more customers, be very clear on what is special about your business and why customers should choose you over the competition. As urban centers grow, more competitors move in. A small business can rarely compete with cheaper prices, so what sets you apart from other businesses?

People are looking to businesses to solve their problems and fill their needs. Think about how your business can meet these requirements. What is special or different about your business? When you decide, this is your **Unique Selling Proposition (USP).** Write down and use your USP as an important component of your marketing messages, as did Jennifer in the Real Life example "Sewing Up Her USP."

What is uniquely yours and sets you apart from the competition ?

_____

_____

_____

Real Life) **Sewing Up Her USP**

Jennifer attended a marketing seminar to find innovative ways to increase business. The economy was slow, as was business. She had purchased a sewing machine and fabric store two years ago in a now sprawling suburban city, and competitors were moving in.

The instructor asked the class to share their Unique Selling Propositions. There was silence. Obviously, no one used one in their marketing. Jennifer thought for a while and then told the class that the business had been established for over ninety years, and that collectively, the employees had over a hundred years of industry experience.

"Well," said the instructor, "that has to be a real USP! Nearly two hundred years between the two."

"I never thought," replied Jennifer, "but yes, the one thing our store has is a well-established reputation, and all those experts! I'll definitely be using that as my USP in my marketing from now on."

CAPITALIZE ON TRENDS
••••••••••••••••••••••••••••••••

Keep abreast of current and predicted consumer trends. For example, if the economy is suffering, how could you address the fact that people have less disposable income and that you could possibly solve some of their problems? Remember that for every adverse reaction, there is a positive action you can take if you put some creative thought into it.

Evaluate changing trends

Realize that trends will directly affect your business. Is the market growing, consistent, or slowly declining? Are prices becoming more competitive? Is technology changing to a point where it may affect your sales in a year's time? Are consumer trends changing? People often become so consumed in their business that they miss changes in the world around them.

Evaluate finances

There is no way around it. Money is a necessary ingredient for increasing your customer base, so you have to calculate how much you can afford to spend on marketing each month.

Underbudgeting is an expensive mistake. Most businesses start on a limited budget, leaving little room for continued marketing costs. By preparing an annual cash flow projection, your figures will indicate how much room there is in your budget for marketing.

REVISE YOUR MARKETING PLAN

To revise your marketing plan, remember that there is more to marketing than just advertising and promotion. This section will guide you through revising your plan, with suggestions for improvement.

The considerations in revising your plan are divided into four categories:

1. Your business image and branding techniques
2. Targeting your market
3. Your marketing budget
4. Your marketing techniques (see Chapters 11 and 12)

YOUR BUSINESS IMAGE AND BRANDING TECHNIQUES

You want to be remembered and referred by customers. Having a sharp and professional image is mandatory. Have you branded your business? If so, how? If it is a little scruffy, refine by revisiting these five important areas.

Name

People remember businesses with clever or easy-to-remember names. Does your name aptly describe what you do? If you have a registered name and don't want to change it, retain the original name and create a subsidiary name. As an example, my business started in 1983 as Eastleigh Management Services, as it was located on Eastleigh Crescent. My website

> ## MAKE YOUR NAME WORK FOR YOU
>
> *One woman who sells therapeutic mattresses calls her business Sleep Matters. Another woman named her mattress store Sleep Depot—short, snappy, and easily remembered. It certainly beats E.D. Enterprises. What is E.D. Enterprises anyway? Make your name market your business and work for you. It's the beginning of low-cost marketing magic.*

domain is *www.smallbizpro.com*. I have now registered Smallbizpro.com Services and use both for different aspects of my business.

Logo and slogan

If you don't have a logo or slogan, consult with a graphics professional to design a corporate image. People recognize logos and associate them with "serious" businesses. One Canadian moving company named their business "Two Small Men With Big Hearts Moving Company." Their name became their slogan and is easily remembered.

I use "The Small Business Specialist," a simple but easy-to-remember slogan. Your logo or slogan can work hard for you if you are creative. A little naughty but never forgotten is the slogan used by one scaffolding company, whose T-shirts read, "Call us for an instant erection." Say no more. If you don't yet have a slogan, jot down some ideas here.

_____

_____

_____

PROMOTE YOUR MISSION STATEMENT

Writing down your mission statement makes you more committed to excellence. Splash it on brochures and promotional material. This reflects a professional attitude to customers. Many businesses hang their framed mission statement in offices or reception areas where customers can see them.

Mission statement

A mission statement is a few sentences that reflect your business goals and commitment to your customers. This written statement reminds you of why you are in business and indicates to customers that you care. It can be short and simple but should capture the spirit of your business. For a service business, it could be a sentence such as, "To always be there for our customers in times of emergency, and to never keep them waiting." This simple statement really says to customers: "I care about you."

Corporate theme

If you don't have a corporate theme, develop one. It should incorporate all of the above: a snappy name, logo or slogan, and mission statement, with clothing, vehicles, promotional material, and stationery all proudly bearing your corporate image.

Staff and business appearance

Take a complete inventory of the physical appearance of your business, including the office, vehicles, staff, and your personal appearance. What looks untidy, dirty, or badly organized? See it from a customer's point of view on their first visit. Would they be impressed?

> # WEAR YOUR NAME
> *Have your logo and name printed on hats, T-shirts, and coveralls. Counter staff or representatives should have corporate shirts, sweaters, or golf shirts laundered so that employees always present a professional business image. The investment in corporate clothing will more than pay off, and it is tax-deductible.*

Real Life Cleaning Up Their Act

Jerry and Stan operated an appliance sales and repair store. They were always getting appliances in to repair, and the store became cluttered over the years. Working in an all-male store, the restroom in particular deteriorated and was usually not that clean. Yet most of their customers were women.

One day, a female shopper asked to use the restroom. Jerry gave her the key, but she returned very quickly.

"That place is disgusting!" she snapped. "I wouldn't use that restroom if it was the last one on earth!" The potential customer stormed out without purchasing, nearly tripping over some hoses lying near the door. Jerry and Stan's apologies fell on deaf ears. They looked at each other guiltily.

They related this story to their accountant, Elizabeth, who looked at them and shook her head.

continued

"From a woman's perspective, what should we do?" asked Jerry.

"Listen, guys, what percentage of your customers are women?"

"Oh, about 75 percent," answered Stan.

"So why wouldn't you clean up the store and restroom and cater to your customers then?" asked Elizabeth. "You may be men in a men-operated store, but you are catering to women shoppers."

The message finally hit home. Jerry and Stan cleaned up their store (and restroom), painted the walls, and put some flowers on the counter. They noticed over a period of time that more women came into the store, because women tend to tell a friend, who tells a friend, who tells a friend...

A dirty or untidy storefront shows customers that perhaps this business is unorganized or doesn't care. Ensure that you and your employees are well groomed. Even a mechanic can wear clean coveralls. Remember—first impressions are critical.

Remember too that women generally control the purse strings and make buying decisions for approximately 80 percent of consumable income. Catering to what women want will help most small businesses grow, as in the Real Life example "Cleaning Up Their Act."

Ten Tips
for Sprucing Up Your Store

1. **Window displays:** What message is your window display carrying? For example, a sterile piece of equipment doesn't attract female shoppers, but if the display incorporates some colorful billowing fabric, the perception softens and makes the display more inviting.

2. **Interior appearance:** Are the wall colors warm and inviting? Has the store had a coat of paint lately? Women notice shabby, scuffed, or dirty walls. If the store needs a paint job, then paint it because it makes all the difference.

3. **Organization:** A well-organized store appeals to women; they are used to being organized. Signs should clearly direct them to products. Women are too busy and get frustrated if they can't find something. Is there enough room to easily move around, or do they have to step over or squeeze past stuff?

4. **Product displays:** Products should be neatly displayed, with clear signage, prices, features, benefits, and information. If you offer numerous services, have them clearly outlined through signs around the store.

5. **One-stop shopping:** Accessories are income-generators, and women need convenience. Ensure that you carry a good selection of accessories so that shoppers don't have to go elsewhere.

6. **Sale and clearance items:** The average woman shopper is first attracted by sale or clearance signs. If you don't have anything on sale, offer *something* that is discounted. Make the signs large and place a small teaser rack at the front of the store and the balance closer to the back so that they have to first walk past regularly priced items.

7. **Staff appearance and manners:** It should go without saying that both you and your staff should be neatly dressed and well groomed (in corporate logo clothing). Always treat customers as VSPs—Very Special People.

8. **Washroom availability:** Have an accessible and clean washroom for customers on the run. It may be a small thing to you, but it means a lot to your customers. Many women plan their shopping route based on where they can find a nice, clean washroom.

9. **Say "welcome":** Women are often busy, stressed, on the run, and missing meals when they shop. Nothing is more tantalizing than a pot of coffee and cookies.

10. **Amuse children:** Parents with children welcome any distraction for their charges so they can focus on purchasing. Have a small play center set up for young children with some special treats on hand.

TARGET YOUR MARKET

If you have a clear understanding of who and where your market is, finding and keeping new customers becomes easier. In many instances, there may be new, untapped, and potential markets that you are not aware of.

Some people start up without researching where and who their market is. As an example, one fashion boutique proprietor felt that her market was all the women in her community, but it wasn't. Her clothes were expensive, and she was located in a small strip mall in a middle- to lower-class community where the average person couldn't afford to pay her prices. There were more accessible fashion stores in a nearby larger mall. The business closed in under a year.

To better target and understand your market, explore these two main areas:

- Defining your market demographics
- Finding niche and secondary markets

STUDY THE POPULATION

Study your geographic selling area and note where the main concentration of each type of dwelling or business is. For example, if there are low-income apartment areas and you cater to middle-income customers, you will know not to market to these areas. This knowledge is helpful for planning your marketing focus. Your municipal hall can help you with many of these statistics and local demographics.

Defining your market demographics

Understanding the demographics of your consumers—that is, who and where they are—allows for focused planning of your marketing campaign. Different methods are needed to target consumers who live different lifestyles. Where people live will determine where, how, and what they buy.

Know your average consumer's age

What is the average age group of people who use your business? Are you in the right location to service them? Many communities have concentrated populations of certain age groups, such as townhouse complexes. Your marketing should be designed to attract the main age group you are targeting.

Understand consumers' shopping habits

If you understand how and where the average consumer shops, you can better target your marketing to accommodate their needs.

Know who you are targeting

Are you targeting residential or commercial consumers? Which generates more profits? Determine which market you cater to and focus on it. Remember—the goal is to become known as the expert in one area rather than being master of none.

Research your community and competitors

Use these avenues to conduct your market research:

- Visit your local government office and ask for information on local demographics—all the statistics you need are usually there.
- Research your competitors using the Yellow Pages. Study their advertisements in the local papers to see what they offer.
- Visit (and join) your local chamber of commerce. They work closely with the business community and have a current business membership directory. Members have access to the directory, which gives a good indication of similar businesses within the community. The staff is usually very knowledgeable and helpful, and knows most of their members' businesses.
- Surf the Internet and browse competitors' websites. You may find some new and innovative marketing ideas.
- Visit trade shows that attract businesses similar to yours. See how competitors and other businesses market their wares. You will come away full of new ideas.

> ## STUDY PREVIOUS CUSTOMERS
> ....
> *Look at past sales records to see where previous business has come from. For example, if over 60 percent is local, then your marketing should focus locally. However, if your service can be offered outside of your community, calculate what physical boundaries are practical. Consider traveling time and your hourly billing rate. Is it profitable to travel farther afield? Or could the networking contacts help you to build both your reputation and the business?*

Know your physical boundaries

If you are a retail outlet or local service business, most of your business will be generated from the local community. Know your physical boundary because it's useless to market outside of this geographic area unless you are a specialized business.

Know your competition

Customer loyalty is often dictated by their wallets. Investigate your competitors regularly. Study pricing, product lines, advertising and promotion techniques, and customer service policies.

Find out: How long have they been in business? Do people travel a distance to their location? Why? How busy are they? How do they treat their customers? Study their displays to see what appeals to the customers. Think of innovative methods that will allow you to compete without resorting to price-cutting.

DON'T MAKE CUSTOMERS WAIT

The average North American spends at least five years of life waiting in lines, and will not wait more than two minutes in a line before leaving the store, and wants to be served by knowledgeable people. Being an expert is important to the consumer, as is prompt service. Compared to the competition, are you offering the same or better service and expertise? Be better than your competitors so that you stand out in a crowd.

Study consumers' incomes

You won't sell antiques to people living in a low-income area. Define the income bracket of the majority of people in your marketing area. If it is 60 percent middle-income and 30 percent low-income, your marketing methods, product mix or service should be geared accordingly.

Understand consumer spending cycles

Consumers spend in cycles dictated by the time of year, their financial position, changing trends, and the time they have for shopping. Families with working parents are usually looking for the quickest way to obtain the best product or service at the cheapest price.

Talk to as many people as you can, tell them about your business, and ask them their expectations of an ideal business. Listen to their answers—you may find some innovative ways to market that will fulfill these needs. Even better, design a short customer satisfaction survey and give every customer who completes one a small thank-you gift.

Service home-based businesses

Over 50 percent of small businesses are now home-based in North America, often operated by busy entrepreneurs wearing sixty different hats. How could you service these people? Office stationers, dairies, dry cleaners, personal coaches, massage therapists, vehicle repairers, and personal chefs all cater to the millions of people working from home who need convenience, so why not your business too?

Build your ideal consumer profile

After the research is completed, you will have an excellent profile of your ideal consumer. Now you can plan how to target this market without wasting valuable dollars.

Finding niche and secondary markets

Many businesses start up with one primary source of income in mind, not realizing that there are also lucrative secondary and niche markets available. As an example, my self-published companion book to *Taking Your Business to the Next Level* is entitled *Business for Beginners*, which to date has sold over 130,000 copies. Traditionally, the primary marketing focus for both publishers and authors has been retail bookstores. After I thoroughly explored marketing to the self-employment and business start-up market, *Business for Beginners* became available as an added bonus with business planning software products. By selling the electronic rights, it is available on

> **THINK OUTSIDE THE BOX**
> ....
> *Think creatively outside of your golden box of opportunity. Can you market to clubs, associations, groups, government agencies, hospitals, schools, other countries, colleges, manufacturing companies or large corporations? You are only limited by your imagination and persistence.*

Intuit's Quicken and Quick Tax programs. It is used by many entrepreneurship programs as either a text or a resource, and is found on most small business reference library shelves. Some colleges and high schools that include an entrepreneurial component in their business education courses also use it. It is soon to be published in six countries, while *Taking Your Business to the Next Level* will be published in five…and counting.

These markets have become more primary than secondary markets because, in many cases, they generate regular, repeat volume orders and sell for a higher profit than through a book distributor. And that's just two books. Find your niche, explore it, exploit it, and be the first—or best—to fill that niche.

Look for multiple and repeat business

Once you have thoroughly targeted your market and niche, think about how you can fulfill their needs. If your consumer market ranges from teenagers to college students, think about where these people spend most of their time. Could you introduce your business to schools, clubs, or colleges? You could offer discounts to special interest clubs or donate part of the profit from sales to schools and associations.

Could your business be tailored to the large population of baby boomers and senior citizens? How could you introduce your business to seniors' complexes, rest homes, or recreation centers? I know of entrepreneurs who teach yoga and fitness or do massages and foot care at seniors' centers and who also offer the service in seniors' homes. My ninety-five-year-old mom has a wonderful woman who comes into her home every six weeks and for $35 gives her a complete foot massage, pedicure, and foot treatment. This solved a great problem for both of us. Her feet get taken care of and I don't have to drive her into town.

YOUR MARKETING BUDGET

Few businesses can survive and succeed without spending money on marketing. As each business requires different marketing strategies, before you plan your marketing budget, read the following four marketing chapters to define the most effective methods for you. After identifying the techniques that may work for you, monitor the results closely to assess their effectiveness, reach, and longevity.

Plan ahead

Timing is crucial for planning and implementing your marketing ideas. There are times when it doesn't even pay to advertise. Do people really want their furnaces serviced in summer? No—but they are thinking about it in the fall, so you should start a strong marketing push when children return to school. You can offer specials during the slow season, but don't expect overwhelming results.

Set a budget

If your business is relatively new, you may have to spend 10 to 15 percent of sales to get and keep your name recognized. A marketing budget should never be less than 4 percent of sales.

If your sales are $5,000 a month, you should be spending between $200 and $750 a month on marketing. Some of these costs have to be paid in advance, such as trade show deposits, so have the funds available. You have to spend money to make money.

Review past sales figures to decide which months need an advertising push. Capitalize on special events and seasons such as Christmas. Your name needs to be consistently in consumers' eyes, so have funds available each month for some form of promotion. If you can't afford to spend the money, consult your accountant for some advice and use a combination of the low-cost strategies discussed in this book.

Combine techniques

One strong push won't bring long-term business, so as you plan your budget, allow for using a combination of techniques. This may include a trade show, seminar, or workshop, coupled with a small advertisement in the local paper and a press release. Set out an annual schedule and use a mixture of techniques that will have their most powerful results during your peak selling seasons.

Figure 8.3 on page 180 shows a four-month marketing plan for a residential air purifier company, using a marketing budget of 5 percent of projected sales. The owner plans to use a well-rounded, low-cost, yet effective mix of marketing techniques.

> ### BOOK SPACE EARLY
> ....
> *If you choose to advertise in newspapers or magazines, be familiar with their copy and camera-ready artwork deadlines. Magazines usually require copy two months ahead of printing. If you are booking a trade show or mall display, obtain their annual program of events, as many of the spaces are booked up to a year in advance. Newspapers and magazines supply annual schedules of publishing themes, and you can usually obtain a copy by phoning or by looking on their website.*

Figure **8.3**

Four-Month Marketing Plan

PERFECT AIR HOME FILTRATION SYSTEMS
JANUARY 20__ TO DECEMBER 20__

	Jan.	Feb.	March	April
Sales and budget:				
Projected sales	$10,000	$12,500	$15,000	$16,000
5% marketing budget:	500	625	750	800
Marketing methods:				
Spring home trade show	—	385	—	—
Chamber networking events	—	—	70	—
Conferences	80	—	—	130
Community newspaper, weekly small display ad	120	120	120	120
Mall display, home show weekend	—	—	—	200
Networking luncheon	15	15	15	15
Chamber monthly dinner	25	25	25	25
Press releases on new product	0	0	0	0
Product evaluation	180	—	180	—
Web site hosting	30	30	30	30
Newsletter to customers and prospects	—	—	250	—
Coupons, cards, gifts, promotional aids	50	50	50	50
Brochure printing	—	—	—	230
Total cost:	$ 500	$ 625	$ 740	$ 800

Monitor results

The key to evaluating each new technique is monitoring the results. When customers call or come into your store, politely ask them where or how they heard of you, then tabulate this information.

DON'T LET 'EM OUT THE DOOR...

Building a solid customer base starts the moment a customer telephones with an inquiry. Of course, you or your employees gave them the royal telephone treatment, and they are now eager to further explore a buying relationship with you.

Once they have come through the doors into your beautifully clean, welcoming, and well-organized business—where they have been politely welcomed and immediately assisted by pleasant and knowledgeable staff—it is now your job to ensure that they love you so much that they will return.

Inform, educate, and tabulate

You can use a variety of marketing methods to help you maintain customer relationships, which will be discussed further in Chapters 11 and 12. Your aim is to make them remember—and refer you. Most important is to get their contact information, which should then be entered into your database. Use the earlier "Ten Tips for Sprucing Up Your Store," coupled with the following low-cost marketing strategies:

> ## USE A SIMPLE LEAD MONITORING SYSTEM
> ....
> *For phone inquiries, keep a two-copy message book by the phone, noting how the caller heard about your business. Add a line "referred by" to your sales invoices and then transfer the information to your invoice. You now have a permanent record of how sales or leads were generated. Review the invoices and messages each month to monitor the results. This is necessary information for formulating future marketing plans and for calculating your return on investment.*

Low-Cost Marketing Strategies

- Have a variety of informative handouts for customers to take home
- Give them your business card
- Have a new customer drawing to gather contact information
- Give them a "first-time customer" time-limited discount coupon
- Ask whether they would like to receive your email or printed newsletter or information on special offers
- Give each customer a little thank-you promotional gift when they leave
- If they purchase a product that needs future servicing, enter the date of the first service on a card for them and also into your database

WHERE CAN YOU IMPROVE?

Part of revisiting, reevaluating, and revising your marketing plan is to assess where you are now and how you can improve. Use the checklist in Figure 8.4 and for each question, determine whether you are satisfied with this area of marketing or whether you could make some improvements.

If you are completely satisfied, check the "satisfied" column. If there is absolutely nothing more you can do, then check the "completed" column. If you find areas needing improvement, check the "needs work" column. When the checklist is completed, you will have a plan ready to put into action. As you complete each stage to your satisfaction, check the "completed" column. This plan may take some time to implement, but each baby step is a step in the right direction.

GIVE SMALL AND BE REMEMBERED BIG

Something usable and as simple as a small fridge magnet, calendar, pen, mints, or a traveling sewing kit imprinted with your business's name is well appreciated by customers. We all love something for nothing and will tell a friend, who, of course, will tell a friend. Fridge magnets are a must for service businesses so consumers can easily find your contact information. Most fridges boast an assortment.

Learn to communicate your message

Once you are more focused on where and who your market is, you have to step up your marketing plans. To grow any business, you must become a competent communicator. Chapter 9 demonstrates how to present a professional written image to your customers and how to use these skills to your advantage.

Figure **8.4**

Improving Your Marketing Plan: A Checklist

	Needs work	Satisfied	Completed
1. I have set long-term goals for the business.	☐	☐	☐
2. I have set short-term goals for the business.	☐	☐	☐
3. I have set personal long- and short-term goals.	☐	☐	☐
4. I have reviewed my marketing strategies.	☐	☐	☐
5. I have reviewed my marketing messages.	☐	☐	☐
6. I have identified and will use my USP.	☐	☐	☐
7. My business name aptly describes what I do.	☐	☐	☐
8. I have an excellent business logo.	☐	☐	☐
9. I have a snappy slogan.	☐	☐	☐
10. My mission statement reflects my business goals.	☐	☐	☐
11. My office or store is clean and organized.	☐	☐	☐
12. My work area is clean and well organized.	☐	☐	☐
13. My staff and I are well groomed.	☐	☐	☐
14. My staff wear clean uniforms or company clothing.	☐	☐	☐
15. All company vehicles are cleaned regularly.	☐	☐	☐
16. I have used the ten tips to spruce up my store.	☐	☐	☐
17. I am familiar with my community demographics.	☐	☐	☐
18. I know the average age of my ideal consumer.	☐	☐	☐
19. I know my average consumer's shopping habits.	☐	☐	☐
20. I know where and when they like to shop.	☐	☐	☐
21. I know the physical boundaries of my business.	☐	☐	☐
22. I am aware of my larger competitors.	☐	☐	☐
23. I am aware of most of my smaller competitors.	☐	☐	☐
24. My prices compare favorably with my competitors' pricing.	☐	☐	☐

continued

	Needs work	Satisfied	Completed
25. I offer better service than my competitors.	☐	☐	☐
26. I have recently visited my main competitors.	☐	☐	☐
27. I treat my customers as Very Special People.	☐	☐	☐
28. I keep informed of changing consumer trends.	☐	☐	☐
29. I keep informed of changing economic trends.	☐	☐	☐
30. I tailor my business to accommodate these trends.	☐	☐	☐
31. I have researched niche markets.	☐	☐	☐
32. I have researched secondary markets.	☐	☐	☐
33. I have set an adequate monthly marketing budget.	☐	☐	☐
34. I monitor the results of all marketing methods.	☐	☐	☐
35. I ask all new customers how they heard of my business.	☐	☐	☐
36. I know the seasonal trends of my business.	☐	☐	☐
37. I maintain a database of all new customers.	☐	☐	☐
38. I offer incentives and/or giveaways to all customers.	☐	☐	☐
39. I attend industry trade shows at least twice a year.	☐	☐	☐
40. I have a website and use the Internet.	☐	☐	☐

CHAPTER NINE

Are Your Written Presentations Professional?

Writing is the opposite of sex. It's only good when it's over.
SIDNEY ZION

By now it should be obvious that you need more than technical and financial skills to be an excellent entrepreneur. You also have to learn to become an engaging speaker and a witty writer. "Oh no!" you sigh. "No one told me this when I started my business." Growing your business will depend on your ability to communicate a variety of messages to a variety of people using a variety of media. ❧

COMMUNICATION IS YOUR KEY TO SUCCESS

If you are shy and lack enough confidence to openly communicate with people, you will have infinite difficulty in taking your business to the next level. The next two chapters are devoted to the art of improving both your written and verbal communication skills.

Think about the variety of people that you communicate with: customers, potential customers, suppliers, associates, the competition, bank managers, government agencies, accountants, lawyers, and members of various associations, to name a few. Each time you communicate with someone, they form an opinion about you, and your competence as a businessperson is always being judged.

We are bombarded with countless communications in our fast-paced, electronic society and some people get sloppy in both their presentations and responses. How many times have you received a letter or some form of advertising, only to toss it aside because the content was grammatically incorrect or it was unprofessionally presented?

Do you use that business, or have you already judged them as unprofessional and recycled their brochure? We are quick to judge others on first and often fleeting impressions. Each time you communicate in business, do so professionally—you are being judged on everything you write, say, or do. Scary thought, isn't it?

The age of speed and cyberspace has changed what was a simple business world into a complex clutter of paper and correspondence. Sometimes it is overwhelming, yet through it all, you must somehow manage to project a calm, professional image and put your best pen forward. This chapter will give you some tips and examples that will allow you to use the written word to your best advantage.

BUILD YOUR COMMUNICATION SKILLS

There is infinite power in both the pen and the ability to hold an impressive and informative conversation. If you lack these skills, start working on them now. Remember—YOU are your business, and of the Eight Essential Entrepreneurial Skills mentioned in Chapter 2, the ability to communicate is near the top of the list.

THE ART OF WRITING PROFESSIONAL LETTERS

Composing a letter, email, or media release is like any other work of art. Just as an artist carefully plans each masterpiece, so should you plan each letter and know exactly the message you want to convey. Address the five "Ws"—who, what, why, when, and where—and don't forget how. What tone do you want to set with each letter? Your letters should be composed to generate the desired responses. Because so many people use email to communicate, a well-written letter will be well remembered.

You use the written word every day of your business life. Some of the more common types of correspondence you will need to compose are:

- letters of introduction
- follow-up letters to potential and existing customers
- quotations
- thank-you letters
- overdue account reminders

HOW TO SET OUT A SMART LETTER

To appear professional, each piece of correspondence requires some careful thought. You will soon develop templates suited to your business needs. With ongoing fine-tuning, letter-writing will take less time as your business grows. Ensure that each piece of correspondence includes all your contact information. Starting from the top, each letter should contain these ten components:

1. date and correct business title
2. correct professional title of addressee
3. correct spelling of all names
4. appropriate opening address
5. suitable opening paragraph

POLISH YOUR WRITING SKILLS

If writing is not your forte, take an evening course on business writing. A course on creative writing is also extremely helpful because as a business owner you will prepare your press releases, compose arresting letters, design your own advertising materials, and contribute articles to magazines. Becoming published will effectively increase your exposure and credibility as an expert for the long term and open many new doors.

6. comprehensive and concise body of letter
7. grammatically correct text
8. suitable closing paragraph
9. correct closing address
10. your business name and writer's title.

Figure 9.1 gives an example of a follow-up letter sent after a customer service manager met with a potential client.

Figure **9.1**

Sample Follow-Up Letter

June 3, 20__
Pacific Northern Overnight Express ⬅ **1**
9331 Suburban Avenue
Winston, CA 90111

Attention Mr. Peter Casey, Operations Manager ⬅ **2 & 3**

Dear Mr. Casey, ⬅ **4**

It was a pleasure meeting with you on May 27 to discuss the potential of Mainline Truck Service Inc. becoming your fleet maintenance contractor. After reviewing both the condition of your fleet and your current rates, I am excited at the opportunity to submit a quotation for your consideration. ⬅ **5**

I believe that our company can increase the life of your fleet by implementing a comprehensive service schedule that will not exceed your budget. Your vehicles are the lifeline to your profits and we are committed to being always available for immediate repairs and service. ⬅ **6**

We pride ourselves on going that one step further by offering the services our clients both need and have come to expect. For example, to start we thoroughly inspect each vehicle free of charge and prepare full maintenance reports, along with the cost of any repairs and a suggested maintenance schedule. I will include this schedule in our quotation.

Please do not hesitate to contact me with any further questions regarding our discussion. I will prepare a detailed quotation by June 15 and will courier it to your office. I personally guarantee you that we will go out of our way to meet your needs. ⬅ **7 & 8**

Yours truly, ⬅ **9**

David Johnson
David Johnson
Customer Service Manager ⬅ **10**

Mainline Truck Service Inc.

Twelve Tips
for **Writing Winning Letters**

Because people are so busy, write letters that quickly catch their attention. Here's how to compose that brilliant masterpiece.

1. If your letter is a cold call, research the company and the correct title of the person you are addressing the letter to.

2. Use tasteful, simple, and professional letterhead. Avoid large logos or heavy, bold print because this detracts from the letter and screams at the reader.

3. First plan your letter in point form, then number each one in the order you want them to appear. Compose your letter around these points. This way, you will not miss any pertinent information and the letter will flow well.

4. Take advantage of word processing tools but don't rely completely on the spell-checker because it accepts any word that is spelled correctly. Change your language setting to suit the country you are writing to.

5. Print out the completed letter and edit it for rambling sentences, punctuation, long paragraphs, and readability. If you stop as you are reading, reread the sentence to discover why. Reword the sentence so it flows.

6. Study the physical aspects of the letter. Use one-inch margins and plenty of white space, as busy letters are difficult to digest. Use shorter paragraphs in long letters. Use a standard font, such as 12-point Times New Roman. Avoid using large, small or fancy fonts.

7. Keep your letters positive unless circumstances dictate otherwise. Start with a pleasant greeting, keep the tone upbeat yet professional, and close with an appropriate salutation.

continued

8. Avoid using block capitals and exclamation marks to stress a point. Capitals scream at readers and exclamation marks look childish. If you must emphasize a point, use italics, but sparingly. Refer to books such as *Write Right,* by Jan Venolia, for more tips.

9. Your letterhead should contain all forms of contact, including phone, fax, and cellular numbers, and your email and website addresses.

10. For a first-time contact, include your business card. Whereas letters may get filed away, most people keep business cards.

11. Although labeled envelopes look neat, if your letter is of a personal nature or a thank-you card or letter, handwrite the envelope—it adds a nice personal touch.

12. Don't write a letter if you are in a negative mood. Wait until you can concentrate all your positive energy on the content, as your mood is often reflected in your writing.

SAMPLE LETTERS FOR ALL OCCASIONS

SAY IT WITH STYLE
Avoid standard closers such as "Looking forward to hearing from you in the near future." Try something different: "I wish you a successful and enriching year and will follow up with you within ten days." If you say that you will follow up, the reader is prepared for your call.

Letters of introduction

Introductory letters can be mailed or emailed and are a low-cost method of introducing your business to potential customers. They can be effective marketing tools if they are well-written, friendly, and informative, telling the reader who you are, what your business is, how long you have been in business, where you are located, and the services you provide.

Many people think that email is a less formal method of communication, and therefore spelling and grammatical errors are acceptable.

They are not. Sloppy emails are acceptable between friends, but not for business.

Figure 9.2 shows an example of a computer repair and maintenance business introducing their services to a potential customer. It can be sent either by email or on company letterhead.

> ### SAVE TIME BUT GET IT RIGHT
> ·····································
> *Using the copy and paste menu, you can send personalized introductory emails without using the broadcast method, which is unprofessional and considered spam. Include the name of the manager of a specific department rather than just addressing the email to "the operations manager."*

Figure 9.2

Sample Letter of Introduction

Attention Mr. James Connor, General Manager

The Internet has created many exciting opportunities for businesses to apply their creativity and expertise in serving the millions of cyberspace customers. Your website design business is important to these people and no doubt relies heavily on the ability of your equipment to remain functional at all times.

Our company has been in business for six years and our purpose is to keep you operational. We understand that time is of the essence when breakdowns occur. We come to your premises to maintain and repair all computer equipment, offering a unique 24-hour emergency service. We have the latest diagnostic equipment and pride ourselves on keeping up with technology.

Our rates are competitive and our service exemplary. We offer free telephone and email support and are happy to provide testimonials from satisfied clients. I have enclosed my business card and brochure, and should mention that we offer a 25 percent discount for your first service call on presentation of this letter.

I will follow up in the near future to answer any questions you may have.
I wish you a successful year.

Yours truly,

Robert McMillan

Robert McMillan
President
Hi-Tech Performance Service Inc.

Letters of quotation

The opportunity to submit a quotation means you are over the first hurdle, so a professional presentation is the next step to closing the sale. If you don't use quotation forms, type the letter. Having done your research, you know your customer's needs and what services you can provide.

Offer an edge over the competition so that your quotation stands out from the others. Include all terms of payment, as attention to these finer details is important. Your customer doesn't want any surprises once you develop a business relationship. Figure 9.3 gives an example of a quotation for janitorial services.

Figure **9.3**

Sample Letter of Quotation

June 19, 20___

Professional Personnel Services Inc.
19947 Springfield Avenue
Suite 203A
Newark, NJ 70132

Attention Ms. Janet Phillips, General Manager

Dear Ms. Phillips,
I enjoyed meeting with you on May 26th to discuss the janitorial requirements for your premises. We understand the need for your offices to look clean, bright and professional at all times. Based on our discussion, I am pleased to submit the following quotation.

QUOTATION FOR JANITORIAL SERVICES:
203A - 19947 SPRINGFIELD AVENUE

The following quotation is based on an annual contract fee, which is subject to renegotiation for any additional requirements. This quotation is firm for a thirty-day period.
Cleaning of all offices and staff areas five days a week (Monday to Friday):
1. Janitorial services provided:
- daily dusting of all furniture and fittings plus waste disposal
- sanitizing and cleaning telephone receivers once a week
- daily vacuuming of all carpets, shampooing every three months
- washing and polishing all linoleum and floors
- cleaning and sanitizing washrooms
- stripping linoleum every six months
- removing marks from walls and doors

2. Cost of services:
    Monthly fee: $875.00

3. Hours of service:
    Service commences at 7:00 p.m. each evening and will be completed
    by 10:00 p.m., excluding evenings when shampooing and stripping are
    scheduled. Please note that we are fully bonded and insured.

4. Payment terms:
    a. Services will be billed weekly and payable within thirty (30) days of
       invoice.
    b. A 2.5% discount is applicable to invoices paid within seven days of
       invoicing.
    c. A monthly 2% service charge will be applicable to overdue
       accounts.

We will contact you the next business day with problems needing attention
and I guarantee that we will take professional care of all your janitorial needs.
I will call you within two weeks, and in the meantime, please contact me with
any further questions. We would be happy to supply you with testimonials
and references.

Yours truly,

Peter Saunders

Peter Saunders, Sales & Service Manager
Corporate Cleaning Services Inc.

Thank-you letters

Always say thank you. My personal philosophy is this: If you aren't sending out at least two or three thank-you cards or letters a week, your business is suffering from your lack of gratitude. Did a supplier go out of their way to deliver a sudden, urgent order? Did a friend refer a new customer to you? Did you complete a job for a new customer? Did a newspaper print your press release?

Don't ever take these things for granted— it's common courtesy to say "thanks." A thank-you letter also gives the customer an opportunity to contact you if there are any concerns. Figure 9.4 offers a short example.

> ## RETURN A FAVOR
> *A thank-you card is usually appropriate, but in some cases, a letter is better. Not only does the recipient appreciate you remembering and thanking them, but your letter can be used as a testimonial or reference when the recipient needs it. One good turn deserves another.*

Figure 9.4

Sample Thank-You Letter

Dear Mrs. Johnstone,

Thank you for using Neat N' Trim Landscaping to prepare the garden for your son's wedding in July. I am pleased you called us in plenty of time, as together we were able to make your ideas become reality. The plants we suggested you add to the garden will produce a mass of seasonal color each year.

I will call you two weeks before the wedding to inspect the garden to ensure everything is in order. This is part of our follow-up service and is free of charge. In the meantime, please call us if you have any questions. Thank you once again for the opportunity to work with you, and I hope the wedding is a wonderful success.

Yours truly,

Kevin Brown

Kevin Brown
Operations Manager
Neat N' Trim Landscaping Inc.

Account reminders

The key to successful collections is to have customers respect your terms and pay on time while still retaining the customers' respect and business (unless you don't want their business anymore). Your first letter should be polite, as there are often extenuating circumstances such as a family emergency, illness, or a lost invoice. Figure 9.5 offers an example of a first reminder letter.

Business letters don't have to be stiff or formal. Make your customers feel that they are important to you by conveying the message that you will bend over backwards to accommodate them. Most people enjoy the personal touch that a letter conveys. Make yours outstanding and express your message personally yet professionally by being creative in your writing.

Figure **9.5**

Sample of a First Overdue Account Reminder

Dear Mr. Waterhouse,

We realize that sometimes accounts are overlooked for various reasons. On reviewing your account, I have noticed that your April invoices still remain outstanding. As they are now 60 days overdue, I am writing to see if there are any problems with your shipment. Please contact our office if you need a copy of the invoices or if there is a pricing or shipping discrepancy, and we will attend to it immediately.

You are important to us, and we value your business. If I haven't heard from you within 10 days, I will call to discuss this matter. If your check is in the mail, we thank you and look forward to serving you in the future.

Yours truly,

Tara Keffer

Tara Keffer
Accounts Representative
Cougar Import/Export Inc.

HOW TO WRITE A POWERFUL MEDIA RELEASE

One of the most powerful promotional tools available to a businesses is a well-prepared media release. Newspapers, magazines, radio, and television media are always looking for newsworthy stories to interest their readers, listeners, and viewers. All it takes is that creative and well-written hook or idea. A hook is what attracts the initial attention of the reader. It could be the way you word the headline or opening paragraph, or an innovative approach to an issue that encourages the reader to continue on.

Editors receive hundreds of media releases each week—by fax, email, and post. Because they work under constant deadlines, plowing through piles of poorly prepared releases becomes a tedious job. One community newspaper editor commented, "I receive hundreds of press releases a week; some are hand-scrawled with no contact numbers and incomplete information. I throw them away," he stated. "I don't have the time or the inclination to read them."

TAILOR YOUR TOPIC
....
A media release must capture the interest of the editor or producer within the first few lines. This is accomplished by preparing a truly newsworthy story, tailored to appeal to the media's audience. Before you send it, study the targeted media to ensure that your release suits their audience.

Nothing beats the widespread credibility that a media release generates. If the story is interesting enough, the editor or producer may assign a reporter to do a story on you, as was done in the Real Life example "Wonder-ful Publicity." Publicity is an invaluable asset to building your media kit and profile.

The media's concept of news will vary throughout the country. What is newsworthy on the East Coast may hold no interest for the West Coast media. Your reception by the press will be based on where you live, the town's size and population, the paper's focus, the timing, space and the competition from other newspapers. For a community newspaper, an article should relate specifically to that community. In areas where the media has its choice of stories, your creativity will have to work overtime to design that compelling angle.

Real Life) **Wonder-ful Publicity**

Two energetic women attending a lunch seminar I presented on low-cost marketing took my advice and approached a female reporter at the community newspaper about their product. They prepared a professional news release, which they hand-delivered to the newspaper, along with a sample cloth. They were distributors of a new environmentally friendly "Wonder Cloth" that cleaned anything and everything without using toxic cleaners, two ideal hooks that sparked the interest of the news reporter.

Ten days later, I was thrilled to see a full-page story about the women and their new business. On calling to congratulate them, I asked how they did it.

"We did what you told us to," was the excited reply. "We went to the newspaper, found a woman reporter, used our hooks, and were hopeful of a few lines, but look at this—a whole page!" They were thrilled. You can't put a monetary value on such positive exposure and the credibility it adds to your business.

Know seasonal trends and keep informed

The media work with a schedule of seasonal themes and most will make this schedule available to you. Look at the topics to decide how you can tie your business to them. At the same time, keep abreast of what is happening internationally, nationally, and locally. If there is a hot topic in the news, think of a creative way to tie your business into it.

Some of these seasonal themes that may be appropriate for your business include:

- Christmas, Easter, Mother's Day, Father's Day, Valentine's Day, Halloween
- back to school, school vacations, traveling, camping, hiking, fishing
- Small Business Week, Secretary's Day, National Women's Business Week
- spring gardening, summer vacations, fall cleanup, winter recreation
- Fire Safety Week, income tax season, influenza season, the weather

---

Ten Tips
for **Preparing a Professional Media Release**

The print media is the most common one used by businesses, so learn how to prepare a professional media (press) release. The rules are:

1. Head the page "MEDIA RELEASE."

2. Use the appropriate subheading: "FOR IMMEDIATE RELEASE" or "HOLD UNTIL..."

3. Include all contact information up front.

4. Include the date.

5. Prepare a subject headline (this will undoubtedly change if printed).

6. Double-space the text; limit your information to one page.

continued

7. Start the text with the place of origin e.g., Louisville, KY.

8. Include some quotations from a key staff member where possible.

9. Answer the six essential questions—who, where, what, when, why, and how.

10. Close with appropriate symbols (either -30-, ###, or [end]).

Figure 9.6 gives a short press release written for a local community newspaper, using an example of a realty company that specializes in selling rural properties. By holding this free seminar, they convey to the public that they care about buyers being well informed before purchasing acreage.

A local newspaper would usually print this type of release because it is of community interest and not too lengthy. The people attending the seminar will become potential customers and think of Brian's company as "the experts." If you think hard enough, you'll generate several story ideas around your business.

Figure **9.6**

Sample Media Release

MEDIA RELEASE ⬅ 1

FOR IMMEDIATE RELEASE ⬅ 2

CONTACT: Brian Phillips   PHONE: (123) 456-7890 ⬅ 3
Country Estates Realty   FAX: (123) 456-7891
DATE: March 19, 20__ ⬅ 4 EMAIL: bphillips@netcom.com

FREE SEMINAR FOR FIRST-TIME HOBBY-FARM PURCHASERS ⬅ 5

Louisville: ⬅ 6 & 7 Spring is here and many suburbanites dream of changing their lifestyle by moving to rural hobby farms. If you purchase the wrong property, this beautiful dream acreage can become a nightmare. Country Estates Realty Inc. is sponsoring a free seminar to help first-time hobby-farm purchasers make informed decisions.

"Many buyers are not aware of the unique considerations in purchasing rural properties," says Brian Phillips, an award-winning realtor with twenty years' experience. "There are many factors to consider, including transportation, schools, neighbors, well water problems, government legislation concerning land usage, and flooding and manure handling, to name a few. We want to help people realize the factors and pitfalls to consider before rushing into signing a purchase agreement." **← 8**

The seminar will be held in room 112 at the Louisville Community Center on Saturday, March 25 from 10:00 a.m. to 12:00 p.m. Coffee and refreshments will be served. For more information or to RSVP, please call Brian at 123-456-7890. **← 9**

← 10

HOW TO PREPARE A PROFESSIONAL MEDIA KIT

To gain more widespread media exposure you need the right tool, commonly known as a "press kit" or "media kit." As the media is deluged with inquiries, ensure you have a topic of real interest and make your kit stand out by its professional presentation. Use a high-quality twin-pocket portfolio that contains all the pertinent, well-organized information you want to convey. It should include the following items:

- a cover letter outlining your topic and confirming your call (see below)
- biographical information about you and your business, including awards, nominations, and committees you represent
- testimonials or letters of reference
- articles demonstrating your credibility on the subject, or a need for your story
- corporate information (brochures, videos, photos)
- published articles you have authored
- anything that validates you or your business's credibility
- a current press release pertaining to your topic

PREPARE A DYNAMITE COVER LETTER

Prepare a cover letter confirming your conversation with the media representative. Thank them for the opportunity of submitting your material, detail the pertinent information, and confirm that you will follow up in ten days to ensure safe delivery. Make the cover letter positive and intriguing enough to capture the reader's interest, ensuring that it answers the six essential questions. Send the kit and follow up by telephone in ten days.

PITCH YOURSELF TO THE MEDIA

Unless you are distributing your media kits at a press conference, before sending the kit, call to ask for the name of the producer of the show or editor of the section you want to contact. Get the correct spelling of their name and the full postal address. Then ask to be put through to him or her. Introduce yourself and your business—making the call as exciting and as positive as possible—and ask if the person would like you to forward a media kit. If your pitch is intriguing, you will be invited to send in your information for review.

The follow-up phone call

Editors and producers are busy people so keep your follow-up call short and to the point. Don't even ask if they have read your material at this stage—they will tell you if they have. Some editors may ask that you only contact them by email. If so, then please respect their wishes. Figure 9.7 gives an example of a follow-up conversation.

Figure 9.7

Sample Follow-Up Call Conversation

"Hello Jennifer, Marlene James calling. I'm following up to ensure that you received my media kit safely in the mail (or by courier or delivered to the front desk).... You did? Please contact me if you need more information, and thank you once again for taking the time to review my package. Have a wonderful day."

Keep a copy of the cover letter in your follow-up file and call back within two to three weeks. Keeping in touch without becoming a pest is called persistence, and it pays off. One reporter commented to me that I was "persistent," but she appreciated it because she was so busy that things often got shoved to the bottom of the pile. Now we have developed a great working relationship, she often calls for small business resource information, which has resulted in further press coverage without even asking.

Build a relationship

The media need resource people to contact for information when they need it. Once you are on file, you may well be asked to provide input for articles or shows. Let your new media contacts know that you are *always* available to help them. Various media organizations are always interested in newsworthy stories that tie into their publishing or production themes. Consider:

- local, state, and national television and radio shows, newspapers and magazines
- specialty, trade, and free magazines
- trade newspapers and journals
- Internet publications
- association and chamber of commerce newsletters
- government training organizations
- college and university newsletters

Real Life) Easy as Pie

Lorna owns the Acme Humble Pie Company, supplying enormous, delectable, beautifully packaged apple pies to corporate clients for gifts. One day I received a copy of nearly a full-page article from Lorna headed, "The pie's the limit," with a subheading: "Never underestimate the power of pastry."

A note was attached: "Frances, I took your advice from the book and got some local exposure. Thank you." Lorna had prepared her media release, approached the local community newspaper with a creative hook, and got her coverage, which resulted in new business for her.

How to source media leads

Who has time to spend countless hours doing research? Save on travel, time, postage, and long-distance calls by researching on the Internet. Search for the media you are interested in using keywords from your industry and geographical

KEEP A DATABASE
....

Print out your search results to keep track of those people you have contacted and those to be contacted. The Internet will give you lists of newspapers, magazines, and radio and TV stations. If your business appeals to a specific market, such as students at postsecondary institutions, there is no better tool than the Internet to locate this information in the geographical area that you want to market to.

market and go to their Web page "contact us" link or staff directory. Peruse their site to become conversant with their focus, format, and content before contacting them.

Use email

Send an introductory email, and if you don't get a reply within a week, follow up with a phone call. Emails get lost and forgotten, but in most cases, you will receive a reply. You have the contact's name and can phone the company switchboard to be put through.

You have a legitimate reason for calling—to see if the email arrived. This can be a comfortable opener to the conversation after you have introduced yourself. If the email was not received, be ready to capture the attention of the listener by having a positive and creative spiel ready. Keep your media release handy as a reference.

HOW CAN YOU IMPROVE YOUR WRITTEN SKILLS?

This chapter demonstrates how using you written skills can help you market your business and increase your profile as the expert in your field. Use your completed checklist in Figure 9.8 as a guide to achieve this goal.

Competent and creative writing skills coupled with a professional presentation are effective and inexpensive marketing tools. This is half the battle. Now you have to ensure you have the ability to express yourself well verbally. The next chapter will help you increase those all-important verbal skills.

— *Figure* **9.8** —

Written Communication Strategies
for My Business

---

1. Currently, I use the following written methods to communicate in my business:

☐ personalized email   ☐ fax

☐ email broadcasts   ☐ fax broadcasts

☐ letters of introduction   ☐ press releases

☐ direct mail   ☐ follow-up letters

2. I experience difficulty with the following:

☐ replying to faxes   ☐ writing promotional copy

☐ replying to email   ☐ replying to letters

☐ account collections   ☐ follow-up letters

3. I could improve my written communications by:

☐ making time to send letters of introduction

☐ sending follow-up letters after meeting potential customers

☐ sending more thank-you letters and cards

☐ sending regular collection letters

☐ using email to introduce my business

☐ using email to correspond with business associates

☐ keeping hard copies of important emails for reference

4. I could improve my communication skills and increase my profile by:

☐ learning how to write effective media releases

☐ marketing my business using the media

☐ taking a course on writing business letters

☐ taking a course on creative writing

☐ submitting articles to magazines, newsletters, or newspapers

☐ using the Internet to locate e-magazines to submit articles

☐ gathering written testimonials and evaluations

☐ informing the community newspaper of my business

☐ hiring some part-time help to allow me to focus on the above

continued

5. Every business is unique in its own right. Write down what sets your business apart from others.

_____

_____

_____

_____

6. Now think of how to use the information in this chapter to promote your business using your writing skills. Which trade publications, newspapers, magazines, or e-magazines could you send a media release to?

_____

_____

_____

_____

7. Research courses, seminars, books, or programs that will teach you how to improve your writing skills. Note the pertinent details and put a deadline on completing them.

a. _____

    I will complete it by: _____

b. _____

    I will complete it by: _____

c. _____

    I will complete it by: _____

CHAPTER TEN

Do Your Verbal Skills Need Enhancing?

———◁◦▷———

*When a man makes a speech, the first
thing he has to do is to decide what to say.*
GERALD FORD

———◁◦▷———

Experiencing a fulfilling and successful business—and life—is all about how we communicate with one another. As the world becomes more overburdened with communication gadgets and technological "time-savers," the sad thing is, people communicate less effectively than ever before. ❧

BUSINESS IS ALL ABOUT COMMUNICATING

The most successful people in business know and understand the importance of superior communication skills. This chapter is devoted to helping you hone your verbal communication skills. From the telephone to a training session to a trade show, your success is totally dependent on how you deliver your messages. So we'll start with the most commonly used communication tool—the telephone.

TELEPHONE TALK

The telephone is a valuable business asset, so use and treat it with respect. Ensure that callers can always reach you. If your business requires that you regularly be absent from your office or cannot always answer the phone, designing a reliable communications system is a priority so that you don't lose business, as was the case in the Real Life example on page 207, "The Too-Big Bank."

The cost of keeping in touch is probably one of the biggest expenses for a small business. Yet with the plethora of bundles, options, and packages available through telephone companies, there is no excuse not to keep in touch. If you aren't taking advantage of call display, call forwarding, call alert, and voice mail, give your phone company a call and get with the program. Whichever features you use, let callers know that messages will be returned promptly. People are impatient and don't like lengthy waits for return calls. They will often call the competition if they need an immediate answer.

USE A TOLL-FREE NUMBER

Even a home-based business can project a "big business" global image by having a toll-free phone number. It utilizes your existing phone number so you don't have to pay for an extra line connection. It's not an expensive monthly fee or toll charges, and customers will often call toll-free, whereas they wouldn't pay the cost of a call. A toll-free number can avoid lost sales, and it's a cheap form of marketing.

Use professional greetings and messages

First impressions are important for building relationships, so always answer the telephone professionally and positively. "Good morning, Doncaster Plumbing and Heating Services, this is Jonathan speaking. How may I help you?"

Greet your caller first, give the company name, and let them know whom they are talking to. You won't go wrong using this professional and courteous greeting. Train employees to be polite, cheery, and helpful, as it is often the first (or last) form of contact by a potential customer. Design a warm and polite greeting like this example, and insist that it is always used.

Many home-based businesses make the mistake of using unacceptable greetings on their voice mail. "Leave a message after the beep," or "You have reached the Smith residence and Bonny's Gift Baskets. We're not home so leave a message" doesn't cut it.

CHANGE YOUR HOME- BASED GREETING

Home-based businesses should leave a professional greeting on their voice mail. Try something like "Thank you for calling Doncaster Plumbing and Heating Services and the Janson residence. Your call is important to us, so please leave a message and we will return it shortly. For emergencies, please call our cellular at 123-456-7890, and have a wonderful day."

Real Life) The Too-Big Bank

A client tried to phone a local bank to confirm a fax number to send information to a loans officer. On looking up the number, there was only one central listing for all branches, which she dialed. She was asked whom she was calling. She gave the name and branch and was informed that the person she wanted wasn't listed.

"But I know she's there," said the client in frustration.

"Well, why are you calling?" asked the receptionist.

"Because I need her fax number!" Now the client was angry. This was none of the receptionist's business. "Please give me the branch number."

"Well, all right then," answered the receptionist reluctantly.

On calling the bank, a recorded voice answered.

"Thank you for calling the Too-Big Bank. Please leave your name and number and someone will get back to you within two hours." The client was now completely disgusted with this runaround and vowed that she wouldn't deal with a bank that couldn't be communicated with. She canceled her loan application and went elsewhere.

If you operate a home office and have children, teach them not to answer the business telephone during working hours. Even though a polite child sounds cute, this does nothing for your business image.

Ten Tips
for Telephone Etiquette

Whether you are calling to collect an overdue account or making a cold call, follow these basic principles and you will generate productive conversations.

1. Write down the important points before calling.

2. Always know whom you want to talk to; ask the receptionist for the appropriate name.

3. Prepare a suitable opening, body, and close for your conversation.

4. Don't call anyone if you are not in a positive mood.

5. Make follow-up calls before lunch, when people are more receptive.

6. Don't call right at business opening or before they have had time for that first coffee.

7. Open with a pleasant salutation and talk on a personable level.

8. Don't waste people's time—try to strike a balance between being both friendly and professional.

9. If the other party appears unreceptive, ask if it would be more convenient to call back at a more suitable time.

10. Close with a friendly salutation, letting them know when you will be in touch again.

COLD-CALL WITH CONFIDENCE

Most people shudder at the thought of making cold sales calls, the main reason being fear of rejection. No one likes a telephone slammed down in their ear. It takes a certain personality to be a salesperson because they face rejection every day and still motor on, undaunted and unruffled. The art of successful cold calls is to develop your confidence and communication skills, coupled with a professional, friendly approach.

Warm up cold calls

No doubt you have received numerous cold calls from people selling anything from carpet cleaning to crematorium plots. These companies usually use telemarketers for soliciting business, relying on volume and the numbers game. Small businesses don't have this luxury, so the key is to target your leads and not use hit-or-miss methods.

Remember—you are offering a valuable service and people need you. You are calling only to introduce your business. If people are interested, you can follow up with either a letter, fax, email, or an appointment. Figure 10.1 gives an example of a landscape company making a cold call.

TRY A SPECIAL OFFER

A special time-limited offer, such as no tax or a 10 percent phone discount can often help close a sale. Start with a friendly opener to the conversation. This allows you to feel out the mood of the person you are calling. If you sense reticence or impatience, keep the call short or ask if they would prefer you to call at a more convenient time.

Figure 10.1

Sample of a Cold Call

"Hello, is this Mrs. Wilkes? I am William Cleary of Gorgeous Gardens Inc. What a lovely day to be in the garden. I hope you're taking advantage of the good weather. I'm calling to let you know that we are a new local business offering a variety of gardening services, including yard cleaning, landscaping, tree pruning, spraying, topping, and lawn maintenance. Do you ever have a need for any of these services?... Occasionally? I would be happy to send you a
continued

brochure detailing all our services and prices. It's actually time for dormant sprays for your fruit trees, and we are offering a special this month. We also offer free quotations.... Send you a brochure? With pleasure. If you give me your address, I will mail it tomorrow. Our number is on there if you would like more information. Please feel free to call us with any gardening questions as we are more than happy to help... Yes, I'll enclose some information about the dormant sprays. Thanks for your time and enjoy your garden."

MAKE FRUITFUL FOLLOW-UP CALLS

This conversation allows the caller to politely follow up in a couple of weeks before the season for tree-spraying ends. Even if no business evolves from the call, the recipient is now aware of the business, has a brochure, and can be added to a mailing list for newsletter or promotional mailings.

William's follow-up phone call with Mrs. Wilkes should sound like the conversation outlined in Figure 10.2.

Figure **10.2**

Sample of a Follow-Up Call

"Hello Mrs. Wilkes, it's William Cleary again from Gorgeous Gardens. I spoke with you two weeks ago and am just following up to ensure that our brochure arrived safely. It did? Good. Can I help by answering any questions about your trees or garden? Some people aren't sure about using pesticides and sprays when they are on well water so I wondered if this was a concern of yours.... No, our sprays are all environmentally friendly as we cater to people living on rural properties. Are you going to spray your fruit trees this year? The season is coming to a close.... Well, if you missed last year, I would suggest it now as it certainly reduces the risk of damage to your fruit crop. Yes, I'd be happy to drop by and give you a quotation. What day and time would suit you?... I'll look forward to meeting you next Tuesday at 2:30 p.m., Mrs. Wilkes. I'll bring some free fertilizer spike samples for you too—your trees will love them. Take care and enjoy your day."

How to tackle tardy accounts by phone

Calling customers to ask for money has to be the worst possible chore. Many procrastinate hoping that the check arrives in the mail, which it usually does. But when it doesn't, you have to call to find out why. Cash flow is the lifeline of your business, so grit your teeth, grab your aged receivable list, and start phoning. Easier said than done, isn't it? Try adapting the sample conversation in Figure 10.3 to make your calls.

Figure 10.3

Sample of a First Collection Call

"Hello John, this is Eva from Office World Stationers. Are you enjoying the sunshine?... Yes, it is too nice to be working today. John, I was calling because I was concerned that there may be a problem with your account. Are any of our invoices missing or incorrect? Your account seems to have slipped into 90 days.... Yes, I'll hold while you have a look.

You're waiting for a credit on one invoice? Please give me the details and I'll fax a copy over to you immediately. Perhaps it got lost in the mail. Could you clear the account for payment when it arrives? We'd appreciate it as you usually pay so promptly. Please don't hesitate to call me if there are any future problems."

Persistence pays off

Customers often experience cash flow problems so you need to be persistent. The old adage about the squeaky wheel holds true, particularly in collections. Those who don't squeak don't get the oil. Remember that businesses go broke overnight and trade suppliers are usually the first ones to suffer. If you know that a business is experiencing difficulties, take a firmer stand on collection calls.

TRY THE "NO BLAME" METHOD

There are many reasons why customers don't pay, so don't assume they are guilty of nonpayment before talking to them. Start your conversation by taking any guilt or blame away from the customer and placing a little on yourself—it will break down their barriers and make communication easier.

Figure 10.4 gives an example of a call to a good customer whose payments have slipped for the second time. This account should be watched closely, and if promised payment terms are not met, stronger action must be taken. See Chapter 5 for more in-depth collections information.

Figure 10.4

Sample of a Second Collections Call

"Good morning Mrs. Pearce, this is Richard Whalley from Fine Oak Furniture. How are you today?... Yes, business is slow during summer, but it'll pick up soon. Mrs. Pearce, I'm calling to discuss your overdue account. I noticed that your payment didn't arrive as promised. Some invoices are ninety days overdue. Your credit record is usually excellent and I see there are orders waiting to be shipped.... Yes, I understand how slow this time of the year can be, and we don't want to put your orders on hold as you have been such a good customer.

Could I make a suggestion? As your order quantities are currently small, could you pay COD for the current orders and divide the balance into four checks, one payable this week and the others every two weeks? You could then keep buying product while reducing the account... That would work? Good, but if there are any problems with the checks clearing, please let me know immediately... It's my pleasure, Mrs. Pearce, and thank you."

SPEAK YOUR WAY TO SUCCESS

A person who develops excellent speaking skills is always in demand. Groups and associations are continually seeking good speakers. If you apply the following "Five Ts" to your presentations, you will be remembered—and referred—as a knowledgeable and professional presenter. Business will come to you. The more you speak, the more your skills increase and the more your name becomes networked as the expert.

Think about how you can apply your business knowledge to developing a twenty-minute keynote address and a couple of seminars. These organizations are always seeking good speakers:

- chambers of commerce and special community events
- radio and TV stations
- networking groups and business associations
- colleges, schools, and universities
- government, corporate, and private training programs
- events requiring a master of ceremonies
- local government committees such as economic development
- corporate, private, and government conferences
- trade shows, home shows, career fairs
- adult education classes

START SMALL

An excellent way to gain experience is to offer to speak to smaller groups or schoolchildren. There are numerous community associations that would enjoy hearing a guest speaker. Smaller groups are easier to build relationships with and are quite forgiving if you are a little nervous, particularly if you don't charge. The thank-you cards, emails, or letters can then be used as testimonials. You can also ask the group for testimonials or feedback for future use in your marketing.

THE "FIVE Ts" OF TERRIFIC TALKING

In addition to public speaking, there are lots of other business situations where you are asked to make a presentation. It may be a spotlight for your business at a chamber or networking meeting, a sales presentation, delivering a toast, presenting an important proposal to a committee, being interviewed by the media, a council presentation, a workshop, or a board meeting.

People will remember you, be inspired by you, and buy from you if you learn the basics of delivering a powerful presentation. Polished speakers inspire and motivate others into action. They are our leaders. One person—examples include Martin Luther King Jr. and Sir Winston Churchill—can change history with their powerful orations.

KNOW YOUR AUDIENCE

Before making any presentation, research the audience's challenges, fears, and concerns and any benefits or advantages that their industry or profession is experiencing. Talk to people within the field so that you can quote relevant statistics, reports, or articles. Find solutions to their problems and remind them of the positives. Tailoring your speech to the audience sets you apart from many speakers who don't bother. You will be remembered—and probably referred.

Learning to speak effectively requires many skills and factors working together like well-oiled cogs to produce a powerful presentation. The Five Ts of Terrific Talking can be applied to all facets of communication in your business, from a phone call to a board meeting:

1. Tuning in: knowing your audience and material

To *connect* and deliver a powerful message, ensure you are knowledgeable about the subject and have passion and conviction. Know:

- *Where you are speaking:* What type of gathering and how many people

- *When you are speaking:* The time of day, who speaks before and after you

- *Whom you are speaking to:* The demographics of the audience, their educational level, professional background, the type of industry, association or group focus

- *Why you are speaking:* Clarify the message you are expected to deliver.

2. Talking: Presenting a dynamic delivery

Let's look at each intricate part of making a winning presentation. If you follow these guidelines, you should be assured of a successful delivery.

Prepare your presentation

Just as an architect starts with blueprints before a house is built, so must each speech be carefully designed and then edited until it is honed to perfection. *It must be organized.*

Your job is to persuade and inspire people to be motivated into some sort of action. You can't do this if you are unorganized in your delivery or unclear about what you are saying, how you are saying it, and the message or call to action that you want to convey. Each speech must have:

- an attention-getting opener relevant to the subject—a quote, story, or question
- a speech body that combines various techniques to illustrate your point
- a strong, thought-provoking close—a challenge is an effective closer

> ## GO FROM POINTS TO PROSE
> ....
> *First write down the relevant points you want to make in the presentation, organize them into sequential order, and then build your speech around these points, incorporating strong opening, body, and closing techniques to keep your audience interested and listening.*

Speak from the heart

You have all heard speakers drone on until you became bored and mentally tuned out. Clearly expressing your knowledge and beliefs is crucial to captivating your audience. Use the following techniques:

- Stress important points and phrases.
- Emote—allow your feelings and passion to show.
- Use the pause for effect.
- Don't "er" and "um." Listeners form the opinion that you don't know what you are talking about and tune out.

Beef up body language

It is said that only 7 percent of what we say is heard by an audience; the other 93 percent is transmitted through body language. There is nothing worse than a presenter who just reads notes, talks in a monotone, and stares vaguely into the audience. A powerful presentation needs:

- *Facial expressions:* Grin, grimace, raise eyebrows, use your face to express your feelings. Let yourself go. *Feel* your speech and express it naturally.

PRACTICE MAKES PERFECT
....

Practice, practice, and practice each presentation. Edit it for superfluous words. Carefully time the length. The less you use notes, the more knowledgeable and sincere you will appear and the better impression you will leave on your listeners.

• *Gestures:* Gripping a podium or notes or having hands in pockets or clasped conveys a lack of confidence to the audience. Use expressive gestures to stress certain points.

• *Eye contact:* Focus on various audience members, holding the gaze for a few seconds. People are more inspired if they feel they are being personally addressed.

• *Use the floor space:* Your feet aren't nailed to the floor, so use the floor space with purpose—without constant pacing. This allows you to gesture and make eye contact effectively and keeps the audience focused on you.

Vary voice tones

A drone is a type of bee or a poor speaker. Use vocal variations to tell a story, stress a point, draw emotions from listeners, and express your feelings.

• Use soft and loud tones in appropriate places.
• Speak slowly to stress a point.
• Emphasize where needed—express anger, elation, or frustration.
• Put pep, passion, personality, and vitality into your voice.
• Speak clearly and audibly; do not race or mumble.

Watch your words

Long or difficult-to-pronounce words, acronyms, and jargon confuse listeners. You are not speaking to impress your verbal mastery on the audience but to deliver a clear, concise, comprehensible message with confidence, so to achieve this goal:

• Eliminate waffling and rambling sentences.
• Use word pictures to enhance descriptions.
• Use simple words and not fillers.
• Be yourself; write the speech as you would speak.

The "Seven Cs" of a Successful Speaker

Sophocles once said, "It is terrible to speak well and be wrong." A successful speaker delivers with:

Clarity: Messages are clearly delivered.

Confidence: The speaker exudes confidence by knowing content and how to deliver it.

Competence: The speech is delivered in a professional manner.

Conciseness: Facts are accurate and words are not wasted in a jumble of fillers.

Correctness: Tasteful humor and political correctness are observed.

Creativity: Creative construction delivers messages that are remembered.

Credibility: The topic is well researched and content delivered as promised.

3. Techniques: Connecting to and inspiring your audience

A good presenter uses a variety of techniques to connect to and inspire their audience, ensuring that they digest the messages. Some effective techniques include:

- *Audience participation:* Involve your audience by soliciting responses or by using applicable exercises to demonstrate points. If well done, audience exercises are a powerful method of driving your message home.
- *Props:* Dependent on the type of presentation, include visual aids such as PowerPoint presentations, video clips, overheads, whiteboards, and flip charts. Be sure that props or techniques are appropriate to your audience.
- *Personal stories:* Successful speakers use personal stories or examples to demonstrate their messages. When an audience relates to how you feel through your own experiences, they will better connect with you, listen, and participate.
- *Humor:* Making your audience smile or laugh helps them connect, relax, and relate. However, ensure that your humor relates to the topic and is not degrading, racial, ethnic, or sexist. Many people are sensitive and easily hurt. You don't have to be a stand-up comic to use humor; draw from personal experiences.

Don't steal other people's jokes and don't use jokes from the Internet. If you are not comfortable using humor, then don't—just be you.

Real Life Be Aware of Your Audience

Charlene was speaking to a women's business group and related some funny situations that had happened between her and her husband. After the event, one angry woman approached Charlene.

"I didn't appreciate your comments about your husband," she said. "Not all of us have opposite sex partners, you know."

Although Charlene hadn't been offensive, she had offended this woman. In every group you speak to, there will be one person from every minority represented, so be careful what you say.

4. Technical preparation: Ensuring a smooth delivery

You are at the podium and the microphone volume is too low, the handouts haven't arrived, and PowerPoint isn't working. Your confidence and professionalism eroded before you began. These things *do* happen. To ensure a smooth and professional delivery, be prepared.

- *Equipment:* Order all your audiovisual equipment, podium, and other requirements well in advance and confirm by telephone before the event.
- *Venue:* Know the size, seating style, and capacity of the room.
- *Freight:* If you are sending materials, phone to ensure they arrived safely.
- *Checks:* Arrive at the venue at least an hour before your presentation to check that everything is working and in place as you requested.
- *Introduction:* Forward your bio or the introduction that you would like used and carry a copy with you.
- *Problems:* If something goes wrong—which it often does—smile and have a sense of humor. Be flexible and always have a Plan B.

5. Timing: Delivering in your allotted time

You are allotted a certain time frame to deliver a promised message. Your job is to honor that commitment. Presenters who rush through presentations or who cannot complete them immediately lose their audience. When you extend your time limit, there are negative repercussions:

> ### BE READY TO "CUT"
> ....
> *If you are presenting after a speaker who is running late, talk to the meeting chair and ask that they inform the audience that your time will be cut short. Always know what can be shortened or deleted in your presentation without losing any important messages.*

- *You upset the planning* of the rest of the meeting or conference and deny other presenters their fair time allotment.
- *People may have to leave* for other commitments. Once one person leaves, the audience is disrupted.
- *Your important message* may not be completed or may lose its impact.
- *You are deemed unprofessional* and may lose future business opportunities.

By applying the Five Ts of Terrific Talking and the Seven Cs of a Successful Speaker to every presentation you make, you will dramatically increase your confidence and reputation each time you deliver. Some business owners are terribly shy, which adversely affects their ability to not only speak in public but to meet people, network, and openly market their business. So let's look at another verbal communication skill, simple networking.

NETWORKING—BREAKING THE ICE

Feeling shy in a room full of strangers can be easily overcome by allowing someone else to speak first. At most networking events, people wear name tags. Approach someone, read their name tag, and say: "Hello Susan, my name is Jennifer Scott. What does your company, Safe and Secure, do?"

Let's be honest, everyone likes to talk about themselves, and Susan will happily launch into a description of her business. Ask a few questions and be a good listener. Of course, ask for a business card and present the listener with yours. This is a networking rule.

The twenty-second infomercial

No matter who you talk to, the question "What do you do?" invariably arises. Be prepared and practice your twenty-second "infomercial." There is nothing worse than asking someone what they do and then listening to an unstructured, rambling spiel. The professional will have a concise, informative answer.

When Susan has finished her spiel, the first thing she will ask Jennifer is: "And what do you do, Jennifer?" Now a relationship has been established. You both feel more comfortable and you can deliver your infomercial. Work on the script carefully and learn it by heart.

Figure 10.5 gives the text of Jennifer's infomercial. She has managed to describe her business in detail mention prices and her success—all in twenty seconds.

Figure 10.5

Sample of the Twenty-Second Infomercial

"Susan, I'm a personal chef and I cook up a storm for busy professionals who don't have time to cook nutritious meals. I come to your home, consult on your meal preferences, shop, cook, and prepare up to four family meals. I also cater and serve dinner parties for up to twelve people and my romantic dinners for two are a hit! My prices are very reasonable and I ease the guilt of serving regular junk food meals."

Build relationships

Selling is all about building relationships, and this is what you are building the minute you start a conversation. Before consumers decide to purchase from you, they are first looking for someone who is trustworthy, experienced, and personable to help them make the right decision. Whether you are networking at a seminar or displaying at a trade show, it is *you* who will sway the consumer either way.

Use nonthreatening openers

Appearance, presentation, body language, and your ability to be a good listener work hand-in-hand with your communication skills to win over consumers. Dress smartly, smile, be attentive, and focus on the needs of the person you are talking to.

If someone stops at your trade show table, don't launch into a sales pitch straight away. First feel out the person's mood—remember, they are just looking and are going to be wary of a strong sales pitch. Here are some examples of openers:

- "How are you enjoying the show today? There's some interesting new products here. Have you had a chance to see the kitchen composting system in aisle three?"
- "Hello, would your child like some candy and a balloon?"
- "Hello, I'm Gerry Taylor of Taylor and Associates Accounting. Would you like to fill in an entry form for our draw prize? It's this beautiful gourmet basket."

Once a comfort level has been established, you can then progress into some business patter:

- "This is a wonderful venue for meeting people and keeping up with technology. Our company has just become the first distributor for this innovative new accounting software. Have you seen it before? I can give you a short demonstration and also a sample CD."
- "We're very excited about being here today. We've just launched an exciting new product line. Do you have an older dog?... You do? Would you like to try a free sample of our new flea control product? You don't have to push pills down their throats or apply sprays or powders. I have a brochure that you may take home."
- "Do you have a garden?... Don't you get sick of edge-trimming and the lawn growing into the flower beds? This colored concrete edging landscape curbing allows you to run the mower along it and keeps the beds neat and tidy—and it lasts forever!"

You should now be able to gauge the person's interest. Describe what you do or show them your products, but ask lots of questions to let the listener know that you care about their needs and are interested in them. Make sure they leave your table with a card or brochure. If there is real interest, make a note on their card or offer to contact them the next week. Follow-up is where the sale will transpire, so be diligent.

IMPROVE YOUR COMMUNICATION SKILLS

Now it's time to review how you can apply the information found in this chapter to enhance your verbal communication skills and build better business relationships. This requires a combination of being available to your customers by using the right communications system and being confident enough to deliver the right words at the right time in the right manner.

Complete the checklist in Figure 10.6. Identify where and how you can improve your verbal communication, and then make a commitment to become a top-notch communicator. Apply these communication skills to enhance your marketing and selling. The next chapter focuses on using these skills to promote, publicize, and advertise your business at minimum cost with maximum exposure.

Figure **10.6**

Verbal Communication Strategies For My Business

1. I could improve my communications system by using:

☐ a toll-free phone number   ☐ a website
☐ more telephone options   ☐ a pager
☐ call-forwarding to my cell phone ☐ a cell phone
☐ email more effectively   ☐ email newsletters
☐ a better telephone greeting   ☐ voice mail

2. I experience difficulty with the following:

    ☐ returning messages   ☐ being away from the office

    ☐ expressing myself clearly   ☐ follow-up phone calls

    ☐ talking to strangers   ☐ selling myself and my business

    ☐ speaking confidently   ☐ making time for the above

3. I could improve my verbal communication by:

    ☐ making regular introductory telephone calls

    ☐ following up by telephone after meeting potential customers

    ☐ trying some cold sales calls and monitoring the results closely

    ☐ following up with after-sales service calls

    ☐ attending to messages and email more promptly

    ☐ making weekly collection calls

    ☐ hiring some part-time help to allow time to focus on the above

4. I could improve my communication skills and increase my profile by:

    ☐ joining Toastmasters to improve oral and presentation skills

    ☐ designing short workshops and speeches

    ☐ speaking to business and networking groups and associations

    ☐ joining more community and networking associations

    ☐ circulating my name as a speaker to related organizations

    ☐ contacting TV and radio stations for interviews

    ☐ applying the "Five Ts" to my presentations

5. Now think of various ways to use these ideas to promote your business. Where could you present seminars or deliver a keynote address? Which TV or radio shows are relevant to your field? Jot down some possibilities.

    _____

    _____

    _____

6. Make a time commitment to tackle two of the ideas in question 5 and put a timeline on them.

    a. _____

        I will start on _____

        _____

continue

b. _____

   I will start on _____

7. If you have checked off any items in question 1 to improve your communications systems, list these below and research the cost. Then commit to
   a date for implementation.

   a. _____   Cost: $ _____   Date: _____

   b. _____   Cost: $ _____   Date: _____

8. If you are not already a member of networking groups or business associations, list two that would be of interest to you. Write down their telephone
   number, next meeting date, location, and cost.

   a. _____   Telephone: _____

      Date: _____   Location: _____   Cost: $ _____

   b. _____   Telephone: _____

      Date: _____   Location: _____   Cost: $ _____

9. Review the "Five Ts" of Terrific Talking and write down five areas where
   you need to improve your presentation skills.

   _____

   _____

   _____

   _____

   _____

10. Create your own twenty-second infomercial for use in networking and
    other situations.

   _____

   _____

   _____

   _____

   _____

   _____

CHAPTER ELEVEN

How Do You Apply Communication Skills to Marketing?

———◄○►———

Don't expect anyone to do your selling. That's your job.
JOHN KREMER

———◄○►———

As you develop your written and oral communication skills as discussed in the last two chapters, you can begin to apply them to some proven low-cost marketing techniques. This chapter is devoted to showing you how to use those skills and techniques to increase both your profile as an expert and your income. If you study highly successful people, you will find that they use many if not all of these methods. ❧

USE LOW-COST OR NO-COST MARKETING MAGIC

You can't just sit back, hoping that customers will come to you. This is deadly for a new small business competing with dozens of others. Even well-established businesses must continually work at marketing. The winner in this race is the one who goes out and makes it happen.

Although the methods in this chapter sound easy, they all take some planning to implement. Don't be impatient. You are not aiming for short-term results but are looking to build repeat business and referrals. Success will be long-term, creating many ongoing and beneficial contacts. I have tackled all of these ideas during my business career, and the results have been overwhelmingly successful. I even had to take my own advice and enlist extra help, because I soon discovered that overwork creates brain overload.

COMMUNICATE IN YOUR COMMUNITY

Most small business sales are generated from within the community. No amount of advertising can replace one-on-one contact for building the personal relationships necessary to grow a small business. So your first step is to use your newly developed communication skills to become an active community participant.

JOIN FOR THE RIGHT REASONS

Join a community organization that will give you personal satisfaction. Don't force your business onto people—you will push them away. Be subtle and low-key when business is discussed. Take an interest in other people's work and lives. The golden rule of networking is to care about and help others besides yourself.

Some business owners make the mistake of not getting involved in their community—the people who give to them—because they feel they are too busy. Become known as not just the expert but also as someone who gives back. You will be referred as you build stronger relationships. Following are some tips to build both your community exposure and your reputation as a community-minded business owner.

Ten Tips
for Reaching Out

1. **Join the chamber of commerce:** Get known in the business community as an active chamber of commerce member. Attend their events and network with other members. Many chambers promote "ring a member first." As both the chamber staff and other members get to know you, they may prefer to use your services rather than a stranger's.

2. **Offer sponsorships and donate:** Consider sponsoring a community organization, a special event, or a children's sports team. These organizations always need funding, and you can usually offer services in kind or door prizes to community events instead of money. In exchange, you can display company banners at events and will be thanked in their advertising and programs.

3. **Get involved in community events:** Offer to help with special community events and projects or join a business group, such as a business improvement association. Build relationships with other caring business people while giving back.

4. **Host a food bank drop-off or Christmas hamper:** Be a drop-off point for the food bank or an annual Christmas hamper. Inform the local press with a press release. Not only are you helping others, you will meet new people who drop off donations—all potential customers or referrals.

5. **Contribute to fundraisers:** Offer your products or services to schools or organizations, donating part of the profits as a fundraiser. They will market for you, with your name being circulated to hundreds of parents, all potential customers.

6. **Be a school guest speaker:** Offer to visit local elementary or high schools as a guest speaker to speak about your type of business as a career option. Such talks are usually promoted through school newsletters, so parents will get to know your business name.

continued

7. **Co-market with complementary businesses:** Join forces with complementary businesses to market. A hairdresser could co-market with a wedding photographer, beauty salon, and bridal store. Carry each other's brochures and cards, advertise together, and refer each other.

8. **Hold a special community event:** Initiate an occasional special event that is community-oriented. You could work with another business and attract some new customers, as in the Real Life example "Cooking Up New Customers."

9. **Participate in business and women's networks:** Women are great networkers, and business network organizations are springing up everywhere. Members usually use each other's services once they get to know each other and also refer other members. If there isn't a network in your town, be a leader and start one.

10. **Hold a free seminar:** A free seminar is an informational event that educates participants but is not openly commercial. For example, a travel agent could hold a free seminar about "The Tricks and Traps of Traveling in Australia." Those in attendance are qualified leads, because they wouldn't come if they didn't have future travel plans and will no doubt call when they are ready to book a trip. Because it is an educational event for the community the local media will probably promote it.

Real Life) **Cooking Up New Customers**

Pat owns a pottery gallery and gift store and has been an active community member for many years. She is a director at her chamber of commerce, serves on the board of the downtown business improvement association, and sits on various arts and community events committees. Her name is well respected and well known in a large community.

Sunanda owns a home-based business where she teaches delicious Indian cooking. She is on the committees of two chapters of the local women's network and is also responsible for collecting, wrapping, and delivering the annual Christmas hamper donations for needy women and their families.

Pat and Sunanda decided to hold a joint Indian cooking event at Pat's gallery, with a percentage of the weekend's sales donated to the local women's transition house. Because both women had a reputation for being community-minded and the proceeds were going to a community organization, they approached the media and got a full-page story in the local paper.

"It was the best weekend since I opened the gallery many years ago," said Pat. "The store was crowded!"

"From the event, I got asked to do a television show on Indian cooking, which was broadcast across the state," said Sunanda.

By being involved in and giving to their community, the women received media coverage—and business—that would not have otherwise come their way.

NETWORK, NETWORK, NETWORK!

What is a networking group? An association of business people who meet for the common purpose of making contacts, exchanging leads and referrals, and reducing their isolation. Some restrict membership to one of each type of business, such as one representative of an accounting company or one realtor. Some are for professionals only, while others cater to a focused membership, such as women's groups or trade associations. With the growing trend toward home-based businesses and many owners feeling isolated, new networking groups are continually emerging.

JOIN A COMMITTEE OR ORGANIZATION

To increase your involvement and visibility, volunteer your services on a community or chamber committee, coach a Little League team, or join a drama group or a service organization such as Big Brothers. Not just an outlet for your individual interests— which you need to relieve the stress of work—your involvement will also provide a sense of accomplishment.

Networking works

Networking groups are designed to help promote members' businesses. There is no marketing tool more powerful than learning—and applying—the art of networking. As an example, in April 1995, a Valley Women's Network chapter was formed in Langley, British Columbia. Fourteen women (including myself) started the group, which was a sister group to three other networks in the Fraser Valley. The network grew so large that currently, nine other chapters have formed, with a combined membership of hundreds. It's like a huge, happy family of women business owners.

Network members develop long-term friendships and business relationships, turning to others within their network to fulfill their consumer needs. The meetings encourage members to increase contacts and try a little public speaking. Members leave these meetings feeling positively charged, no longer alone, and ready to tackle the world.

PARTICIPATE
....
When you become involved in a networking group, don't expect business to come to you. It won't. Use your communication skills and join a committee, help out, introduce yourself to people, and exchange business cards. Give to other members, and they will give back to you. The time spent will reap rewards.

Reap the many benefits

By becoming *involved*, you will learn valuable information about your community and how it operates plus have an opportunity to contribute directly to decision- and policy-making. You may have some fresh and innovative ideas that will benefit your community. As an active committee member or director, you can have direct input in formulating and implementing these ideas.

COMMUNICATE THROUGH SPEAKING

As you develop enough confidence to speak in public, some exciting opportunities become available, and the networking benefits are excellent. Each time you speak, someone will tell someone else about your presentation, and on it goes. Your credibility as the expert builds until you are in demand and able to command reasonable fees for your presentations. Here are some ideas on how to achieve this.

Teach adult education classes

Adult education organizers are always interested in new subjects and presenters. Classes are usually small, ranging from eight to twenty-five participants. This is an excellent training ground to practice your speaking skills. Smaller groups are usually friendly and quite forgiving if you are a little nervous.

Preparation involves planning the course material so that you teach within a given time frame. Courses can be as short as two hours or as long as a term. Your basic requirements are handouts, perhaps some audiovisual backup, and a presentation that is both interesting and informative. Initially, you will spend time in preparation, but materials can be repeatedly used and updated as required.

> ## GET PAID TO NETWORK
> ....
> *You get paid to teach adult education classes, with hourly rates ranging from $20 to $100. What an added bonus! Students are all potential customers, so this is a win–win situation. When the course is finished, you will have developed that necessary trust with your students. If they need help in your field, who will they call first?*

After teaching a three-hour, ten-week evening bookkeeping course for three years, my business blossomed partly as a result of my new contacts—regular classes of twenty-five to thirty participants. I finally had to employ a full-time bookkeeper. When that business was sold, it paid off the house mortgage. Most of the increased business came from the evening classes and community exposure as a weekly business columnist for a local newspaper.

Become a speaker

It is said that only five percent of adults can comfortably face a crowd with a microphone in hand. Of that five percent who do appear to speak effortlessly, probably four out of five have experienced butterflies, sweaty palms, and a good attack of nerves before speaking. Given time and experience, this nervousness is replaced by feelings of excitement and anticipation.

Eight terrific benefits of being a good speaker

Master the art of public speaking and these benefits can be yours:

1. You become considered an expert in your field.

2. Listeners become customers.

3. The more you speak, the more your confidence grows.

4. Your new skills can be applied to sales and public relations.

5. You can earn excellent money as you become more professional.

6. Organizations network your name to other groups.

7. Organizations are always looking to hire you to speak.

8. You can receive valuable press coverage through media releases.

Speaking opens new doors

Previously closed doors will open wide once you polish your speaking skills. There is no better feeling than being in demand for the knowledge which you professionally impart. Speakers can earn $3,000 to $5,000 per day—and then there are the exceptional ones who command up to and over $20,000 a performance. Your enhanced communication skills will serve you well.

Present workshops and seminars

Once you become an expert in your field and polish your communication skills, put these skills to work for your business. Offer your expertise in the form of public workshops or seminars. By building on a variety of topics within your field, you can market your services to numerous organizations.

To gain confidence, start locally and ask for written references, then market your seminars to other organizations. Expect to give some of your time free of charge or for a small honorarium. Whenever you appear in public, you usually receive free publicity, and people will refer you without you even asking.

Get creative

There aren't too many businesses that couldn't offer some form of relevant public education. A website designer could present a seminar about selling on the Internet. A retail fashion store could host seminars on wardrobe coordination for business women. A vitamin store could deliver a seminar on the benefits of using natural supplements during pregnancy. Be creative and make the effort; you'll have to work hard at building your communication skills as you grow your business. Market yourself with passion and persistence.

> ## JOIN TOASTMASTERS INTERNATIONAL
> ....
> *Public speaking skills can be learned by joining Toastmasters International. Local groups usually have small memberships who encourage you to learn in a supportive and non-critical environment. Nervous wrecks quickly develop into excellent, confident, informative speakers. You also learn other valuable business communication skills, including being more articulate, setting agendas, how to chair meetings, and handle difficult situations.*

COMMUNICATE THROUGH THE MEDIA

Contrary to popular belief, it isn't usually hard to get your name in the news, although it can be more difficult in larger cities. Newspapers are always looking for interesting stories about local people. You need to be creative—find a unique angle to your business or something timely or of interest within your community or industry, something that will capture the interest of an editor or reporter. See the Real Life example "Front-Page News."

Get your name in the news

Think about the reader appeal in a simple yet unusual story. You can't put a price on this type of publicity. Not only is it free, but readers are influenced by what they read in newspapers, and your credibility is immediately enhanced. Compare what you pay for a small advertisement in a newspaper to the benefits of free media coverage.

Real Life Front-Page News

On attending a seminar called "Getting Your Name in the News," I learned of a warehouse storage company that landed the whole front page of the business section of a large Seattle newspaper. How? By using a unique story angle.

The company rented one storage locker to a writer, who couldn't find peace and quiet at home. At the other end of the complex, another locker was rented to a young rock band, who couldn't find anywhere to practice because of the noise. The company saw the humor in this surprisingly peaceful arrangement, wrote it up in a snazzy press release and used it to their advantage with the media. This media exposure had their phones ringing off the hook.

CONTACT RADIO AND TV SHOWS

Exposure on television or radio greatly adds to your credentials and credibility. Once you have polished your speaking skills, approach producers with an idea that will pique their interest for a segment that is related to your business. Is there some controversy within your industry or a new product that listeners or viewers need to know about? Is it time-saving or environmentally friendly? Could you educate people with this information? Be creative and find that appealing "hook."

How many small but interesting businesses have you seen publicized in local newspapers? These people have found a way to get their name in the news. You won't find a reporter beating down your door to interview you, so you need to start applying your newly honed writing skills with a professional press release. If you can't write one, hire an experienced writer to prepare it for you. Use the checklist in Figure 11.1 to identify events that could get your name in the news.

Figure 11.1

What Is Newsworthy About Your Business?

1. Have you recently won any awards or gained any special recognition? ☐

2. Has something innovative happened within your industry? ☐

3. Are you holding a special community event or free seminar? ☐

4. Are you going to teach an adult education class? ☐

5. Are you going to be a guest speaker? ☐

6. Are you going to offer a new or unique service or product? ☐

7. Can you use your USP to interest a reporter in a story? ☐

8. Do you have a business anniversary coming up? ☐

9. Have you made a large donation to a community organization? ☐

10. Are you joining the board of a local or national organization? ☐

COMMUNICATE, DEMONSTRATE, AND EDUCATE

An integral component of marketing is continued exposure. You must also keep up with industry changes to keep in step with or ahead of the competition. To achieve these goals, attend industry trade shows, conferences, and seminars—seriously networking at the same time. This is where those strong communication and presentation skills discussed in Chapter 10 need to work overtime.

Participate in trade shows

At trade shows, not only can you showcase your business, you can also see how others organize and promote theirs. Assess the competition and leave with some new creative ideas, customers, and leads. If you are shy, attending these shows and using the principles described in Chapter 10 will help to increase your confidence as you talk to people and "get your lines down pat."

TARGET THE RIGHT SHOWS

There are shows for every interest. Books, gardens, homes, vehicles, technological gadgets—you name it, there is a trade show or fair for it. But carefully select where you display to ensure that you are hitting a focused market and not wasting valuable marketing money. There is no better venue to meet customers one-on-one in a targeted environment.

Show off at shopping malls

Retail malls are excellent local venues for promotion and exposure, as is demonstrated in the Real Life example "See It, Feel It, Touch It." Malls usually work to a schedule of theme weeks, and the managers will send you an annual schedule of events. The few hundred dollars invested will give you more publicity than a dozen full-page advertisements. It's no use just sitting there and waiting for people to come to your display; say "hello" as they pass by and give shoppers candy and brochures. Use those persuasive communication skills to draw them to your display. As malls are open for extended hours and at weekends, you may need extra staff to work the booth. Select your representatives carefully.

Real Life — See It, Feel It, Touch It

A landscape curbing company had difficulty finding the best marketing method, so they tried a mall display during Home Week. Using a colorful but inexpensive display with samples, plants, pictures, and bright signs, they got shoppers interested in these attractive, labor-saving products. The opportunity to talk to homeowners and demonstrate their product was exactly what was needed. Using similar openers and communication techniques to those described in Chapter 10, they generated more leads in a week than they could handle and now use these venues regularly.

Eight Excellent
Trade Show Tips

Use your refined communication and presentation skills to interact with potential customers. Here are some additional tips to ensure a winning presentation and successful trade show or networking event:

1. **Know what to expect:** People come to trade shows to browse and compare products and prices. Welcome, inform and give brochures and cards to those who stop by your display; don't pressure them to close a sale. If you leave with a few leads each day and your brochures are reaching potential customers, you have done well.

2. **Offer "freebies":** Attract people to your booth by offering candies, pens, and novelty "freebies." People look for them. Demonstrations always attract a crowd. Have you ever noticed the people watching cooking or makeup demonstrations?

3. **Offer something different:** Develop a skill-testing questionnaire, offering a prize to the winner. I used one of these at an entrepreneurial trade show, offering a free consultation for the worst score. This piqued people's interest plus it was a comfortable opener for a chat about their business.

4. **Offer draw prizes:** No table is complete without a drawing, if legal in your state. Most people love to enter drawings, so splash lots of "win" signs around your booth. Ask on the entry form if the contestant would like a free quotation or more information. This qualifies leads for follow-up. Check federal competition legislation at *www.ftc.gov* and state legislation through your Department of Consumer Affairs office.

5. **Converse professionally and politely:** Don't pounce on people as they approach your table. Use the appropriate opener. Ask if they would like a drawing entry form and whether they would like to take some information with them. Be professional, polite, and interested in their questions.
continued

6. **Distribute brochures and handouts:** Count cards and brochures before putting them on the table so you can monitor the interest level. Give out informative handouts with all your contact information as this enhances your credibility as an expert. For example, a garbage disposal company could prepare handouts about the benefits of composting and recycling.

7. **Dress presentably:** Dress to suit the occasion as first impressions *always* count. Golf shirts with your logo look smart and convey your professionalism. If you don't have corporate clothing, wear a suit or smart casual clothes. Jeans and sneakers are out unless you sell jeans and sneakers.

8. **Follow up:** During the following week, contact those who were interested in your business. Tell them that it was a pleasure to meet them and ask if they need more help or information. If you don't follow up after a trade show, you will lose valuable business.

GIVE YOUR BRAIN A BOOST

Participating in these events takes you away from the day-to-day routine of doing business and reduces isolation. It is a mini mind vacation. Learning new information and meeting new people helps to remotivate you. Even if you learn only one or two pertinent facts to apply to your business, the time has been well spent.

Attend conferences and seminars

Conferences, seminars, and workshops are not only necessary education, they provide invaluable networking contacts and exposure. When networking, use the twenty-second infomercial incorporating your USP. Radiate confidence in who you are and what you do.

Learn about new products, marketing on the Internet, management, changing marketing and selling techniques, or motivating employees and yourself. If you think you could present a relevant workshop at their next event—which will help to cement your expert reputation—contact the planners during the event, introduce yourself, give them some information, and follow up the next week.

COMMUNICATE THROUGH WRITING

Nothing helps to build your reputation as an expert more than getting published. If you've been developing your writing skills, why not prepare some short articles and shop them around? E-magazines, websites, local newspapers, trade magazines, free newspapers, and magazines are always looking for new material. If they don't pay, you can often trade the article for an advertisement.

The articles are an excellent addition to your résumé, brag book, and media kit. The publicity from being published is far superior to any form of advertising. However, nothing is worse that a poorly written article, so have a professional check and edit your work. Here are some low-cost ways to utilize your writing skills.

Write columns

Contact your community newspaper or industry publications and offer to write a weekly or monthly column. Most publications allow a byline on the column with all your contact information. Some will trade the column for an advertisement. Once you are published, you cement your name as the expert. You can then use these columns for other promotions.

Give customers informational handouts

Have some handy tips, hints, and articles that you have written photocopied to give to customers. People love information and will pass them on. Use them anywhere that you are marketing your business—at trade shows, networking events, in media kits, and in mail-outs.

Have a "wall of fame"

If you have articles published and clippings about your business from newspapers, frame them and put them up on your wall, along with testimonials from satisfied customers and community awards. Customers can't help but be impressed. It builds their relationship of trust with you, and they will tell others.

Post articles on your website

Direct your website visitors to your library of published articles. Link the latest article on your front page to the archives. To keep visitors returning to your site, add new information each month. Contact other sites that are compatible with yours and ask to cross-link (see page 254). Let them know that you have articles available and offer to post a couple on their site.

BUILD CREDIBILITY USING TESTIMONIALS

Testimonials are one of the most powerful marketing tools—and they're free. When people choose a book, they are strongly influenced by the back-cover testimonials. When employees are hired, references play an important role in the final selection process. There is credibility in references from a third party. In most cases, all you have to do is ask for a testimonial in that confident, persuasive, friendly manner that you have developed.

How to obtain testimonials

Satisfied customers shouldn't mind preparing a testimonial for you. Ask: "Gordon, are you happy with the work I did for you?... You are? Would you mind doing me a great favor? I would really appreciate a testimonial from you to use for promotional purposes." If you have made a presentation at an event or delivered a workshop or seminar, ask for a testimonial. If you did a good job, people usually always oblige. These testimonials can then be used if you are looking for other speaking business or can be added to your media kit.

Obtain a letter of permission

When you receive a testimonial, send a thank-you card along with a nice note, asking for their signed permission to use the letter. Enclose a permission form and a self-addressed stamped return envelope. The permission form should read as in Figure 11.2.

Where to use testimonials

Wherever you are marketing, testimonials can be used to enhance most of your promotional materials. Use them:

- in brochures and flyers
- in newspaper advertisements
- in press releases
- in media kits
- framed on walls at your office
- on your website

Figure **11.2**

Sample Letter of Permission

October 19, 20__

Competent Computer Repair Services
19307 - 148th Street
Sunny Hills, TN 60119

PERMISSION TO REPRODUCE TESTIMONIAL LETTER

I, Gordon Miller of <u>The Accurate Accounting Company</u>, hereby give permission for my testimonial letter, dated September 21, 20__ , and written to Competent Computer Repair Services, to be used in part or in full in written or oral media promotions, brochures, and any other form of promotional material. This permission shall remain in effect until rescinded in writing.

Signed: Gordon Miller
Title: President
Date: October 19, 20__
Business: The Accurate Accounting Company Inc.

Evaluations

If you are introducing a new product or service, use your verbal presentation skills to deliver a powerful pitch to a well-known company, offering a free test period in return for a testimonial. For example, if you are marketing a new computer security product, offer to install a system into a large corporation's computer network, free of charge for a three-month period, in exchange for a written testimonial. Once introduced to your product, the corporation may even want to purchase it.

START A BRAG BOOK

Have you ever seen an interior decorator's brag book or a model's portfolio? These are their most important selling tools. Start a brag book of your own. Carry it with you to events and leave it in your reception area. Where applicable, include some "before and after" photos.

APPLY YOUR COMMUNICATION SKILLS TO MARKETING

Think about how these methods in this chapter could apply to growing your business. Research and complete Figure 11.3, "Where and How Can I Use Low-Cost Marketing Magic?"

These low-cost marketing magic techniques will increase your exposure, expertise, and credibility. Use them along with the marketing plan strategies described in the following chapter as you continue to grow your business.

Figure 11.3

Where and How Can I Use Low-Cost Marketing Magic?

1. Which community organizations could you join that are of interest to you?

_____

_____

_____

2. Which networking groups or business associations would be most beneficial to join?

_____

_____

_____

3. Of the "Ten Tips for Reaching Out," pick three that you'll commit to using.

_____

_____

_____

4. Write down the names of three businesses you could co-market with.

_____

_____

_____

5. If you are not a member of your chamber of commerce, note their phone number and the date by which you will call them for information.

Phone number: _____ Date: _____ Cost: $ _____

6. Define then write down three areas in your industry or profession where you consider yourself an expert.

_____

_____

_____

7. Think of topics in your field of expertise that you could build a short speech or a workshop around.

_____

_____

_____

8. Research adult education facilities or colleges in your area with regards to offering a course in your field of expertise.

_____

_____

9. Question 5 in Figure 9.8, Chapter 9, asked you to identify what is unique about your business. Now think of some hooks or unique angles highlighting your USP that could be used to interest the media.

_____

_____

continued

10. Research annual trade show events where it would be suitable for your business to exhibit.

_____

_____

_____

11. Note which customers you could ask for written evaluations or testimonials.

_____

_____

_____

12. Research free magazines and Internet e-magazines. Which ones could you approach to write articles for? Note all contact information.

_____

_____

_____

CHAPTER TWELVE

What Else Should You Know About Marketing?

---◄○►---

*The spirit of self-help is the root of
all genuine growth in the individual.*

SAMUEL SMILES

---◄○►---

Using communication skills to market is a highly successful technique, but you can't be everywhere at once. In order to grow your business, you need to develop affordable yet effective methods of keeping your name in the marketplace. Because consumer trends change quickly, what works one time may not work the next. This means trying different techniques, adapting to trends, and, of course, carefully monitoring the results. ❧

DEVELOP A MARKETING MIX

This chapter explores using service as an effective marketing tool, marketing on the Internet, and advertising using more traditional methods—their advantages and disadvantages. You'll learn what marketing mistakes to avoid and how to prepare a marketing plan. It is up to you to put everything you have learned into practice.

BUILD A DATABASE—BUILD CUSTOMER LOYALTY

From the first phone call to a potential customer walking in to your business, your goal is to build long-term customer loyalty. Start by maintaining a detailed customer database that conforms to privacy legislation. Being technologically terrific helps, but manual systems work just as well. Combining this information with your excellent service policies will generate repeat business.

Use one of the methods described in Chapter 8 to get new customers' contact information. Many retail stores using computerized systems ask for full contact information before processing a sale. Some customers consider this an invasion of privacy, although most comply. If you offer after-sale services and incentives, most customers are happy to supply the information. Once you have made a sale, you usually include their information on the sales invoice.

EXPLAIN YOUR SERVICES AND INCENTIVES

Always explain in detail to customers the various services and incentives that you offer; it makes them feel special that you have taken this time. Give them a handout to take home that lists all these services. They may even pass it on to their friends.

If you intend to keep the customers you already have, plan who will be responsible for maintaining the database and ensuring that mailings, email, and follow-up phone calls are made in a timely manner. If you need extra staff to do follow-up work, hire a part-time marketing student from a local college. They are usually keen and computer-literate. Businesses that value customer service consistency develop a loyal customer base. Here are some ideas to put this information to use.

Seven Tips
To Build Loyalty—and Sales

1. **Say thank you:** Send a thank-you card to new customers or to a customer who referred another to you. People who take the time to write personal thank-you notes are always remembered.

2. **Keep detailed personal information:** Listen to customers, remember their faces, know their family's concerns. Ask about family members or subjects that are personally important to them. Keep notes in a file for future reference.

3. **Go that extra mile:** If a customer has experienced family illness, death, a new arrival, marriage, or has won a special award, send an appropriate greeting card, letter, or flowers. Let them know that you really care.

4. **Send special occasion cards and birthday discounts:** Send customers seasonal greeting cards with a personal note. Start a birthday club and send customers cards with a special discount coupon to be used during that month. People will bring in their card to receive the discount.

5. **Make an after-sales follow-up phone call:** Within a few days of customers purchasing from you, follow up with a phone call to see if they are satisfied. This way, problems can be quickly rectified and your call will be remembered.

6. **Start a service reminder system:** We expect it from our car dealership, and they are assured of repeat business. Take care of the customers you already have. When a serviceable product is purchased, note the service details in a service database and call or email the customer to remind them. If they are busy, offer a pickup service.

continued

7. **Send newsletters and announcements:** Send a regular newsletter by either mail or email to existing and potential customers. Incorporate informative and educational items of interest or updates about industry developments, and include a competition or coupon to monitor the response. A short email announcing a special event is a fast, cost-free way to reach the e-connected.

OUT-SERVICE THE COMPETITION

As the huge upsurge of baby boomers become more affluent, they are able to dictate to business their greater purchasing needs. Those needs boil down to competitive pricing, hassle-free shopping, a friendly buying environment, knowledgeable staff, and—most important—quality service.

This is where the smart small business owner should recognize that they *can* compete by incorporating an extra level of service. Cater your services to busy self-employed people—many of them home-based and understaffed—and working parents on the run; they represent a large percentage of the buying population.

Give what your competitors can't

In most cases, big-box and chain stores can't afford to give personalized service. You can't afford not to. Here's how to improve your customer service and to fill those gaps left by larger competitors.

OFFER A "LOANER"
....

If a product breaks down or needs servicing and the customer is inconvenienced, offer a loaner service, just as car dealerships do. This can apply to vacuums, computers, certain appliances, lawn mowers, and sewing machines, to name a few. Customers won't forget the inconvenience you saved them and will tell others, who will tell others...

- *In-home servicing:* If your products require servicing or repairing, where practical, offer in-home servicing. For example, vehicle oil changes and computers can be serviced in the home.
- *Pickup and delivery:* Cater to busy moms and home-based business owners. Offer a twice-weekly pickup and delivery service. Office Depot offers a twenty-four-hour delivery service for office supply orders over $50. Pay a high school student instead of doing it yourself.

- *Sweeten the pot:* Some small businesses offer extras including free lessons on purchase of certain machines and equipment, a no-limit warranty, and interest-free terms for ninety days. Consider in-home product demonstrations when a customer purchases a product that they don't know how to use.
- *Those little added touches:* They are small things but important to your customers—offering draws and competitions, candy (and balloons for children) at the front counter, customer discount cards, complimentary coffee, free samples, and a suggestion box. Each one silently says "We care about you."

Don't compete—work with the big-box chains

Retailers continually worry about price-cutting big-box chains and larger stores. There is no way they can compete on price. And there are many consumers who shop for price only, rarely considering the consequences when their product breaks down or needs servicing.

Some larger chains offer extended warranties, which of course are a great income-generator for them, because few people ever use them. What started as a "cheap computer" soon costs hundreds of dollars more. Have you heard this line before? "But it'll only cost you 38 cents a day for three years to have the added security of the warranty." That three-year warranty costs the customer over $400.

Consumers continually buy products at large chains that they don't know how to correctly use. Often, the salesperson knows little about what they are selling. This is where the smart retailer or service company will jump in feet first and take advantage of the situation. How?

Build big-box relationships

Meet with managers of large chain stores that sell the same brands of products as you or products that you can service or repair. Let the manager know that you are an expert and can offer the following services to their customers:

- a free lesson or product demonstration
- free assembly and testing
- warranty service
- product service reminder calls
- a discount off their first service or purchase

- a full range of accessories
- any of the other suggestions previously mentioned

Leave cards and brochures with the manager and touch base regularly. You are doing the chain stores a favor by offering these services. Then, when a customer comes to your business who has been referred by the larger store, you will win them over with your excellent customer service and expertise. They may have purchased an inferior product that they are not satisfied with. You now have the opportunity to educate them on the benefits of trading up to one of your quality lines.

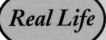 ## Coaxing in the Chain Store Customers

Gary owned a small fitness equipment store. Catering mostly to the home gym market, he began to feel the pressure when another huge new chain store moved into town. It seemed that nearly every chain store now sold treadmills and gym equipment much cheaper than he could.

He was a fitness trainer and expert, knowing both the equipment and the body intimately. Rather than give up the store, he approached four of the large chain stores selling home-gym equipment, offering to give their customers a free fitness lesson and equipment demonstration, plus be a depot for servicing and repairing their brands.

The managers were very happy to work with him. Gary left cards and brochures, keeping in touch by phone regularly. He started to get sales calls from chain store employees who couldn't answer customers' technical questions. He was always polite and helpful.

Then customers started calling Gary, asking him questions about the equipment. Some came into the store for advice, often buying small accessories. Over a period of a few months, he realized that he had gained a base of new customers who had evolved from the chain store referrals. By putting them onto his service and customer appreciation programs, within twelve months, Gary wasn't worrying about business anymore. He had enough to handle.

MARKETING AND THE INTERNET

There's no getting away from it—if you aren't using the Internet for research, knowledge, and marketing your business then it's time to get with the program. Before you race off to have a website designed, research sites of businesses similar to yours. Decide what you want your site to achieve and how you will entice visitors to return. If you need more in-depth information, there are countless reference books available on this subject. However, following is some basic information to help you make a more informed decision about your business website.

Design and cost

The average person surfing the Net is impatient, so your site should be designed to load quickly. Extras such as audio, complex graphics, or video clips can frustrate the average visitor if they are not using a high-speed connection. They won't wait for information to download unless they are extremely interested in what you have to offer. A small business doesn't need massive amounts of fancy tricks on their site, just enough content to inform, educate, and generate interest.

Hire a reputable designer to put your site together, because it requires both graphic and programming talents. You can pay as little as a few hundred dollars for a basic site to many thousands of dollars, depending on the bells and whistles. Once it is up and running, a monthly fee is paid to your Web designer to "host" or look after the site. This can vary from $25 to $50 a month, depending on the site's size and how often you make changes.

Your designer can amend your pages as required. You will pay approximately $75 to have your domain name registered annually, your monthly Internet Service Provider (ISP) fee runs about $20 to $30 a month, and the hourly rate for your designer to make changes to your Web site can vary from $30 to $75 an hour. Many Web page designers who host

MAKE YOUR SITE INFORMATIVE
....

People look for information on the Internet so your site should contain more than just advertising. Include helpful and educational material that can be printed out. It's another way of getting your name out there. An automotive dealership could include some helpful road safety or vehicle maintenance tips. Or try a quiz that can be completed online and offer support by email for people with questions.

MONITOR SITE VISITORS

Make sure your contact information is on every page for monitoring purposes. Most hosting companies offer a statistical service which gives you access to a detailed daily log, including what search engines found you and what search phrases were used. "Hits" are not important statistics; the number of home-page visits are. Ask your Web designer how to access this information and use it to monitor site usage, and understand why people visit your site.

your site are happy to answer unlimited email questions and make monthly alterations and updates (within reason) as part of their service. If you have an efficient designer, changes can be made within twenty-four hours.

Make surfing easy

Your home page should be easy to navigate, with clear directions to the rest of the site. Drop-down menus are a nice addition. Pages shouldn't be cluttered. Use a good-sized font that will readily adapt to a variety of computer monitors. Remember that baby boomers and older people usually suffer from failing eyesight. If fonts are too small or too light or the background is too busy, your site will be difficult to read. People will give up and go elsewhere.

What's in a name?

Your domain name has to be easy for people to find. Many companies use their business name—for example *www.microsoft.com*. Others prefer to use a name relevant to their business. My domain name is *www.smallbizpro.com*. It's getting harder to register popular names because of the millions in use, so you have to be creative. Of course, now we have .net and .org plus a few other dots, just to confuse the issue. However, search engines such as Google are pretty reliable at finding people and their sites.

What are the advantages of having a website and using the Internet?

It seems that if you don't have a web address, people think you aren't a real business. These days, many people prefer to first check a business's website before picking up the phone. A website silently markets your business 24/7.

Unfortunately, your site can get lost among the millions, so if you want to be at the top of the search engine listings, you can either pay the search engine company "per click" or for a search engine placement service. Neither strategy is guaranteed and each can cost hundreds or thousands of dollars. Otherwise, *you* have to promote your site. As rates and pricing packages vary, be sure to compare prices.

Some of the advantages of having a website and using the Internet for your business include:

- **Credibility:** Many people make their decision to use a business after visiting their website, so include testimonials from satisfied customers and a detailed personal or corporate profile.
- **Global exposure:** Your business is showcased universally. If you are seeking national or international business through introductory emails or phone calls, suggest that people look at your site for company credentials.
- **A research tool:** Using the Internet, you can keep up with world and industry news, technology, and your competitors. Look at other sites that appeal to you and incorporate some of the better ideas into yours.
- **Easy sourcing of leads:** By using search engines, you can locate businesses on the Internet that may require your services. Then, send an introductory email, suggesting that they look at your site. Of course, ensure that you comply with spam regulations.
- **People-finding:** If you are looking for a specific person, such as the purchasing agent for a particular business, you can locate their website and then correspond by email. It sure beats calling directories or looking in the Yellow Pages.
- **Cost-effectiveness:** Once established, your site's ongoing maintenance costs are relatively low in return for the twenty-four-hour-a-day silent marketing that it can achieve. Results will be strictly dependent on how you market and utilize your site.

> ## PROMOTE YOUR WESITE
> ....
> *Many people launch their site, then sit waiting for "hits." It doesn't happen that way. You must actively promote your site by including your web address on every form of promotion— business cards, stationery, trade show signs, brochures, advertisements, vehicles, your voice mail greeting, and the Yellow Pages. Tell everyone about it.*

Link, link, and cross-link

To drive traffic to your site, contact other compatible and reputable businesses that you feel comfortable recommending to others. Ask to cross-link sites, ensuring that you both give a detailed description of your site. Have a section on your menu for Useful Links. If you check your Web statistics, you will discover that a greater portion of your visitors come from these links. Submitting articles to other sites with a link back to your website is another effective way to drive traffic to your site.

For most businesses, a website is a complementary form of marketing which works in conjunction with other marketing tools. Unless your business is built entirely around e-commerce or you are prepared to spend a lot of time promoting it from your keyboard, don't rely on it for total marketing exposure, and always ensure that you project a professional image.

Real Life) **From Russia with Love**

In January 2004, my first book, *Business for Beginners*, was adapted for and published in Russia. Everything regarding its publication was done quickly and efficiently using email and my website. In fact, a contact of the publisher, a Russian gentleman living in the east, initially discovered the English language version of my book through my website, *www.smallbizpro.com.*

He purchased a copy and took it to his Russian publisher friend, who wanted to publish a Russian version. The only transactions that were not done through electronic media were signing of faxed agreements and, of course, sending me a royalty check. Now all my book files are sent globally by email. It's great!

So when you have a website, your business immediately becomes global from the comfort of your home office.

"HIT-OR-MISS" MEDIA ADVERTISING

Throughout these last few chapters, the marketing focus has been on utilizing verbal, written, and customer service skills. Now it's time to look at the various media and how they can help implement your marketing strategies. My personal term for media advertising is "hit-or-miss" marketing, because you are not usually targeting a focused market.

Different methods work for different businesses. Here are the advantages and disadvantages of the more common methods of media advertising, which you can assess for growing your business.

Direct mail

Direct mail refers to bulk mailings sent to a list of prospective customers. Most of it, as you know, ends up in the recycling bin, so be selective about who receives yours. Some companies experience a higher rate of success because they have the resources to produce a professional product and mail in high volumes.

Advantages:
- You can better target by using selective mailing lists.
- Because you know who received the materials, you can follow up by telephone.
- Bulk postage rates reduce mailing costs.
- You can use a limited-time offer to solicit a faster response.

Disadvantages:
- The success rate is low, with a response of around 1 to 2 percent.
- Preparation is expensive and time-consuming, with most of the mail recycled.
- You are not targeting a focused market.

Radio and television

Although buying trends are created through television and radio commercials, the average small business cannot even contemplate the high cost of this advertising. Don't undertake it without careful research and planning.

Advantages:
- Commercials are seen or heard by thousands of people.

- This form of advertising increases your credibility as a business.
- Costs of advertising on local (as opposed to national) stations are more affordable and target specific communities.
- Viewers and listeners tend to use certain channels and will hear or see your advertisements regularly.

Disadvantages:
- The key to success is repetition, which is costly.
- It is momentary, non-targeted advertising and easily forgotten.
- You need enough inventory and staff to cope with a successful response.

Coupon books

Although coupon books work well for some businesses, such as restaurants, dry cleaners, and fast food outlets who offer "two-for-one" coupons, studies show that less than one percent of recipients respond to these offers.

Advantages:
- Mass distribution makes the cost per household economical.
- Results can be monitored by using limited-time offers.
- Your business is exposed to tens of thousands of people.

Disadvantages:
- You could be swamped with calls and unable to meet demand.
- You could get very little response and lose money.
- If you make "two-for-one" or similar offers and solicit a good response, you could lose substantial profits.
- You need to repeat the advertisement for consistency.

Newspapers and magazines

Local newspaper advertising is one way to keep your name in front of the community. People enjoy their community newspaper, although it is usually brimming with flyers, and your advertisement could get lost.

Be prepared to advertise regularly. This can be costly, sometimes with disappointing results. Magazine advertising is usually expensive, so choose one that specifically targets readers who use your type of business. Specialized businesses often get a satisfactory response from selective magazine advertising.

Advantages:

- Your business is exposed to your whole community.
- Advertising in the classifieds section is an affordable option.
- For newspapers, copy isn't needed until a week before publication. (Magazines need copy up to ninety days in advance.)
- Special advertising features focus on certain types of businesses.

Disadvantages:

- People usually skip advertisements unless shopping for a specific item.
- Large, display, and "one-shot" advertisements are expensive and often don't solicit the expected response.
- A small advertisement can get lost.
- Newspapers and magazines have a short life.
- Community newspapers are often loaded with flyers and readers receive too much advertising to read it all.

> # MONITOR ADVERTISING RESULTS
> ....
> *Design an advertising campaign to intrigue readers and capture their attention. Use a limited-time offer or clip-out coupons to monitor your results. Always ask customers how they heard about you. Seek professional help to design eye-catching copy so that your advertisement has impact.*

Yellow Pages

More a hit than a miss: if you are in business, you should be in the Yellow Pages. When people don't know who to use, they usually refer to either the Yellow Pages or their local newspaper.

Advantages:

- People trust businesses that advertise in the Yellow Pages.
- Your advertisement is working for you 24/7, twelve months a year.

- You can use a cell phone number to advertise.
- Everyone receives a copy of their local Yellow Pages directory.

Disadvantages:

- Large advertisement costs are prohibitive for the average business.
- There is no way out of the annual contract.
- Your competitors advertise there.
- You need a business line or cell phone to advertise.

DESIGN AN AD YOU CAN AFFORD

....

Yellow Pages advertising works particularly well for service businesses, because people don't use them regularly and often don't know who to use. Keep the size of your advertisement affordable because you are tied to an annual contract. Study competitors' advertisements to see what attracts you to read them.

Flyers

Attract customers with special offers printed on brightly colored paper. Keep the message simple and uncluttered. Use a time-limited offer to monitor responses. Circulate small quantities in a selected area and monitor the results before embarking on large flyer drops. Flyers also make useful handouts at trade shows and special events.

Advantages:

- Your local newspaper or neighborhood teenager will deliver them for a reasonable cost.
- You can monitor the results almost immediately.
- They are inexpensive to produce and multifunctional.

Disadvantages:

- The response rate is low compared to the number circulated.
- People are inundated with flyers and advertising materials.
- Flyer delivery can cost up to 10 cents each.
- Consumers have to need and be able to afford your product at the time of advertising.

There are other ways to advertise your business, including ads on transit, benches at bus stops, billboards, posters, coupons, and free samples in mailboxes. For the average small business, many of these methods are outside their budget. Plan your marketing strategies carefully and make every dollar work for you.

DON'T WASTE MARKETING TIME AND MONEY

It seems that everyone is trying to sell everyone everything, and quite frankly, consumers become tired of being solicited. Remember a few rules as you plan your marketing campaign. Rule number one is "Don't upset the customer." Rule number two is "Don't waste your time and money." To save bad feelings and wasted efforts, avoid the following methods.

---

14 Marketing Mistakes
to **Avoid**

1. **DON'T** delay in returning messages. A good percentage of business is lost through phone calls and emails not being returned. Stay connected in our disconnected "e-society."

2. **DON'T** drive people away by being too persistent, a nuisance, or aggressive in your follow-up. Do not force appointments or keep people talking if they are busy. Ask if you can follow up at another time.

3. **DON'T** miss appointments. A forgotten appointment is lost business and a slur on your reputation.

4. **DON'T** make phone calls if you are feeling irritable, stressed out, negative, or depressed. Wait until you are feeling more positive, as your mood will be reflected during the call.

continued

---

5. **DON'T** put the competition down even if you know they have a bad reputation.

6. **DON'T** trust your memory and scraps of paper. Follow up on important deals or customers with a confirmation letter or email.

7. **DON'T** phone people at home after 5:30 p.m. This is family time; people are going crazy cooking dinner and organizing the family or just returning home from work. Your call will not be appreciated.

8. **DON'T** send unsolicited "junk mail" faxes or spam email. Don't send faxes at night as home-based business phones are either connected to the residential line or situated near a bedroom area, and you will wake people up.

9. **DON'T** waste money on large, non-targeted newspaper and magazine advertisements.

10. **DON'T** distribute flyers where you have not targeted your market.

11. **DON'T** blow your whole marketing budget on one form of advertising.

12. **DON'T** do any form of marketing without closely monitoring results.

13. **DON'T** use just one form of marketing. Combine different methods and media until you know which works better for you.

14. **DON'T** hide in your office relying on advertising. Get out there and meet people. Remember—*YOU* are your business.

NOW PLAN YOUR MARKETING APPROACH

These last two chapters have given you many ideas to ponder. Think how each one could be applied to your business and over what time frame. Because many involve only minimal cash outlay, you could implement some immediately. Others take time, but the efforts will reap you long-term business.

To help you plan your marketing, review the ideas in Figure 12.1. This worksheet allows you to plan up to two years ahead, so you can monitor your progress to see if you are staying on target. Use the sample marketing budget in Chapter 8, Figure 8.3, to help put your budget together.

Now that you have learned how to revamp your marketing plan, increase your communication skills and effectively market your business, the next step is to learn how to complete the sale. Chapter 13 guides you through the selling process and helps you to better understand what customers expect from you during and after the sale.

Figure **12.1**

Marketing Strategies for My Business

STARTING DATE: _____

	PROJECTED TIME FRAME			
Marketing idea	**Under 3 months**	**3–6 months**	**One year**	**Two years**
Join a community organization	☐	☐	☐	☐
Join a networking group	☐	☐	☐	☐
Join the chamber of commerce	☐	☐	☐	☐
Host a special community event	☐	☐	☐	☐
Be a food bank or hamper drop-off	☐	☐	☐	☐
Co-market with other businesses	☐	☐	☐	☐
Learn the art of speaking	☐	☐	☐	☐
Join Toastmasters International	☐	☐	☐	☐
Hold a free seminar	☐	☐	☐	☐
Teach adult education classes	☐	☐	☐	☐
Guest-speak at schools and associations	☐	☐	☐	☐
Participate in trade shows/networking events	☐	☐	☐	☐

continued

Marketing idea	PROJECTED TIME FRAME			
	Under 3 months	3–6 months	One year	Two years
Participate in conferences and seminars	☐	☐	☐	☐
Present a workshop or seminar	☐	☐	☐	☐
Use press releases or radio/TV interviews	☐	☐	☐	☐
Write columns and articles	☐	☐	☐	☐
Obtain evaluations and testimonials	☐	☐	☐	☐
Build a "wall of fame"	☐	☐	☐	☐
Start a brag book	☐	☐	☐	☐
Build a customer database	☐	☐	☐	☐
Implement after-sales follow-up calls	☐	☐	☐	☐
Implement a service call system	☐	☐	☐	☐
Offer a pickup and delivery service	☐	☐	☐	☐
Work with large chain stores	☐	☐	☐	☐
Offer free demonstrations and lessons	☐	☐	☐	☐
Market using email	☐	☐	☐	☐
Launch a website	☐	☐	☐	☐
Produce a newsletter	☐	☐	☐	☐
Offer discount cards	☐	☐	☐	☐
Send thank-you cards	☐	☐	☐	☐
Send birthday and seasonal greeting cards	☐	☐	☐	☐
Use draw and suggestion boxes	☐	☐	☐	☐
Sponsor a community organization	☐	☐	☐	☐
Support fundraisers	☐	☐	☐	☐
Offer complimentary coffee	☐	☐	☐	☐
Advertise on community notice boards	☐	☐	☐	☐
Use direct mail	☐	☐	☐	☐
Use radio or television commercials	☐	☐	☐	☐
Advertise in a coupon book	☐	☐	☐	☐

Marketing idea	PROJECTED TIME FRAME			
	Under 3 months	3–6 months	One year	Two years
Use newspaper advertising	☐	☐	☐	☐
Use speciality magazine advertising	☐	☐	☐	☐
Circulate flyers	☐	☐	☐	☐
Design a brochure	☐	☐	☐	☐
Design informational handouts	☐	☐	☐	☐
Other: _____	☐	☐	☐	☐

CHAPTER THIRTEEN

How Do You Improve Your Sales Skills?

—◄◦►—

Buying and selling is essentially antisocial.
EDWARD BELLAMY

—◄◦►—

Armed with an array of new ideas for marketing your business, now it's time to brush up on your sales skills. Once your marketing efforts bring in potential customers, the next step is to complete the sale. Many people fear the word "selling," yet it is not a difficult process as you do it all the time. ❧

SELLING IS AN EVERYDAY EXPERIENCE

Everything you do in life is motivated by the sales process. Think about the many decisions you make. Which house do I buy? Which trip do I take? Do I take this job? These choices involve a decision and the process of selling yourself on the answer.

Everything you want someone else to do is also motivated by you selling them on the idea—going for a job interview, applying for a loan, or being elected to public office. These situations all employ the same techniques as selling a product or service.

This chapter will convey the message that the concept of selling should not be foreign to you. In fact, we use it each day and are already quite effective at the technique. If you understand the overall sales concept, how the consumer thinks and the more formalized sales process, you will feel more confident in your selling abilities, which will help in growing your business. Harness your passion, communication skills, confidence, and expertise to help build your sales skills.

DEVELOP WINNING SALES QUALITIES

Learn to recognize and develop the qualities of a winning salesperson. An ideal salesperson can empathize with customers and is sensitive to their needs. This person is dedicated, competitive, energetic, and usually self-driven. Quick thinking, good communication skills, good understanding of figures, being a team player, being outgoing, and having charisma are all key to becoming a winning salesperson. You must be willing to learn, able to work independently, and above all, be honest with your customers, and they will come back.

What is selling?

Selling is the process of transferring goods or services from one person to another. Other definitions may include "for the transference of money." Almost everything we do involves the sales process, although selling doesn't always involve the transfer of funds.

You can already sell

Most people have the ability to sell. For example, in the morning you have two choices—you can get up or stay in bed. We automatically condition our minds to "sell" ourselves on one of the two choices. Whichever choice is appealing is the choice we make. You may decide that you need to go to work so you won't lose business, or that you have put in extra time and can afford to stay in bed. Either way, you have sold yourself on this choice.

DISPELLING THE SALES MYTH

Many salespeople make the mistake of trying to sell something to someone who really doesn't need or want it. This is referred to as high-pressure sales, the type of stereotypical sales process that we all detest. No doubt certain salespeople come to mind when "high pressure" is mentioned. Some have earned their bad reputation.

> ## READ THE SIGNS
> ·······································
> *To convince customers that they should buy from you, learn to recognize their needs. Allow them to discover the benefits of your product, while showing them the value and illustrating how easy it is to buy.*

Have you been pressured at a holiday time-share presentation or been hounded by an aggressive appliance salesperson? You probably didn't use or return to these businesses. Hopefully you vowed not to use those tactics on your customers.

A good salesperson's goal is to assist customers in making the right decision that will fulfill their needs and expectations or solve their problem. The key phrase here is "solve their problem." Always look upon your job as one of helping people, which is the real goal behind this cooperative or nurturing selling style.

CONSUMERS ARE FILLING A NEED

Think of selling as filling a need, because fundamentally, that is what selling is about. People buy because they have a need at that time, whether it is physical or psychological. When partners argue, one may go on a shopping spree or buy comfort food. Why? Because they are filling a need for some positive reinforcement.

Few people think they want or need a hydraulic jack, but if their car had just broken down, the story would be different. Knowing your customers' needs and wants—and the difference between the two—will help the aspiring salesperson to make a successful sale.

Develop a positive relationship with your customers. A happy customer will tell their friends and acquaintances about your business and will return in the future. An angry customer will also tell everyone about your business, but not in the manner that you would like. Everyone has a dissatisfied sales story to tell; I'm sure you have heard many over the years.

USE THE SIX-STEP SALES PROCESS

To effectively sell, understand the following six-step sales process, which works integrally with the "Five Ws" of selling which follow.

1. **Prospect:** finding and identifying potential customers

2. **Planning:** knowing how you will approach the presentation

3. **Presentation:** presenting your sales strategy to the prospect

4. **Problems:** being ready to competently handle customers' objections

5. **Purchase:** knowing the right technique to use in closing a sale

6. **Public relations:** following up after the sale to ensure customer satisfaction

THE "FIVE Ws" OF SELLING

You need to understand and use the "Five Ws" of selling. Ask yourself these five questions before you attempt to close a sale. You will be pleasantly surprised at how much easier it is to complete the sale.

1. **Who** is buying?

2. **What** do they need and want?

3. **Why** do they need it?

4. **Where** do they need it?

5. **When** do they need it?

1. Know who is buying

Don't assume that the person standing in front of you is the one making the buying decision. Many salespeople try to convince a prospect that an item is exactly what they need, when that person isn't the actual purchaser. Ask who is the decision-maker and who is the user.

For example, a husband often accompanies his wife when she shops for plants. He is approached by a salesperson who informs him that the tree he is looking at is low maintenance and beautiful when it blooms. The husband doesn't need this information.

If the salesperson had asked the husband what he was looking for, he would have been told that his wife was the purchaser. The wife would appreciate the service, the husband would appreciate being left alone, and the salesperson would appreciate the sale. Know who is buying before you start your sales presentation.

2. Know their needs and wants

The difference between needs and wants can only be ascertained by asking the prospect. There is a distinct difference between the two that cannot be evaluated any other way. You may decide that you need a vehicle to get to and from work. A poor salesperson will decide that a certain vehicle is the one that you need and start the sales process for that vehicle. A good salesperson will question you to find out your exact needs and then build the sales process around those needs as in the Real Life example on page 278.

You *need* a vehicle that gets excellent mileage as you drive 60,000 miles a year. You also need a good sound system, plus air conditioning due to your asthma. Unless you were asked about these requirements, the salesperson wouldn't know. You may want a vehicle with cruise control that looks sporty. You don't necessarily need these, but if the price were right, you might consider them in your purchase decision.

3. Know why they need it

Now you must be more specific and ask for what purpose the goods are to be used. Using an alarm sales company as an example, if a customer only wants to scare off possible intruders, an alarm sign may suffice. If valuable merchandise is being stored, then a complete system would better suit their needs. By finding out why the customer needs (or wants) a certain product, you can more clearly define how to assist them.

4. Know where they need it

Knowing where a product or service will be used is important sales information, as the sale may depend on other associated costs. This knowledge is especially essential for service businesses. When you quote on a project, you need to know where you will be working, as this directly affects the cost. If the work is not local, evaluate whether subcontracting is necessary, which could affect the final contract price.

This knowledge can also help you to determine the appropriate product or service quality. A customer will pay a higher price for a premium product if the situation warrants it. For example, purchasing a department store alarm might suffice for the average homeowner but might not be suitable for a business, which will pay a higher cost for a more dependable alarm.

5. Know when they need it

Most people research before they purchase and enjoy the browsing process. Ask the customer when they need the product or service. This information can assist you to specifically fill the customer's needs. If a customer was going to buy a computer next month, you could inform him or her that it will be on sale then, or that a new model will be available. The customer appreciates your honesty and concern, will not feel pressured, and will most likely return to purchase from you. Don't feel that you have lost a sale because the customer didn't immediately buy from you. Some people spend months browsing before making a purchasing decision.

Always ask

These examples demonstrate why you must ask customers these five questions. By being better informed before attempting to close a sale, you won't make the mistake of under- or over-selling them. Customers will appreciate your attention to detail and the fact that you listened to their needs and didn't try to sell them something they didn't want or need. If you are still unsure of any facts, ask—customers are usually happy to tell you.

Ten Tips
for Relationship Selling

Small Investments for Big Payoffs

A longtime performance, innovation, sales, and customer service trainer and consultant to many large corporations, Lorne Kelton, CEO of ThinkShift, offers these tips for building long-term and profitable customer relationships.

1. **Make the relationship matter:** Connect with your customers to get to know them beyond the sale. Establish honest and open dialogue that fosters trust. This strategy encourages growth and reduces customers' concerns.

2. **Develop your personal sales competencies:** You can no longer just hope for the sale. Arm yourself with a wide range of talents, from solid questioning skills to understanding how to effectively use technology. Acknowledge where your greatest personal sales challenges are and spend time developing them.

3. **Become a master communicator:** Your voice is your primary selling advantage. How you speak—from intonation to syntax—impacts the sales process. Join Toastmasters to brush up on your speaking skills.

4. **Know the business inside out:** People still pay a premium for expertise, so be the expert by knowing the makes, models, colors, sizes, options, and benefits of your products and services better than anyone else in the industry. Regularly analyze your competitors' offerings.

5. **Hire and train the best and brightest salespeople:** Don't skimp on your sales team. They are your ambassadors. Train them to represent your business as if it were their own. Pay them well or offer incentives so that they make a deeper commitment to your business.

continued

6. **Read your customers' buying signals:** Tune in to your customers' nonverbal buying cues before they tune out. Body language reveals as much about buying intentions as words. Study cues such as eye contact, arm folding, deep sighing, finger tapping, and hand placement. Learn how to decode these subtle messages and leverage them as a sales advantage.

7. **Develop your negotiation skills:** Find common ground to build a mutually beneficial sale. Customers won't always like what you present to them, so you have to be flexible and ready to deal with changing expectations. Negotiation is all about striving for outcomes that can serve as a catalyst to further the sales relationship.

8. **Shut up and listen:** Listen in order to learn. Your customers' words will educate you about their true needs, so close your mouth and open your ears.

9. **Involve your customers in your business:** Continuously solicit your customers' input. As end users of your business, they are well placed to make insightful suggestions that will strengthen the relationship. Invite them to board meetings, focus groups, special events, and trade shows.

10. **Give back more—they will be back for more:** Offer added value—it's highly prized. Repeat business is the highest form of flattery. Follow through on promises, keep appointments, don't make excuses, and maintain the personal touch; you will be rewarded tenfold.

THE "SIX Ps" OF SELLING

Now that you better understand how to assess a prospective customer's needs, the next step is to continue with the sales process—referred to here as the "Six Ps" of Selling. Knowing this process enables you to better understand how to recognize your prospect through to after-sales service.

I. Prospect

People new to selling often ask: "Who is a good prospect and how will I recognize one?" The simple answer is that everyone is a prospect. Not everyone will become a customer but everyone is a prospect.

Webster's Dictionary defines a prospect as "a potential client or customer." A prospect is anyone who has the ability or opportunity to use your products or services. This doesn't mean that they *will* use you, but only that they have the opportunity. As an example, a grandmother shopping for clothes mistakenly could go into a children's store. She doesn't need children's clothes, but the salesperson doesn't know this. At this point, the grandmother is still a prospect, because she may be looking for her grandchildren.

The salesperson should approach the grandmother and, on being informed of the error, direct her to a women's clothing store. The grandmother now ceases to be a current prospect. But because the salesperson assisted her, she may become a future prospect.

> ## GENERATE MORE LEADS
> ●
> *You have to use your creativity to continually generate sales leads. Be organized and keep a lead file of both prospective, current, and old customers. Contact old customers, and ask neighbors and friends for referrals. Use business and personal associations to generate leads. Try advertising, using mailing lists, and, when you feel comfortable, cold-calling, using the techniques explained in Chapter 10.*

2. Planning

Before you launch into any sales presentation, plan your approach and the sales strategy to use. Every customer is different and many will present you with unforeseen challenges. Know what constitutes a successful presentation and how to handle diverse situations.

Your confidence and expertise will build with practice, so rehearsing various approaches and sales demonstrations will help you feel more at ease. Have the appropriate sales aids ready and ensure that the setting is comfortable for the customer. Know how to handle different cultural and ethnic values.

Planning which approach to use involves standard sales techniques. Learn how to be personable, how to appeal to the customers' emotions and senses, and how to involve them in the conversation. Strike a balance between demonstrating the product and relating its features and benefits. Explain each feature slowly and thoroughly. These techniques are all necessary to ensure a successful presentation.

USE THE "FEATURES AND BENEFITS" TECHNIQUE

Study any advertising flyers from large stores and you will notice that they stress the features and benefits of their products. This is a strong sales tool that must be used. A feature is a characteristic of a product or service. A benefit is the value of the feature and what it does for the customer. One feature of a gas dryer is the self-timer. The benefits are that it turns itself off and conserves energy. Where men are usually more interested in a product's features, women often prefer to know the benefits.

3. Presentation

Once you have identified a prospect and believe that there is an opportunity for him or her to become a new customer, start your sales presentation, extolling the virtues of your product or service and explaining why a buying decision would be in the prospect's best interests. Never deceive a prospect into believing that your product is infallible. A good salesperson will tailor the presentation to meet the prospect's needs while emphasizing the benefits and downplaying the drawbacks.

Your sales presentation is the process of influencing your customer and starts the moment he or she enters your doors. It continues until the sale is either made or lost, or the customer makes a decision to return. It includes planning and after-sales follow-up, which sometimes means going that extra mile to ensure a successful presentation.

The problem of perception

One problem you may experience is clarifying the difference between a business' physical appearance, what it can do, and what you say it can do. Let's use an automotive repair business as an example. You drive into a garage to be faced with rusted vehicles, beer bottles, and garbage piled against the wall and a dirty, ill-kept shop. You are starting to make a decision about the quality of service that can be delivered.

On entering, you step in some old oil. The filthy washroom has no toilet paper. A scruffy, unkempt mechanic with nicotine-stained fingers approaches you. He uses language unfit for children's ears. Would you trust this man with your vehicle?

Contrary to these external appearances, he is recognized as one of the best, award-winning mechanics in the region. His abilities are unquestionable yet his presentation is appalling. The message to this analogy? How customers perceive your business on first impression is how you are being judged. Ensure that your sales presentation is perceived exactly as you intend it to be and that you always present a professional image.

4. Problems

It is surprising how many salespeople struggle to prevent their customers from voicing their problems or concerns. You need customers to voice their problems before you complete the sale. It is your job to ensure that all problems or objections are satisfactorily answered before you try the closing process. Objections are those reasons why customers feel that they should not buy your product.

As a prospective buyer, if you mention to a salesperson that a vacuum cleaner is too expensive, yet they can demonstrate how it can save you money over the years, is it still too expensive? Was this really your objection, or was there another underlying problem that you didn't mention?

> # DELIVER A DYNAMIC PRESENTATION
> ....
> *A dynamic presentation takes preparation, so do your homework and know your product or service thoroughly. Use effective sales tools and have brochures or take-home information readily available. Spend time getting to know your customer and dress smartly. Remember those first impressions. If you need others to help, ensure they are available and have any paperwork accessible and ready to complete the sale quickly and efficiently.*

Clarify the objection

Objections voiced by customers often don't truly express the real problem. Clarify concerns and have suitable answers. This isn't as complicated as it sounds. Quite simply, be prepared. Before you can address an objection, you must fully understand it, so ask the prospect.

After your wonderful presentation to a customer who wants to purchase a vehicle, he or she answers you with "I'll think about it." Ask them: "Is there anything I have missed or that you are not sure of?" If the prospect answers, you can be sure there is something holding them back. Your job is now to work with them to identify that objection. Once identified and dealt with, you are in a position to close the sale.

If the customer doesn't answer your question or reiterates the first answer, you probably failed in your first attempt to complete the "Five Ws." If he or she is the decision-maker, wants and needs a reliable vehicle immediately, and your suggested vehicle fills this need, plus you addressed other problems, the customer should purchase the vehicle, providing he or she has the financial ability.

If finances were the only reason that the customer is hesitating and you offer a suitable financial arrangement, then the sale will be finalized. Sometimes people just want to browse. In the "Five Ws," you should have identified this and geared your presentation to suit. By helping now, you will encourage the customer to return when he or she is ready.

If the purpose of your presentation was to bring them to the point of making a buying decision, you must now handle all the objections. You need to show them why they should buy from you.

EMPATHIZE WITH YOUR CUSTOMERS

People like to know that you have been listening to them and that you empathize with them. The "Feel, Felt, Found" technique demonstrates that other customers have expressed similar concerns with satisfying end results. Because you use the word "feel", you connect with their emotions. This is of particular importance to women.

Use the "Feel, Felt, Found" technique

There are many ways to handle objections, including the "Feel, Felt, Found" and "Averting" techniques. The "Feel, Found, Felt" technique is helpful when you are dealing with an emotional customer.

As an example, a customer in your clothing store is at the point of making a buying decision, but mentions that the suit he or she likes is too expensive. Reply using the "Feel, Felt, Found" technique, but with the utmost sincerity. If the prospect feels that you are not sincere, this method will backfire and you could lose not only the sale, but the customer. It's very effective when used correctly. Try empathizing with your customer using the "Feel, Felt, Found" technique as illustrated below:

"I can understand why you feel this way, as many of our long-term customers felt the same way when they first shopped here. What they have found is that by buying our top-quality-workmanship suits, the suits have lasted and kept their appearance for twice as long as our nearest competitor. It really depends on what you want." (This should have been identified during the "Five Ws" stage.)

Use the "Averting" technique

This second technique is more preemptive, to be used before an objection is even raised. When as a salesperson you repeatedly hear the same objection, incorporate your response into the presentation, thus completely averting the objection. If you sell computers, you might use the following:

> "Even if the speed of computers doubles in the next six months, this computer allows you to use this installed software for many years to come. If an upgrade is necessary, we can easily do that for you. It's no trouble at all, and we can do it free of charge when you buy the unit."

By using the "Averting" technique, you have circumvented this common objection about the speed of technological change while allowing the customer to focus on the features and benefits. A competent salesperson can time the averted objection to minimize its effect and maximize the benefits, then continue the sales pitch to stress how this software will help to solve the customer's problem.

5. Purchase

The purchase, or the close, is the most important part of the sales process, because if you don't close the sale, your efforts were in vain. This section explores what a trial close is, how to use it, why people find it difficult to close, how to overcome these problems, and when it is time to close. If you use these techniques, your success rate is bound to increase.

What is closing a sale?

"Closing a sale" is the specific point during your presentation that confirms a buying decision by your customer. It only occurs after all your prospect's objections and concerns have been satisfactorily answered. Closing the sale is the question that you ask to complete this part of the sales presentation. Remember—once you have closed, don't continue to close.

How do you close?

Imagine a salesperson making a presentation to a customer about a trip to Mexico. She has given a detailed account of what the customer can expect, places to go, and things to do. There is not much more to say.

TRY A VARIETY OF TRIAL CLOSES

....

Trial closes do not specifically ask for the sale, but give the salesperson an indication of how close they are. During a sales presentation, try to use as many trial closes as possible. It's not uncommon to use between ten to fifteen trial closes before the actual close. The more trial closes you use, the easier the sale becomes.

Before closing the sale, the salesperson may ask questions such as "Will we book an early September or a fall departure?" or "Will we be booking a reservation for you alone or will you be traveling with a friend?" Trying to close a sale by asking these questions is called a trial close.

Use trial closes

You are attempting to solicit a positive response from your prospect on their intent. A trial close uses phrases that should always imply a close. Questions such as "Would you prefer the metallic color or something a little more adventurous?" "When did you need this by?" "Will you want Picture in Picture in your new television?" are all examples of trial closes that are leading up to and cementing the final close.

Real Life) Filling a Want and a Need

A few years ago, my rusty 1981 Oldsmobile needed replacing. One of my biggest fears is buying from a used car lot. After researching and browsing many lots, I drove to Willowbrook Motors in my old sports car, parked, and started looking at sedans. The salesman approached.

"Hi, I'm Dave, how can I help you?"

I explained what I was looking for, then Dave asked me how I used my vehicle.

"I carpool schoolchildren, take my mom shopping, carry one or two bales of hay at times, use it for business, travel, and shopping, and I live in the country so I need something economical and safe to drive in the snow."

"What would you want from a vehicle?" asked Dave.

"I want a standard shift, coffee-cup holder, makeup mirror, electric windows and nothing over $20,000," I replied, smiling.

"I have the perfect vehicle for you," said Dave after I further defined my needs and wants. "Follow me." He took me to a 1998 Jeep Cherokee two-door truck.

"I don't do trucks," I said. "I like to drive small, sporty cars. Trucks are for men."

"It'll drive like your sports car, and it's four-wheel drive, which you need," answered Dave. "It holds two bales of hay, five passengers, your mom can get in, it has two cup holders, two lighted makeup mirrors, gets up to 28 miles per gallon on the highway, and parks like a small car. Just drive around the block with me."

Well, everything Dave said was true. The little sporty truck has been a godsend. In fact, my ex-husband bought his pickup from Dave. Because Dave listened carefully to our needs and wants and did not over-sell, I refer his dealership to others and will probably buy my next vehicle from him. I might even get ambitious and buy another sporty SUV.

Some salespeople mistakenly believe that the trial close can replace the actual close. If you don't ask for the sale, it's likely that your customer will walk away and buy from someone else. They have already made the decision to buy based on your presentation, they just haven't decided from whom. It's not enough to believe that the close will happen—*you* must make it happen.

When do you close?

Gauging the right time to close is difficult because only you can sense this from your conversations. Generally, it's time to close when your customer shows a genuine interest in your product. If he or she nods affirmatively, agrees with your answers, or if there are verbal or body language indications that your customer is ready to get down to business, this is the time to close.

Salespeople must continuously observe the customer for subtle signs that a purchase is imminent. Salespeople are often better talkers than listeners, thus missing these most important signs. If a customer is ready to make a purchasing decision, stop talking, start observing and listening, and close the sale.

6. Public relations

The message has been stressed throughout this book that follow-up and service keep your customers returning. Once the sale is completed and the satisfied customer leaves, how will you follow up to ensure that he or she stays happy? My car dealership always calls within twenty-four hours to ensure that the vehicle is operating properly, plus they send regular service reminders. I not only appreciate it, I have come to expect it.

You have many options to choose from, depending on your type of business. Letters, thank-you cards, and follow-up calls all build relationships. For some products or services, a further follow-up call may be in order to ensure long-term customer satisfaction. By building these relationships, customers will refer you to others.

CAN YOU IMPROVE YOUR SALES SKILLS?

If you learn to use the basic sales strategies and principles as outlined in this chapter, combined with a winning marketing plan and your excellent communication skills, your sales will increase by leaps and bounds. Learning all these skills may take some time and practice.

Figure 13.1 provides a checklist for you to ensure that you don't miss one important step. If you have sales staff, let them take the test as well. Can you answer yes to these twenty questions?

WHAT IF...

This book has taken you from assessing where you are now right through to operating more efficiently and profitably. It has explored all the important factors that contribute to growing a strong, successful business. If you use all this advice, you will become a multifaceted entrepreneurial success.

IMPROVE YOUR LISTENING SKILLS

There is a vast difference between hearing and listening, and successful selling requires that you listen to your customer's needs. A good listener treats each customer as a VSP and tries to think like that customer. The salesperson listens for ideas and makes notes, concentrating on what the customer is saying without interrupting. A good listener is polite, asks questions, limits talking, and is sensitive to the customer's concerns.

But what if you feel that there is still no apparent solution to your problems? Chapter 14 guides you step-by-step through how to operate in crisis mode and explains the available options. It includes a detailed worksheet and checklist to help you to assess your current situation and make a decision on your next course of action.

Figure 13.1

Can I Improve My Sales Skills?

	Yes	No
1. I avoid using high-pressure sales tactics.	☐	☐
2. I am sensitive to my customers' needs.	☐	☐
3. I am always honest with my customers.	☐	☐
4. I understand the importance of recognizing customers' needs.	☐	☐
5. I use the "Five Ws" of selling when assessing these needs.	☐	☐
6. I maintain a customer leads file.	☐	☐
7. I contact old customers and ask for referrals.	☐	☐
8. I first plan my sales presentation.	☐	☐
9. I often rehearse my sales presentations.	☐	☐
10. I have a variety of sales tools available.	☐	☐
11. I always dress appropriately.	☐	☐
12. I understand how to clarify objections.	☐	☐
13. I use the "Feel, Felt, Found" technique.	☐	☐
14. I use the "Averting" technique.	☐	☐
15. I use the "Features and Benefits" technique.	☐	☐
16. I use trial closes during my presentations.	☐	☐
17. I am a good listener and ask the customer many questions.	☐	☐
18. I allow the customer to talk and don't interrupt.	☐	☐
19. I understand and use the six-step sales process.	☐	☐
20. I always follow up each sale to ensure customer satisfaction.	☐	☐

CHAPTER FOURTEEN

How Do You Operate in Crisis?

———◄○►———

Nothing fails like success because we don't learn from it.
We only learn from failure.
KENNETH BOULDING

———◄○►———

Once starry eyes are now blurred from worry and lack of **sleep.** The "bounce-out-of-bed" attitude has been replaced with dragging your butt out from under the covers because the doors have to be opened—darn it! The passion and dreams feel more like pain and nightmares. What happened to the enthusiasm, the big picture, the great entrepreneurial dream? ❧

DO YOU STILL HAVE PASSION?

Anyone who has owned a business for more than a year will understand how easy it is to lose enthusiasm as the harsh realities of owning a business set in. I find it only marginally easier after twenty years than the first day I started, because there are always new challenges to contend with.

I lost my passion for accounting, taxes, and bookkeeping a few years ago and knew I had to do something. Luckily, I had found a real passion in speaking and writing, but then there were the new challenges of making a living at both. By selling my accounting practice, refocusing, setting goals, staying positive, flexing with change, and working hard each day I am surviving and succeeding. The lesson I have learned over the years? *The minute you stop working on your business, the business stops working.*

Apart from obvious mismanagement, why do people lose passion for their business? Because as soon as you lose your passion, you might as well close the doors. Often, life gets in the way of the great entrepreneurial dream. Here are some of the more common threats to the health of your business:

- illness or injury
- boredom
- too much competition
- constant stress to make ends meet
- family and their related problems
- partner loses their job and financial pressures increase
- divorce
- midlife crisis

Any one of these factors can have a devastating effect on your business. Yet every year across the nation, thousands of businesses start with the universal dream of succeeding. You hear of the success stories through media and from friends. Rarely do you hear of the failures. No one likes to think about failing—so most people don't. There are thousands of self-employment programs and courses, and an abundance of resources to help businesses through start-up and growth—but not enough people utilize them. The message has been said before in this book and bears repeating: work *on* your business not just *in* your business.

Unfortunately, statistics tell us that 80 to 90 percent of new businesses don't make it. This book was written with the hope of making a dent in these depressing figures by analyzing the main causes of failure and offering workable, practical solutions. If you put these suggestions to work for you, your chance of failure will be much diminished—if not erased—and you will be on your way to growing a healthy small business.

"LET'S NOT TALK ABOUT FAILURE"

"What if your business doesn't make it?" I have asked many clients. "What will happen to the financial stability of the family unit?"

"Let's not talk about failure" is a standard reply. "I didn't go into business thinking about not making it. I haven't even considered those consequences."

"Perhaps you *should* think about it," is my reply.

Someone has to talk about those people who don't make it, so please read this chapter and take the information to heart. After consulting many struggling businesses since 1983, I have found the failure stories far outweigh the successes. What breaks my heart the most is seeing the resulting divorces and the innocent children who suffer in the process.

Psychologically, the main reasons for failure are that people don't want to admit they are wrong, they don't like the work involved in doing it right, or they think that they know it all. We all make mistakes.

One of my favorite quotes comes from an article in an old Toastmasters magazine. "Flops are part of life's menu. Everyone makes mistakes. High achievers learn by their mistakes. By doing that, an error becomes the raw material out of which future successes are forged. Failure is not a crime. Failure to learn from failure is."

FIND A MENTOR

Many successful people owe their success to having guidance from a mentor. A mentor is anyone who is prepared to take an interest in helping you and who can offer experienced advice and support. If you don't know where to find one, ask your chamber of commerce or a successful community member. Most successful people have had a mentor themselves and will usually go out of their way to accommodate you.

HEED THE WARNING SIGNS

Buried in the day-to-day operation of your business, the warning signs of crisis can pass unnoticed. The more obvious signs will be there, but because no one likes admitting to possible failure, many take the ostrich approach and ignore them. Others know that something is wrong but are too scared to face the reality. If you are aware of some of the effects that indicate a potential crisis looming, you will be better prepared to take immediate action. See Figure 14.1 for a list of the warning signs.

On the positive side, many people have failed at one or more businesses before making a roaring success of the next one. So if this business doesn't succeed, don't feel ashamed—you will have learned some valuable lessons. Take a moment to think about your business, as Jim and Linda did in the Real Life example "Traveling Back to Success." Then complete the checklist in Figure 14.1 by checking off the warning signs that apply to you.

Real Life   **Traveling Back to Success**

Jim and Linda started a travel agency ten years ago. Linda managed the store, also working a couple of days a week at another job while Jim worked a full-time day job, helping out on weekends and in the evenings. They both loved to travel, taking advantage of the many travel opportunities that the business offered. Now someone had to mind the store, so they employed staff to help out. Each year, the financial figures told a grim story: the business wasn't making the money it should, and debts were not diminishing.

There were costly problems with the employees, and Linda realized that she needed to get back into the business and be there for her clients. The employees were laid off, and she started taking better care of her accounting and administration. But there were always challenges that could not be changed or controlled—a reduction in commission from travel suppliers and airlines, and then 9/11, followed by ongoing threats of terrorism, followed by the SARS episode. Linda's health began to suffer.

"There was nothing we could do to change these situations," says Linda. "I have learned that you have to learn to work with them and restructure around them. But I was getting so tired." The couple seriously discussed closing the agency; it was just too much work.

Jim and Linda took a weekend away to refocus, armed with a copy of *Taking Your Business to the Next Level*. With a bit of work, the idea of a travel café started to evolve. They had a brilliant location; both their accountant and clients had mentioned that a coffee shop would do well in this spot. They also realized that for many years, they had been working in their business and not on it.

Their enthusiasm for the business was rekindled, and with careful research and planning, they redesigned the whole premises around clients being able to have coffee and browse in a relaxed and comfortable atmosphere, without any sales pressure. Positive press coverage about their grand opening day gave the coffee shop a wonderful boost.

Jim and Linda were fortunate. They found a unique way to re-market their business and operate it as astute managers. But for some, the challenge of toughing it out and turning it around seems too huge a task to tackle.

Figure **14.1**

Warning Signs that Your Business Is In Crisis

Your payments to tax agencies are behind and are incurring penalties. ☐
You cannot meet payroll commitments. ☐
Suppliers are becoming more aggressive in their collections. ☐
Your accounts payable are increasing, and payments are falling behind. ☐
Sales are decreasing. ☐
Profits are not supporting overhead commitments. ☐
Inventories are decreasing. ☐
Accounts receivable are decreasing. ☐
Cash in the account is decreasing. ☐
You are reducing prices too often to stimulate sales. ☐
You are reducing the wage you take from the business. ☐
Employees are being laid off or their hours reduced. ☐
Suppliers are asking for cash-on-delivery payment terms. ☐
Banks won't give you a business loan. ☐
You keep injecting capital into the business. ☐
You are constantly depressed and irritable, with feelings of futility. ☐
Consumer or economic trends are adversely affecting your business. ☐
Losses are increasing. ☐

TEN STEPS FOR OPERATING IN CRISIS

As each business differs in their problems, there is no one-size-fits-all solution. In many cases, a business can be salvaged. In other situations, the most practical answer is to close shop before the situation gets any worse. This is where sitting down with your accountant to review your past and current fiscal history is essential. Ideally, you devised an exit strategy on start-up. If not, include an exit strategy in your future planning process.

It's no use constantly pouring money into a leaky pail if there is no way to plug the holes. On the other hand, some decisive action could well get you through this situation. Take these steps to ease the mental stress while you regroup and decide on a course of action. Once you have assembled the required information for each of the following steps, transfer it to the corresponding section in Figure 14.3, the worksheet at the end of this chapter.

Step 1: Review gross profit margins

As previously discussed, healthy gross profit margins are necessary to sustain overhead commitments, and it's easy for them to decrease unnoticed if they are not constantly monitored. Review your cost of goods and all related costs to see which ones are contributing to decreasing margins. Estimate through your accounting records how much these costs have increased this year. Review the detailed list of cost of goods expenses at the end of this chapter in Figure 14.3, step 1, and write your answers on the worksheet.

Inefficient management in any one of the areas of materials, packaging, equipment, or staff will lead to lost profits. One client reviewed their annual discounts, only to find that they had doubled while sales had increased by only 10 percent. Over a year, this made a difference of $8,000. A new discount structure was put into place that satisfied the customers and reduced this expense to an acceptable level.

Step 2: Review overhead expenses

If you haven't already studied your recent overhead expenses in previous exercises, now is the time to do so. Print out a detailed general ledger report for the year and examine each expense account. Take five different colored highlighters and as you review each account, use them to track these categories:

1. One-time expenses that will not reoccur within the next twelve-month period.
2. Expenses that were unnecessary or frivolous.
3. Expenses that have increased in the last fiscal year (example: wages).
4. New and ongoing expenses (example: extra telephone line).
5. Expenses that could be reduced (example: travel).

Then complete step 2 in Figure 14.3. You have now identified increased overhead costs, one-time expenses, and frivolous expenses and are better able to prepare a "bare bones" budget.

CALCULATE THE COST OF LAYING OFF

....

If your budget involves laying off employees, calculate the amount of severance, vacation, and any other wages due, including the tax remittance portion. Be sure you include this amount in your cash flow calculations. Laying off long-term employees can be an expensive exercise, and you need the available funds to pay them out.

Step 3: Prepare a bare-bones budget

Next, you need to calculate a conservative budget. Prepare monthly projections for six to twelve months, using statistical sales history combined with expectations from future marketing strategies to see how much profit can be generated. See step 3 in Figure 14.3 for an example. You will need this information to negotiate with suppliers and various tax agencies. If the new budget reflects losses or little or no profit, this will be addressed later on in this chapter.

Step 4: Review marketing strategies

Although you have to be frugal at this stage, a business will not sustain sales without some aggressive marketing. Review how your marketing dollars were spent and how effective the results were. Complete the exercise in step 4 of the Figure 14.3 worksheet to ascertain unproductive marketing costs.

Step 5: Review cash flow

Projecting future profits doesn't take care of paying the current bills, so your cash flow situation needs some attention. Once again, your accountant should help interpret your financial statements or accounting records and assist with your decision-making.

SEEK MARKETING ADVICE

••••••••••••••••••••••••••••••

If your methods are not working, seek some free marketing advice from your chamber of commerce, Small Business Development Center, or Small Business Administration office. There are locations in every state and a website loaded with information at www.sba.gov. Information, help, and suggestions are usually free of charge. You may even have to spend money hiring a reputable marketing consultant to help.

Use the following list of parameters to analyze your current cash position and then record this information in Figure 14.3, step 5.

• How much of the accounts receivables are collectable and in what time frame?
• What inventory levels must be maintained to meet future projected sales?
• Which slow-moving inventory items can be turned into cash through a clearance sale?
• What equipment needs repairing?
• Does any major asset need purchasing in the next few months?
• Which accounts payable, loans and taxes are delinquent and by how much?

Next calculate your current working capital position by totaling current assets and current liabilities. If current liabilities exceed current assets, you now know the amount that you are short to meet your obligations and can plan a course of action based on your sales and expense projections. This exercise allows you to plan how you will approach the various creditors and to what level you may have to further reduce expenses.

Step 6: Deal with tax agencies

If you are open and honest in dealing with the various tax departments, they are usually cooperative. First know how much you owe them and how late the accounts are. Before you contact them, prepare a budget to estimate how much you can pay monthly. At the same time, you must commit to maintaining current payments.

This can be achieved by transferring the tax portion of each bank deposit into a tax savings account. In fact, always use this system to ensure that tax monies are available. Don't put suppliers ahead of taxes—you collect taxes in trust and the various government agencies make this quite clear. In step 6 of the Figure 14.3 worksheet, list the agencies you owe, the amounts you owe, and the agencies' phone numbers.

Before you call the various tax agencies, have all your information and account statements on hand. Be polite, stress your intention to pay, don't tell lies, and write down their instructions. Have your accountant review any correspondence to them.

If you have accrued a huge sum of interest, visit www.irs.gov/appeals to find out how to have the interest portion reduced and download their Publication 3605, *Fast Track Mediation.* This has worked quite successfully for past clients of mine, with no appeals being denied. Even the tax department has a heart, as shown in the Real Life example "Tackling a Tax Crisis."

CONTACT TAX AGENCIES

If taxes are behind, call the collection department of each tax agency to explain your financial situation. They will ask for a payment plan, financial figures, and your budget. They also require that current payments be kept up to date. If you miss one payment or the check bounces, don't expect any sympathy. If you don't honor your promises, expect your bank accounts to be frozen or the money taken from them.

Real Life) **Tackling a Tax Crisis**

Although Diane worked full-time for one employer for ten years, the terms of her employment were to work as a subcontractor—take it or leave it. When she started under these terms as a new self-employed business owner, she had no prior business knowledge. She came to me desperate—the only way she could pay a huge tax bill of nearly $140,000 was to sell her property. She was a nervous wreck.

A series of traumatic events over the past ten years had included a huge barn fire that killed all her breeding animals and the death of her husband from cancer. During her ten years as a "business owner," she had effectively lost well over $50,000 in unpaid employment benefits, plus she had to pay someone to do her work when she took time off. In all the turmoil, Diane didn't quite get around to filing her taxes.

continued

Her fear of the obvious mounting tax bill kept her from facing the situation until it seemed almost insurmountable. The tax bill was well under $100,000, but the penalties and interest were nearly as much as the tax portion.

I prepared a long letter of explanation to the tax department, accompanied by a detailed budget and the promise that she would ask her employer to put her on the payroll. After three months of negotiating, the current year's taxes were added to the bill and reduced penalties and interest by $55,000.

Diane's employer finally put her on the payroll, and her bank cooperated with a term loan. Fortunately, Diane only had a small mortgage. Although her debt is now larger, she still has her home, saved $55,000, and has peace of mind.

WORK WITH YOUR SUPPLIERS

Review each supplier's account to see what payment terms you can offer, as you need their cooperation in maintaining your supplies to continue business. Look at the situation from their perspective—they can't keep supplying you with products or services without a structured repayment plan. Perhaps you can offer to pay a small amount each month off the old debt, with new purchases being paid for COD. Call them before they call you—turn a negative into a positive. In most cases, they are happy to work with you.

Step 7: Deal with suppliers

Suppliers are well aware that businesses go bankrupt overnight. Struggling businesses mistakenly tend not to communicate with suppliers, hoping to drag payments out until "things get better." You must inform your suppliers that the business is experiencing cash flow problems and is working on solutions. Otherwise, they will hound you for payment and create more undue stress.

If you honor your commitments and pay the overdue accounts, credit is usually restored. If not, and you are an incorporated company, trade suppliers usually lose any outstanding debts on bankruptcy. If you are a proprietorship, they can take you to court. Your personal assets are then at risk.

On Step 7 of the Figure 14.3 worksheet, list those pressing suppliers, the amounts you owe, and the date you promised to pay them. You will need this information for your cash flow projections.

Step 8: Turbocharge collections

Some of your problems may be the result of lax collection procedures. Many small businesses suffer because one large customer went belly-up. So review your current outstanding accounts receivable, breaking them down into current, thirty, sixty, ninety days and over. Transfer these totals to step 8 of the Figure 14.3 worksheet. Starting with the ninety days and over, call each overdue customer—get the potential bad debts before they are not recoverable. Use the suggestions in Chapter 10. Decide which accounts need further action and start immediately.

Seven Tips
to Speed Up Collections

1. Call all customers with debts due over thirty days; a personal phone call goes a long way.

2. Let customers know that there has been a change of credit policies and that due to restructuring, thirty-day terms is your new limit.

3. Call and offer a discount for current accounts paid within seven days.

4. Phone tardy customers and offer to pick up their checks, or ask that the debt be transferred to their corporate credit card.

5. Be more aggressive with customers who stall payment—they may be experiencing problems similar to yours.

6. Be honest with your customers; those who can pay will pay if you ask.

7. Ask.

Step 9: Assess yourself

Continuing a business in crisis mode is both mentally and physically exhausting. It takes great courage, determination, persistence, and hard work to turn a floundering business around—but it can be done. Many struggling businesses have made successful transitions because owners have made concerted efforts.

The process takes time and energy. You have to be ready to face the challenges ahead and be confident that you can do it. Without this commitment, it won't happen. You have come this far in making your entrepreneurial dream a reality. Are you ready to fight to keep your dream alive, or ready to let it go? Only you can make that choice.

Take the test

Before you make any final decisions, assess whether you are ready to move forward. Answer the ten questions in Figure 14.2, then transfer your answers to step 9 of the Figure 14.3 worksheet and review your score. Be honest with yourself when you answer—these are important questions requiring careful consideration. You should discuss them with your partner or spouse.

Figure 14.2

Am I Committed To Continue?

	Yes	No
1. Am I ready to commit to a concentrated effort?	☐	☐
2. Do I have the support of my family?	☐	☐
3. Do I realize how long this may take?	☐	☐
4. Do I feel physically ready to cope with the extra work?	☐	☐
5. Do I feel emotionally ready to cope with the extra worry?	☐	☐
6. Am I currently feeling positive about the future?	☐	☐
7. Am I willing to follow professional advice?	☐	☐
8. Am I willing to learn from past mistakes?	☐	☐
9. Could I further endanger our financial stability?	☐	☐
10. Am I currently feeling depressed?	☐	☐

Step 10: Know your options

Finally, you must understand all the available options. A business that has experienced sudden and unexpected growth will face different challenges than one that is struggling to survive. A growing business with long-term potential has many opportunities to seek external help to work through problems.

A business heading for failure can often survive and succeed by seeking professional help before it is too late. When the worksheet is completed, discuss your situation with your accountant. Your options are summarized in step 10 of the Figure 14.3 worksheet.

> ### SEEK FREE CREDIT COUNSELING
> *Credit Counseling Centers of America are a non-profit organization that can help you to consolidate debts and explore bankruptcy alternatives. Their website is at www.consumercounseling.org. More information and locations of centers is found at www. creditcounselingresources.com.*

FAILURE OF A SOLE PROPRIETORSHIP

If the most viable solution appears to be closure of the business, know the ramifications. Research the alternatives before making this decision. Meet with a bankruptcy lawyer to discuss resolving your financial difficulties. The lawyer will advise you on:

- debt consolidation/settlement arrangements
- preparing an informal proposal for creditors
- filing a state court receivership proceeding
- filing for reorganization in federal bankruptcy court to allow the business more time to pay creditors
- credit counseling services
- filing in federal bankruptcy court to discharge debts on liquidation of non-exempt assets.

Understand your liabilities

A sole proprietorship or partnership usually carries more liability than an incorporated business. If you have signed any promissory notes or personal guarantees for loans or guarantees with other creditors, you are held personally responsible for these debts, all trade creditor debts, loans, government taxes, and leases.

Your personal assets are at risk, as creditors have the right to take you to court. Liens can be placed on bank accounts or assets, both personal and business. Tax agencies can freeze your bank account or take funds directly from it to repay taxes. Working with a bankruptcy lawyer can often negate a portion of this debt, or a payment-free period can be negotiated.

Bankruptcy—the last alternative

When there seems to be no light at the end of the tunnel, bankruptcy may be the final alternative. While bankruptcy results in the elimination of the majority, if not all of your debts, it isn't a pleasant alternative. Whenever a business or an individual files for bankruptcy, there seems to be a stigma attached for the person involved and their family. It is a difficult and emotionally shattering time for the whole family, so choose this route with professional guidance.

The effects of bankruptcy will vary based on whether the business is intended to survive bankruptcy, but in a nutshell, assets are liquidated to repay debts, with certain personal possessions being exempt from the bankruptcy order. Exempted items usually include clothing, furniture, income-generating tools or equipment, motor vehicles, a principal residence to a certain value, food, and necessary household effects. Visit the website *www.bankruptcyaction.com* for some very helpful information, including how to prepare for your meeting with a bankruptcy lawyer, FAQs, a statewide bankruptcy lawyer locator, and state bankruptcy exemption details.

How long does bankruptcy apply?

Subject to certain restrictions, a bankruptcy is usually discharged after nine months. If you have been previously bankrupt, you may be required to appear before a judge before the discharge is made. The bankruptcy will remain on the Credit Bureau's records for seven years from the date of discharge for a first-time bankruptcy and fourteen years for a second bankruptcy. You may apply for credit once the bankruptcy is discharged, although the decision to grant credit rests with the creditors.

The steps in a sole-proprietor bankruptcy process can be summarized as follows:

1. Contact a bankruptcy lawyer.
2. Attend the Meeting of Creditors, if required.

3. Make payments to the Trustee while awaiting discharge, if required.
4. Attend court for the discharge hearing, if required.

FAILURE OF AN INCORPORATED BUSINESS

There is more protection for an incorporated company that is experiencing insolvency problems. By incorporating, the shareholders, officers, and directors ensure a degree of limited liability. Unless you have signed personal guarantees or promissory notes, trade creditors are forced to take what is left over after business assets are liquidated. Government departments and banks have first priority. Even though it is the business bankrupting, emotionally, it is most stressful for both the directors and employees.

A business can be saved by filing a petition in bankruptcy. Filing the petition enables a debtor to reasonably rearrange their finances without the fear of creditors taking legal action. Proposal terms may allow for payment of less than 100 cents on the dollar to unsecured creditors. An informative article on small business bankruptcy can be found at *www.cato.org/pubs/regulation /regv24n2/white.pdf*.

WHAT ARE DIRECTORS' LIABILITIES?

Apart from any personal guarantees that directors have signed, they are responsible for the payment of fiduciary debts (funds held in trust), such as excise taxes or employee withholding taxes. In some cases, an incorporated business has declared bankruptcy, and directors have then had to file for personal bankruptcy due to their inability to personally repay these agencies.

When a business either closes or bankrupts, if there are outstanding shareholders' loans, they can be claimed on your personal income tax return as a business investment loss. You can also claim the value of shares lost in the incorporated business as a capital loss. As there are restrictions and varying parameters, talk to your accountant. Also, read the IRS's Publication 550, *Investment Income and Expenses,* which can be downloaded at the website *www.irs.gov/publications/p550/index.html*.

THINK ABOUT YOUR FAMILY

If you are reading this for information only and are fortunate enough not to be in crisis, it should reinforce the message that astute business management is crucial—not just for the success of the business, but for your family's health. Small business failures cause a multitude of divorces. I have witnessed too many cases where marriages break down due to business failure or bankruptcy.

Is any business worth risking a marriage? It's not just the broken marriages; next come the threats, sometimes violence, the turning of children against parents—and their long-term psychological suffering—and the battles over child custody and support payments. The emotional effects are long-lived and traumatic. No one escapes unscathed. Promise both yourself and your family that you will work hard to succeed at this business—and your relationships.

WHAT WILL YOUR DECISION BE?

Although somewhat depressing, this is a necessary chapter to read. It should convince you to become more financially conversant with your business and committed to success. Speaking of success, the final chapter is devoted entirely to this subject.

Figure **14.3**

Ten Steps for Operating In Crisis Worksheet

The information required to complete steps 1 through 10 will document your current financial position and guide you through the necessary action. If you complete this worksheet, then you have the right attitude and are serious about turning your business around.

Step 1: Review gross profit margins
Write down the increase over normal costs in each applicable area for this current year.

   1. Production systems $_____

   2. Raw material costs $_____

  3. Wages $_____

  4. Freight $_____

  5. Customs, brokerage, duty $_____

  6. Equipment repairs $_____

  7. Inefficient equipment $_____

  8. Packaging materials $_____

  9. Packaging methods $_____

10. Selling costs (commissions) $_____

11. Discount structure $_____

12. Employee unproductiveness $_____   Total: $_____

Step 2: Review overhead expenses

When you have reviewed the general ledger and carefully categorized each of the expenses, total each category. Add together the expenses in items 1 and 2. You have now separated one-time and frivolous costs from your figures.

Re-total each general ledger account minus these expenses to give you a better indication of normal operating costs. Study this amount to see how it has affected your profits.

Then total the expenses in items 3 and 4. You will need this information to plan your revised budget as overhead increases must be properly accounted for. How can you reduce these costs?

The expenses highlighted in item 5 need to be reviewed to see how they can be reduced without affecting the efficiency of the business. Calculate the total of these extra expenses to see how much they contributed to reduced profits and cash flow.

1. One-time expenses $_____

2. Unnecessary expenses $_____   = $_____ subtotal

3. Increased expenses $_____

4. New and ongoing expenses $_____   = $_____ subtotal

5. Expenses that could be reduced $_____   = $_____ subtotal

       Total extra overhead expenses: $_____

continued

Step 3: Prepare a bare-bones budget

Prepare a six- to twelve-month no-frills budget using the sample following as a guideline. Next, prepare a cash flow projection to estimate cash shortages.

	Month 1	Month 2	Month 3	Month 4	Month 5	Month 6	Total
Sales:							
Direct costs:							
Purchases							
Production wages							
Freight and duty							
Packaging							
Discounts							
Sales commissions							
Other							
Total:							
Gross profit: (%)							
Overhead:							
Accounting fees							
Advertising							
Bad debts							
Bank charges							
Couriers & postage							
Depreciation							
Employee benefits							
Fees, licenses, taxes							
Insurance							
Loan interest							
Management salaries							
Marketing							
Office salaries							
Office supplies							
Rent							
Repairs & maint.							
Shop supplies							
Telephone, Internet							
Vehicle gas							
Vehicle repairs, ins.							
Workers' comp.							
Total expenses:							
Net profit (loss):	$	$	$	$	$	$	$

Step 4: Review marketing strategies

1. Marketing strategies that did not increase sales

   a. _____ Cost: $_____
   b. _____ Cost: $_____
   c. _____ Cost: $_____

   Total: $_____

2. Estimated cost of hiring a marketing consultant $_____
3. Estimated cost of increased marketing strategies $_____

Step 5: Review cash flow

List the current amounts in each category.

1. Cash in bank accounts $_____
2. Accounts receivable $_____
3. Inventory: Estimated revenue from clearance sale $_____
4. Funds required to increase inventory $_____
5. Fixed assets: Estimated repair and maintenance costs $_____
6. Estimated new asset purchases $_____
7. Accounts payable: current month _____

               30 days   _____
               60 days   _____
               90 and over   _____ $_____

8. Taxes: Federal   _____

           State/local   _____
           Payroll   _____
           Personal   _____
           Corporate   _____ $_____

9. Loan payments: Total due in next _____ months $_____
10. Working capital: Current assets $_____

        Current liabilities $_____
        Working capital position: $_____

continued

Step 6: Deal with tax agencies

List the amounts owing to each agency and their phone number. Keep a detailed log of your conversations.

1. Federal $_____   Phone: _____   Called: _____
   Person spoken to: _____   Action: _____

2. State $_____   Phone: _____   Called: _____
   Person spoken to: _____   Action: _____

3. Payroll $_____   Phone: _____   Called: _____
   Person spoken to: _____   Action: _____

4. Personal $_____   Phone: _____   Called: _____
   Person spoken to: _____   Action: _____

5. Corporate $_____   Phone: _____   Called: _____
   Person spoken to: _____   Action: _____

Step 7: Deal with suppliers

List the most urgent suppliers, the amounts you owe, and the date you promised to pay them.

Supplier	Amount	Pay by
1.		
2.		
3.		
4.		
5.		
6.		
7.		
8.		
9.		
10.		
Total:	$	

Step 8: Turbocharge collections

List all current outstanding accounts receivable totals.

1. Accounts overdue 90+ days $_____
2. Accounts overdue 60 days $_____
3. Accounts overdue 30 days $_____
4. Current accounts $_____

                Total: $_____

Start by listing and contacting the accounts over 90 days. List the oldest debts on the worksheet first and the action to be taken.

Name	Invoice date	Amount due	Action
1.			
2.			
3.			
4.			
5.			
6.			
7.			
8.			
9.			
10.			

Step 9: Assess yourself

Complete the self-assessment test in Figure 14.2 and note your results below.

Questions 1 to 8:   Yes _____   No _____

Questions 9 and 10:   Yes _____   No _____

Ideally, you should have answered yes to questions 1 to 8 and no to questions 9 and 10. Any other answers mean that if you continue, you could experience significant problems. To turn your business around, you need a positive attitude, total commitment, professional help, and family support without further risking your financial stability.

continued

Step 10: Know your options
Discuss with your accountant which of the following options currently apply to your business. You now have a plan of action.

		Yes	No
1.	Gross profit margins must be increased.	☐	☐
2.	Overhead expenses must be decreased.	☐	☐
3.	The budget reflects that a turnaround is possible.	☐	☐
4.	The budget reflects further future losses.	☐	☐
5.	Cash flow projections show the need for a loan.	☐	☐
6.	The business can survive without a loan.	☐	☐
7.	Current loans may have to be refinanced.	☐	☐
8.	The working capital is in a positive position.	☐	☐
9.	The working capital is in a negative position.	☐	☐
10.	Marketing strategies need to be changed.	☐	☐
11.	I need professional help with marketing.	☐	☐
12.	Aggressive attention is needed for collections.	☐	☐
13.	I need the services of a collection agency.	☐	☐
14.	Inventory levels are too high/too low.	☐	☐
15.	I can currently meet accounts payable liabilities.	☐	☐
16.	I cannot currently meet accounts payable liabilities.	☐	☐
17.	I can meet all tax requirements.	☐	☐
18.	I must contact tax agencies to formulate a payment plan.	☐	☐
19.	I must contact suppliers to organize payment terms.	☐	☐
20.	I am mentally and physically ready to handle all this.	☐	☐
21.	I do not feel capable of facing all this work and worry.	☐	☐
22.	There is no viable financial solution for continuing on.	☐	☐
23.	I understand my liabilities as a sole proprietor.	☐	☐
24.	I will contact a credit counseling agency.	☐	☐
25.	I will meet with a bankruptcy lawyer.	☐	☐
26.	I understand the ramifications of personal bankruptcy.	☐	☐
27.	I understand my liabilities as a director.	☐	☐
28.	I understand the ramifications of corporate bankruptcy.	☐	☐
29.	I could lose my home and family if I continue operations.	☐	☐
30.	I could lose my home and family if I declare bankruptcy.	☐	☐

Summary: Priorities and worksheet checklist

Next list the three main priorities that require urgent attention.

1. _____
2. _____
3. _____

As you chart your way through the ten-step worksheet, check off your progress.

If you complete the ten steps, you deserve to succeed.

Step	Completed	Date
1. Review gross profit margins	☐	_____
2. Review overhead expenses	☐	_____
3. Prepare a bare-bones budget	☐	_____
4. Review marketing strategies	☐	_____
5. Review cash flow	☐	_____
6. Deal with tax agencies	☐	_____
7. Deal with suppliers	☐	_____
8. Turbocharge collections	☐	_____
9. Assess yourself	☐	_____
10. Know your options	☐	_____

CHAPTER FIFTEEN

Are You Ready to Succeed?

---◆◇◆---

*There is only one success—to be able to
spend your life in your own way.*
CHRISTOPHER MORLEY

---◆◇◆---

If you asked a thousand people what success means to them,
you would probably get a thousand different answers. Success
means something different to everyone. By asking people who
are considered successful, you may be surprised to learn that in
most cases, money is quite a long way down the list. ❧

WHAT DOES SUCCESS MEAN?

For many, success is simply achieving their dreams, reaching a goal, feeling content with life, and looking forward to every day. For some it may mean the opportunity to enjoyably explore their creativity, putting talents to work at their business to make enough money to pay the bills, or it may mean the silver Mercedes coupe (slightly used) that you always dreamed of at the end of the rainbow.

Those who are considered successful don't necessarily have a great deal of money. What you will find successful people have in common is that they are usually the volunteers, the mentors, the pillars of the community who give copious time—and sometimes generous dollars—to their community and other worthwhile causes. They voluntarily sit on boards as directors; they help make things happen; they take dreams and turn them into reality; and they are prepared to sweat to achieve a unified goal.

The inner rewards of success

When you ask successful people what success means to them, they use a language full of beautiful "life" words. Read and absorb some of their inner values, the wonderful words of which they speak. They are the real reason—apart from making a living—that you are in business:

• achievement	• happiness	• balance
• feeling good	• excitement	• passion
• satisfaction	• helping others	• freedom
• hard work	• reaching goals	• focus

If you are experiencing some or all of these feelings, then you are well on your way to building a successful business. Doesn't it feel great?

Success is...

When you peruse books of quotations, it becomes clear just how intangible and finite success really is. Most quotations have one common thread; if you just sit on the fence watching the game, you will never get to play. It's the playing that counts, not the winning. Here are some examples:

> *Success is never final and failure never fatal. It's the courage that counts.*
> **GEORGE R. TILTON**
>
> *Only those who dare to fail greatly can ever achieve greatly.*
> **ROBERT F. KENNEDY**
>
> *To follow, without halt, one's aim: That's the secret of success.*
> **ANNA PAVLOVA**
>
> *Successful men and women...don't consider the odds. They just sneak up at night and cut their own holes in the fence.* **WELLS ROOT**
>
> *Success makes us intolerant of failure, and failure makes us intolerant of success.*
> **WILLIAM FEATHER**
>
> *Most successful members of society have broken the traditional age rules. They have done things when they wanted to do them and have ignored any imagined limitations on them.* **DESMOND MORRIS**
>
> *No one knows what he can do till he tries.*
> **PUBLIUS SYRUS, 42 BC**

Forget the money—remember the "Five Fs"

Successful people talk a lot about the importance of the "Five Fs" that were mentioned in Chapter 3: fitness, food, family, friends, and fun. One of the biggest lessons I have learned —and also live by—is that money isn't so important. Yes, you need enough to live, but without a loving, cohesive family unit, your health (watch what you eat and practice regular fitness), some special friends to lean on, and the ability to have fun and enjoy life, you might as well be kicking up daisies. So forget making money your first priority; it seems that if you get these other priorities straight, success—and money—follow.

START A "THINK" GROUP

You need others to inspire, motivate, teach, and support you. Start a group with four to five associates from varying businesses who meet weekly for an hour or so. Share ideas, exchange contacts, review and set new goals, brainstorm, and problem-solve. It works! That's how my first book came to be. Without this peer support, it would not have happened as quickly as it did.

Ten Simple, Happy Tips
to "Make Your Day"

It doesn't take much effort to turn a bad day into a good day, either for yourself or for someone you love. It's the small things in life that give the greatest happiness. Here are some simple happy things you can do.

- Praise your children instead of chastising them—there's always a positive *action* to replace a negative *reaction*.
- Put an "I love you" card on your spouse or partner's windshield.
- Even better, if you pack lunches for the family, take a bite out of a sandwich and replace the bite with an "I love you" note and a smiley face.
- Go for an evening walk with the family.
- Call a friend or family member and tell them you have been thinking of them.
- Send someone a thank-you card. There is always something to be thankful for.
- Listen to your partner or children instead of doing something else while they talk.
- Pull weeds, get some dirt under your nails, and breathe some fresh air.
- Find a quiet place; listen to and watch the sounds and sights of nature.
- Start the day with a smile. Answer the "How are you?" phone question with "I'm great!" Pass on that positivity.

LOOK FOR A POSITIVE IN EVERY DAY

When the going gets rough, there is even more reason to find something positive in every day. The endorphins generated from positive thinking help you to focus more clearly. Being positive can actually become a great habit.

What does "success" mean to you?

Now is a good time to reflect for a few minutes and think about what success really means to you. It helps you to better focus on where you are going and why. In Figure 15.1, write down your five top indications of the success you are striving for. Copy or photocopy this sheet and put it where you can see it. Then read on about why men and women succeed in business and the challenges they face. This chapter also provides some tips to help you reach your goals.

Figure 15.1

I Feel Successful When...

1. _____

2. _____

3. _____

4. _____

5. _____

WOMEN MOVE INTO THE BOARDROOM

Women have stormed into the business world. They represent the fastest growing sector of the small business economy; nearly 40 percent of small businesses in North America are owned by women. Statistics show that between 1981 and 2001, the number of women entrepreneurs in Canada increased 208 percent, compared to 38 percent for men. In the U.S., there are 9.1 million women entrepreneurs contributing 3.6 trillion dollars to the economy. That's impressive.

Women now hold top positions in politics and the corporate environment, although they *still* hold a minority percentage in the boardrooms. There are many dynamic, successful woman entrepreneurs, and it's not surprising, as women have some wonderful inherent talents that can be adapted naturally to owning a business.

WHY WOMEN SUCCEED

After working closely with a broad spectrum of entrepreneurs for over thirty years, I've assembled some thoughts on what sets men and women apart in the business world and the challenges they face.

Women...

- are committed to seeing their business succeed as every dollar invested must work for them

- see the benefits of joining networks to make business contacts
- take more courses and seminars and buy more self-help books to educate themselves (70 percent of book purchasers are women)
- are budget-conscious; they can make do without the frills
- are quick to learn how to prepare their own accounting
- are willing to seek professional advice—and take it
- are multifaceted; they have innate creative and artistic talents and incorporate some brilliant ideas into their businesses
- can multitask several jobs at once without "losing it"
- are usually organized; running a family requires fanatical time-management and juggling skills
- are better suited to repetitive tasks, a substantial part of business management
- welcome change and are eager to explore opportunities
- are usually honest and straightforward in their business approach

These wonderful qualities explain why so many women-owned businesses succeed. At the same time, women face many unique challenges that often inhibit them from reaching their full potential.

THE CHALLENGES WOMEN FACE

Women *do* have to work harder to be recognized and to grow their businesses. Many feel that they must always be proving themselves in the business world—which holds true. Banks now realize that lending money to women isn't such a crazy idea, although it's still difficult to get financing. Most businesses owned by women are started with a personal capital investment of under $10,000.

Because of a lack of funding or capital to market or grow, women go about it the best way they can. Often, there is little chance to seriously devote themselves to taking their business to the next level. They struggle to juggle business with family life and to please everyone except themselves. By putting themselves last, they put their business last.

Some women experience guilt for attending evening or weekend business-related functions, often canceling them to keep the family peace. Business owners or not, they are often still expected to play the role of wife, mother, cook, nurse, and chauffeur and have dinner on the table by 6:00 p.m.

Success—at what price?

What price do some women pay for success? One woman informed me that her business succeeded only after a second attempt. "I'm my own boss now," she laughed, "and it only took ten years of hard work and a divorce."

More women are choosing the workplace over having a family or marrying, realizing that combining the two may not bring the success they strive for. Many return to the workforce after the family has left the nest. Some become more aggressive, hardened, and selfish to compete and "succeed." These days, when I talk to women business owners, they seem to have one complaint in common; they are not making time for the "Five Fs" and are always "too busy." Each woman must make her own choices.

> # UNDERSTAND THE DIFFERENCES
> ....
> *The best book I have ever read that clearly explains why men and women are so different is called* Why Men Don't Listen and Women Can't Read Maps, *by Barbara and Allan Pease, ISBN 0-7679-0763-9. It would have saved a marriage and a few relationships had I read it sooner. Don't read it if you don't have a sense of humor.*

Ten Tips
for Women In Business

1. **Choose the right business:** Many women become involved in business opportunities promising low start-up costs, part-time hours, no experience necessary, with great financial rewards. These rarely succeed. Be sure you choose the right business for the right reasons.

2. **Learn to say NO:** Women constitute a greater percentage of the nation's volunteers. Giving is an important part of owning a business, but be discriminating about how much time you give and whom you give it to. Learn to say NO to requests for your time and energy and focus only on commitments that you feel comfortable accepting.

continued

3. **Build your confidence:** Many women lack confidence, but by choosing the right business, developing communication skills, and becoming the expert, confidence builds. Don't let overbearing spouses or family members make you feel guilty about owning a business. Be proud of your accomplishments. Having the freedom and family support to do what you want is a great confidence builder.

4. **Reduce isolation:** Isolation is the most common problem for women in business. Join networking groups, business groups, and/or special interest groups. You will make the contacts and friends you need to bounce ideas off and to turn to when you are feeling alone. Many women form lasting friendships through joining women's networking groups.

5. **Put yourself first:** Women tend to put themselves last. Family is, of course, our most treasured asset, but so is a happy, healthy, and fulfilled mom who has been given the opportunity to do something she has dreamed of. Make you and your business a priority—you will feel happier and pass these good vibrations along to your customers and family.

6. **Don't sell yourself too cheaply:** Women are notorious for undervaluing their services. Know your worth and let customers know what free services you offer, what will be charged for, and what your rates are. They will appreciate your honest and straightforward approach. If a customer tries to beat you down, stand firm or walk away from the sale.

7. **Monitor your business:** Don't become too busy to take financial care of your business. Learn to read financial figures, update your books monthly, and review the results regularly with your accountant.

8. **Stop trying to be perfect:** Does it really matter if you sweep dustballs under the refrigerator or that dinner was delivered in a box? Spoil yourself with a few hours of regular hired housekeeping help. In case you didn't know, Superwoman died from overwork.

9. **Take your business seriously:** If you don't take your business seriously, then don't expect your family to. Set your goals and focus, then sit down with the family with a set of rules. Work toward demanding the respect you need to successfully operate the business.

10. **Delegate household chores:** Even if you work part-time, send younger children to a babysitter so that you have focused time. Trade sitting time with a friend or join a babysitting co-op. Delegate chores to family members. Involve children by paying them to help with office chores. Remember, we work to live, not live to work.

BUT MEN HOLD THEIR GROUND IN THE BUSINESS WORLD

Throughout history, men have been the leaders, heroes, and conquerors while women have been the silent strength behind them. The last few decades have seen an incredible swing toward more equality, and in some cases, total role reversals. No doubt the surge of women in the workplace has been quite an adjustment for men, and generally, they have coped admirably with this change.

In the North American business world, both sexes now work hand in hand. Gentlemen, over the centuries you have built this wonderful world with your strength, innovation, courage, and determination to succeed, so keep up the good work. Let's look at some of the reasons why men are so successful in business.

WHY MEN SUCCEED
Men...
- excel in fields requiring technical and spatial abilities
- can look at the bigger picture as a challenge and without fear
- are excellent at delegating tedious chores
- can focus on one issue, steadfastly working at it until the job is done
- are usually confident and able to express this confidence
- run with the entrepreneurial spirit and are risk-takers
- excel at confidently communicating their ideas
- become impassioned and dedicated to their work

- are willing to travel and spend long hours away from home
- network well and conduct extensive business where women often can't (the golf course or the pub)
- can schmooze well with associates and customers
- are adept at closing sales
- are competitive and aggressive at reaching for their goals
- work exceptionally well in team environments.

These qualities have won wars and built empires and huge conglomerations, although not every man is born with them. The technician leaving a corporate environment after twenty years is often ill-equipped to face the entrepreneurial challenges, and some don't succeed.

After presenting a seminar on starting a business to downsized corporate upper and middle management, one male computer programmer of many years said, "But I don't want to do all that administrative and marketing stuff. I don't really like people. I just want to sit at my computer and design Web pages." He will no doubt experience infinite problems adjusting to self-employment.

THE CHALLENGES MEN FACE

DON'T GO IT ALONE
....

You won't build your empire by yourself. There are many resources available to help a small business to grow. At www.smbiz.com and www.msnbc.com there are links to hundreds of sites. A mentor is a wonderful asset, as is a professional business coach, who acts as a guide and a mentor. Co-marketing is another way to work with others.

Self-employment is difficult for some men because there are few teammates to bond with, bounce ideas off, or compete with. Because men don't cope well with multitasking, many jobs are put aside in favor of being "the operator." For some, doing the job and earning an income is far more important than monitoring the financial progress of the business.

Tedious chores are not given priority nor do they hold any challenge. Men often choose a business for the love of money, rather than the love of their work. They tend to make more impulsive decisions without performing the required research, and are impatient to succeed. Many men are inflexible to change. Others are high burnout candidates as their stress tolerance is often lower than that of women. They are more driven to succeed—often at the expense of their personal and family health.

Image is an important consideration. Men tend to spend more on clothing, toys, gadgets, technical equipment, socializing, and vehicle upgrades, often without first consulting the budget. The term "But it's a write-off!" is heard more from men's lips than from women's. These problems and attitudes often hinder business growth and are contributing factors to failure.

Ten Tips for **Men In Business**

1. **Become budget conscious:** If you don't have a head for figures, learn about budgeting, projecting, planning, and cash flow. Before making a financial commitment, be sure the item is needed and is affordable. Keep your checkbook up-to-date and the bank account reconciled.

2. **Work with your accountant:** If you don't enjoy figures, employ a reputable bookkeeping service and build a comfortable relationship with an accountant. Confer regularly and heed your accountant's advice.

3. **Pay attention to details:** Small and "inconsequential" chores are often overlooked in favor of completing billable work. Use the systems in this book and make time for the paperwork. Or pay someone to do it.

4. **Look at the smaller picture:** Have the everyday picture in mind as well as the big future-success picture. Don't ignore what is happening around you, as small problems quickly escalate if they are ignored.

5. **Be a compassionate boss:** Everyone can learn from their employees, so talk to them, listen to their ideas, concerns, and complaints, and implement the good ideas. Encourage, motivate, and respect them—they often have experience in areas that you don't.

   continued

6. **Don't forget your family:** It's too easy to become a workaholic and forget the family. Without a happy family life, work becomes empty and meaningless. Plan to spend quality time together—pencil time in your organizer and don't ignore them.

7. **Include family in decision-making:** Don't let the business alienate you from your family. Tell them how the business is going, warn them if you are stressed, and tell them why. Discuss important decisions that may affect them and listen to their input.

8. **Be open to change:** The older we become, the more frightening change can be. Be open to new ideas and technological changes. Learn to bend the rules and be a little more flexible and patient.

9. **Limit working hours:** Men tend to throw themselves wholeheartedly into their businesses and burn out faster than women. Adequate sleep, a healthy diet, and relaxation time are all important for keeping the work machine finely tuned. Learn when to stop.

10. **Listen to your partner:** No one knows you better than your partner, so if you are getting strong messages—listen. Partners don't normally say anything unless there is an obvious concern. Don't ignore the warning signals.

MANAGE WELL

A successful business meets both your growth and profitability expectations and is efficiently managed. It utilizes cost-effective systems, has productive marketing techniques, is regularly monitored, and has a positive team environment. You reap both personal and financial satisfaction.

WHAT IS GOOD BUSINESS MANAGEMENT?

To determine if you are managing your business effectively, use Figure 15.2. On this final checklist, check "yes" to the questions about areas where you feel confident that you are operating your business efficiently. For those that you answer "no," you know what to do—now all you have to do is do it.

PLAN TO SUCCEED

This book has been written because I have a personal passion in seeing each small business thrive and grow. All businesses experience growth problems through various stages of their life. The information in this book will help you through many of those problems if you use it. The formula for success isn't simple, but the rewards are well worth striving for. There is no substitute for being your own boss, watching a dream become reality, and growing with your business. Never stop learning and always be open to change. Be organized, positive, motivated, passionate, confident, expert, persistent, and never lose sight of your goals.

You have to work long, hard hours, market aggressively, administer, account for, be detail-oriented, and have control of the financial reins. Yet there are no words for the feeling of personal fulfillment you experience as obstacles are overcome and your business grows to the next level. Never forget to always work *on* your business, not just *in* your business.

And when it's time to turn to something else, you have a viable, saleable business that has not only given you a satisfactory lifestyle, but has provided some nice perks. You have built goodwill that can now be exchanged for dollars. You have the luxury of deciding what to do next—retire, travel, or turn your hand to another challenge.

You can do it. I wish you good luck, good judgment, sound management, and great happiness.

Figure **15.2**

Good Business Management Checklist

Good business management is:

Developing and using a combination of skills and techniques to keep both your business and yourself operating at peak performance at all times. Check off how you measure up and total your "yes" answers for your score. In my business, I feel confident that I am...

	Yes	No
Staying industry-educated:		
1. Understanding all aspects of my business and the industry	☐	☐
2. Attending industry-specific seminars, trade shows, conferences	☐	☐
3. Aware of changing economic and consumer trends	☐	☐
4. Regularly reading trade, Web, and business publications.	☐	☐
Keeping control of the financial and administrative reins:		
5. Monitoring my financial progress, reviewing concerns	☐	☐
6. Understanding how to read and use financial statements	☐	☐
7. Being organized, motivated, and focused	☐	☐
8. Using a business plan, reviewing, and updating it regularly	☐	☐
9. Using financial information before making financial decisions	☐	☐
10. Knowing and monitoring my break-even point	☐	☐
11. Having an exit strategy and contingency plan	☐	☐
12. Planning for personal goals with regular tax planning	☐	☐
13. Consulting with my accountant throughout the year	☐	☐
14. Keeping employees motivated	☐	☐
15. Keeping up with technology and time-saving products	☐	☐
16. Staying physically and mentally fit; practicing the "Five Fs"	☐	☐
17. Diversifying—not putting all my eggs in one basket.	☐	☐

Staying on top of the competition:

18. Providing better service than the competition ☐ ☐

19. Identifying and filling a marketplace niche and need ☐ ☐

20. Becoming known as the expert in my field ☐ ☐

21. Reviewing marketing messages and strategies ☐ ☐

22. Using low-cost, long-term marketing strategies ☐ ☐

23. Following up regularly with customers and leads ☐ ☐

24. Continually networking with others ☐ ☐

25. Being an active part of my community. ☐ ☐

Score: ____/25. The five most important areas that I need to immediately focus on are:

1. _____

2. _____

3. _____

4. _____

5. _____

INDEX

9/11, and surviving change, 22

A

Accenture Institute for Strategic
    Change, 39
Accountants
    as advisors in financial crisis,
        288–289
    consulting regularly, 320
    need for, 10
Accounting system
    accounting cycle, 61–63
    accuracy, 60
    balance sheet, 63
    general ledger, 62–63
    importance of, 60–61
    journals
        accounts payable, 65
        cash expense, 64
        cash receipt, 64
        check disbursements, 64
        and financial record-keeping,
            62–63
        general, 65
        sales, 64
    record-keeping, 92
    software, 63
    source documents, 64
    systems inventory of, 90
    tips for, 66–67
    trial balance, 62, 63
    See also Financial management
Accounts payable
    aging, 91

definition, 81
filing, 65
journal, 65
Accounts receivable
    delinquent accounts, 81,
        107–109
    monitoring, 105–106
    month-end receivables
        procedure, 107
    tackling tardy accounts by
        telephone, 211
    See also Bad debt
Act (contact management
    system), 47
Address Book (Microsoft Works)
    (contact management system),
    47
Administration
    efficiency checklist, 110
    and entrepreneurial success, 4
    and growing a business,
        113–118
    monthly functions, 52
    See also Office management;
        Organization
Advertising
    combining techniques, 179
    coupon books, 256
    definition, 165
    direct mail, 255
    files, 46
    flyers, 258
    "hit-or-miss," 25, 255
    magazines, 256–257

monitoring return on
    investment, 92
newspapers, 256–257
Yellow Pages, 257–258
See also Marketing; Promotion
American Psychological
    Association, 39
Appointments
    managing lunch and coffee
        meetings, 49–50
    weekly time planner, 40–41
Assets
    current, 81
    fixed, 81
Attention Deficit Disorder
    (ADD), in business, 39
"Averting" sales technique, 277

B

Backing up computer files, 47
Bad debts
    credit and collections strategy,
        90
    handling, 107–109
Balance sheet
    current assets, 81
    current liabilities, 81
    deciphering, 79-82
    as financial statement, 67–68
    fixed assets, 81
    long-term liabilities, 82
    shareholder's loan, 82
    and six-step accounting cycle,
        61–63

Banking
deposits, as accounting source documents, 64
efficient, 90
financial files, 45
securing loans for business growth, 123–125
Bankruptcy
business, 296–297
personal, 295–296
Basic 7(A) Loan Program, 123
Beck, John, 39
Big-box chain stores
building relationships with, 248-249
complementing, 249
Branding techniques
business appearance, 169–171
corporate theme, 171
logo, 170
mission statement, 170
name, 169
slogan, 170
staff uniforms, 171
Break-even point, 73–78
Breaking Into the Trade Game: A Small Business Guide to Exporting, 131
Budget, reviewing, 289, 300
Business. *See* Business failure; Entrepreneurial skills; Growing a business; Real Life examples
Business consultants, need for, 10
Business cycle, 38–39
Business failure
and the economy, 22
incorporated business, 297
learning lessons from, 285
losing passion for the business, 284
operating in a crisis, 298-305
sole proprietorship, 295–296
warning signs, 286–287
See also Crisis management

Business for Beginners, 177

C

Case studies
Snappy Lawn Equipment Services Inc., 68–73
See also Real Life examples
Cash expenses
and accounting source documents, 64
recording, 64
Cash flow
reviewing, 289–290, 301
sustaining, 8–9
Cash receipt journal, 64
Cash register tapes, 64
Cash theft, 159
Chambers of commerce
and cheaper credit card rates, 92
joining, 227
as venues for public speaking, 213
Change
addressing, 22–23
researching industry trends, 25
seven tools of, 24–26
turning adversity into opportunity, 25
Checklists
administration
Administrative efficiency checklist, 110
Is my business growth out of control?, 112–113
Monthly administrative functions, 52
Your daily task list, 29
communication skills
Verbal communication strategies for my business, 222–224
Written communication strategies for my business, 203–204

employees
Additional employer expenses, 154–155
The dos and don'ts of team building – "Good Boss, Bad Boss" quiz, 157–158
Skills priority list, 144–145
Your hiring checklist, 161
entrepreneurial skills
SCCOPPED (essential entrepreneurial skills), 18
Tools of change needed for my golden box, 27
Your entrepreneurial wardrobe (A to Z), 28
financial management
Bad debts and your accounting records, 109
Calculate your break-even point, 78
Financial control checklist, 88
Gross profit erosion factors, 83
Month-end receivables procedure, 107
Six-step accounting cycle, 61–63
Twenty-question profitability checklist, 84–85
growing a business
"Are you ready for growth?" checklist, 115
"Going for growth" action plan, 135-137
Seven tools of change, 24–26
Top ten mistakes in growing a business, 7–10
marketing
14 marketing mistakes to avoid, 259–260
Improving your marketing plan: a checklist, 183–184
Low-cost strategies, 181

Marketing strategies for my
business, 261–263
operating in a crisis
Ten steps for operating in
crisis worksheet, 298–305
organizing yourself
Daily task list, 29
How to use a weekly time
planner, 40–41
"Operation: Get Organized"
checklist, 57
Organize for the "Five Fs,"
43
public speaking
"Seven Cs" of a successful
speaker, 217
selling
"Five Ws" of selling,
268–270
Six-step sales process, 268
succeeding
Good business management
checklist, 320–321
See also Tips
Checks
disbursements journal, 64
employee theft by, 158
tips for managing, 66–67
Children's play area, in retail
businesses, 173
Cleanliness, of stores, 171–173
Cold calls, 209–210
Collections
persistence pays off, 211–212
tackling tardy accounts by
telephone, 211
techniques, 291
Communication skills
and business, 206
checklist, 203–204
first impressions, 186
improving, 222–224
media kits, 199
media releases, 197–198

necessity of, 186
professional letters, 187–195
testimonials, 240
writing articles, 239–244
See also Public speaking;
Telephone
Complaints, as favor to a business,
5
Computers
backing up, 47
computer skills, and new
employees, 147
computer theft, 159–160
defragmenting hard drive, 47
email, organizing, 48
files, organizing, 45–46
virus protection, 47
Confidence
building, 19, 314
as essential entrepreneurial skill,
18
Contacts
contact management systems,
47
managing lunch and coffee
meetings, 49
marketing files, 46
organizing email, 48
See also Customers; Networking
Cost of sales, analyzing, 70
Coupon book advertising, 256
Creativity, and entrepreneurial
success, 4–5
Credit
business, and bankruptcy, 296
customers
credit applications, 103–105
credit limits, 105
credit policies, 102–103
personal, and bankruptcy,
295–296
working with suppliers in a
crisis, 292, 302
Credit cards

cheaper rates, 92
receipts, recording, 66
statements, as accounting
source documents, 64
Crisis management
assessing yourself, 293–294
collections, 293
dealing with suppliers, 292
dealing with tax agencies,
290–292
financial steps, 288–289
options, 295
reviewing marketing strategies,
289
steps for operating in a crisis,
288–295
Current assets, 81
Current liabilities, 81
Customer loyalty, 246–248
Customer service
as basis of business, 5–6
building loyalty and sales,
246–248
and customer loyalty, 246
following up, 247
free lessons on equipment, 244
importance of, 5–6
in-home servicing, 248
keeping customer files, 46
and marketing strategy, 166
personalized service, 248–249
See also Big Ideas; Customers
Customers
contact database, 246
credit policies, 102–103
and entrepreneurial success, 4–5
needs, and selling, 267–268
relationship selling tips,
271–272
word-of-mouth referrals, 5
See also Accounts receivable;
Customer service
Cycle, of business, 38–39

D

Damaged goods, and inventory costing, 99–100

Davenport, Thomas, 39

Defragmenting computer hard drive, 47

Demographics, defining
average consumer's age, 174
community research, 175
competitor research, 175
consumer shopping habits, 175
residential or commercial, 175

Direct mail advertising, 255

Discipline
as essential entrepreneurial skill, 19
and organization, 19–20

Distribution businesses, break-even point, 76–78

Domain names, 252

Dreams
defining, and creating goals, 21–22
as essential entrepreneurial skill, 21–22
and reality, 2

E

The E-Myth Revisited (Gerber), 32

Economy, and surviving change, 22–23

Email
announcements, 248
organizing, 48

Employees
benefits, 153–155
and changing social conditions, 142
cost of, 153–155
and customer service complaints, 5
determining skills required, 144–145

employment options
casual labor, 143
commissioned employees, 143–144, 152–153
contract labor, 143
full-time, 144, 153
part-time, 144, 153
self-employed commission agents, 143
expenses paid by business, 154–155
fun in the workplace, 156
giving responsibility to, 156
incentives, 155
interviewing, 149–150
keeping, 25, 155–157
LIFER strategy, 155–156
payroll withholdings, 81
recognition, 156
recruiting, 145-148
reference checks, 150-151
résumés, reviewing, 148
selecting, 144–148
staff appearance and manners, 171, 173
testing, 152
theft by
example, 150
types of, 158–160
training, 155

Employer's responsibilities, 153–154

Entrepreneurial skills
and addressing change, 22–27
eight essential skills (SCCOPPED)
communication skills, 18
confidence, 19
dreams and goals, 21–22
expertise, 21
organizational skills, 19–20
passion and a positive attitude, 20–21
persistence and perseverance, 21

self-motivation and discipline, 19
and entrepreneurial success, 4–5
obtaining professional help, 32–33
See also Big Ideas

Entrepreneurs
and all-around business skills, 3–4, 17–18
burnout, 30–31, 32
definition, 17
entrepreneur or operator, 30
entrepreneurial wardrobe (A to Z), 28
tasks, 29

Expertise, as essential entrepreneurial skill, 21

Export Working Capital Program (EWCP), 123

Exporting
benefits, 128–129
challenges, 129
goods versus services, 130
information resources, 131–132
loan program, 123
readiness checklist, 130–131

F

Family
and business goals, 119
effects of bankruptcy on, 296, 298
and fitness activities, 44
making time for, 43
and men in business, 318
as supportive, 314, 315, 318
ten simple, happy tips, 310
and women in business, 311
and working from home office, 52–53

Fast Track Mediation (IRS Publication 3605), 291

"Feel, felt, found" sales technique, 276

Filing system
  20-second filing system, 44–45
  cabinets, organizing, 46
  files, organizing, 45–46
  important documents, 45–46
Financial management
  accounting system, 60–67
  accounts payable, 91
  balance sheet, 79–82
  billing and collections, 90
  break-even point, 75, 77–78
  budget, reviewing, 288, 299
  checks, 91
  comparing results to projections
    using spreadsheets, 126–128
  and entrepreneurial success,
    4–5
  and filing system, 46
  financial statements, 67–68
  financing needs for growing a
    business, 122–126
  learning financial skills, 8
  marketing budget, 178–180
  and marketing reevaluation, 166
  overhead, 82
  payroll, 91
  steps for operating in a crisis,
    288–295, 298–305
  sustaining cash flow, 8
  undefined financial resources,
    8–9
  working capital, 82
  See also Accounting system; Big
    Ideas; Payroll
Financial statements
  balance sheet, 67
  as financial barometer of
    business, 67–68
  statement of income and
    expenses, 67
  understanding, 67–68
  year-end, 63
Fitness
  and family activities, 44

  finding time for, 43
Fixed assets, 81
Flyers as advertising, 258
Food
  eating properly, 43
  managing lunch and coffee
    meetings, 49
  promotional meal costs, 93
Friends
  advice against hiring, 147–148
  interruptions when working
    from home office, 53–54
  making time for, 43
  and your business, 32–33
Fun
  and keeping employees, 156
  making time for, 43

G

General ledger
  as key to business information,
    65
  and six-step accounting cycle,
    61–63
Gerber, Michael, 32
Goals
  defining, 119
  as essential entrepreneurial skill,
    21–22
  and growing a business, 113,
    121–122
Golden box of opportunity, 24
Goldmine (contact management
  system), 47
Gross profit margins
  analyzing, 70
  erosion factors, 83
  reviewing, 288
Growing a business
  and business plans, 7, 112,
    121–122
  commitment, 115–116
  comparing progress to
    projections, 126–128
  deciding to grow, 116–118

  definition, xvii
  employees, 118
  evaluating where you are now,
    114–115
  exporting, 128–132
  financial considerations,
    117–118
  goals, 119
  growing with a business, 3
  incorporation, 132–134
  overcoming problems, 11
  planning financing needs,
    122–126
  relocation, 117
  six-step growth analysis plan,
    113–126
  ten top mistakes, 7–10
  uncontrolled growth, signs of,
    112–113
  you are your business, 3

H

"Hit-or-miss" advertising,
  255–259
Home office
  ensuring uninterrupted work
    time, 55–56
  organizing, 56–57
  overcoming geographic
    isolation, 54–55
  sharing home with shift
    workers, 54
  space for, 53
  telephone calls, 206–208

I

Incorporation
  benefits, 132–134
  challenges, 134–135
Insurance, reviewing costs of, 92
Internal Revenue Service (IRS)
  claiming business losses, 297
  self-employment tax, 143
  tax appeals, 290
Internet. *See* websites

Inventory
 computer system, 96–97
 costing, 99–100
 managing, 93–96
 manual system, 96, 97–98
 and profits, 93–94
 stock, 93–101
 systems, 90–91
Investment Income and Expenses
 (IRS Publication 550), 297
Invoices
 as accounting source
  documents, 64
 posting, 46
 with preprinted account codes,
  90
 receiving and checking, 44–45

J

Journals, in accounting system
 recording in, 63
 sales, 64
 and six-step accounting cycle,
  61–63

K

Kelton, Lorne, 271

L

Lawyers, need for, 10
Letters
 components of, 187–188
 samples
  account reminder, 194–195
  follow-up letter, 188
  letter of introduction,
   190–191
  letter of quotation, 192–193
  permission letter to use
   testimonial, 241
  thank-you letter, 193–194
 writing winning letters,
  189–190
Liabilities
 current, 81

long-term, 82
LIFER strategy, for employees,
 155–156
Lists. *See* Checklists
Loans
 for growing a business, 123–126
 lowering interest rates, 92
Location, importance of, 7
Logo, of business, 170
Long-term liabilities, 82

M

Magazine advertising, 256–257
Managers
 multitasking, 39
 time management, 39–44
Manufacturing businesses, break-
 even point, 77
Market research
 building ideal consumer profile,
  182
 and business plan, 9
 competition, 176
 consumer spending cycles, 176
 consumers' incomes, 176
 home-based businesses, 177
 importance of, 9
 multiple and repeat business,
  182
 niche and secondary markets,
  178
 physical boundaries of market
  area, 181
 researching industry trends, 25
 target market, defining market
  demographics, 182
 using the Internet, 251–254
 See also Marketing
Marketing
 budget, 9–10, 182–184
 business image
  corporate theme, 171
  logo, 171
  mission statement, 170
  name, 182

  slogan, 182
 combining techniques, 184
 community participation as,
  226–228
 compared with promotion and
  advertising, 169
 files, 46
 low-cost techniques, 185–186,
  226, 242–244
 marketing mix, 246
 mistakes to avoid, 259–260
 and overhead costs, 84
 planning, 182–183
 reviewing strategies, 289, 301
 at shopping malls, 236
 skills, 8
 to small business owners,
  248–249
 strategy, and service, 166
 trade shows, 236–238
 under-projection of costs of,
  9–10
 websites, 251–256
 See also Advertising; Market
  research; Marketing plan;
  Networking; Promotion
Marketing plan
 budget, 178–180
 business image and branding
  techniques, 169–171
 example, 180
 monitoring results, 180
 planning ahead, 178
 reevaluating, 166–167
 revising, 169
 revisiting, 165
 strategy checklist, 261–263
 USP (Unique Selling
  Proposition), 167–168
Maximizer (contact management
 system), 47
Media
 building a relationship, 201
 communicating a unique angle,
  233

email introductions, 202
getting your name in the news, 233–234
pitching to the media, 200
sourcing leads on the Internet, 201
Media kits
following up, 200
preparing, 199
Media releases
criteria for, 197–198
preparing, 195–196
sample, 198–199
seasonal trends, 197
Meetings, managing, and planning, 50
Men in business
challenges, 316–318
reasons for success, 315–316
ten tips for, 317–318
Mentors
finding, 285
for men in business, 316
mentoring at lunch and coffee meetings, 49
Merchandise theft, 159
Microloan Program, 123
Mission statement, of business, 170
Motivation, as essential entrepreneurial skill, 19
Multi-tasking, 39

N

Name, of business, 169–170
Networking
becoming involved, 229
breaking the ice, 219–221
building relationships, 220
at conferences, seminars, and workshops, 237–238
and the golden rule, 226
groups, 227–228
how it works, 229
importance of, 312, 314
twenty-second infomercial, 220, 238
using USP (Unique Selling Proposition), 238
Newsletters, and marketing, 248
Newspaper advertising, 256–258

O

Office management
filing systems, 44–46
home office, 52–57
Operating a business. *See* Administration
Opportunity
changing adversity into, 25
metaphor of golden box, 24
Organization
and business cycle, 38–39
computer files, 47
definition, 19–20
and discipline, 19
email, 48
and growing a business, 116
need for, 38
paper files, 44–46
scheduling tasks, 38–44
time management, 48–57
Overhead expenses
analyzing, 70
reviewing, 84, 288–289, 299

P

Passion
as essential entrepreneurial skill, 20
losing passion for the business, 284–285
Payroll
and employees, 153–155
monthly salary calculation, 154
payroll services, 91
Pease, Barbara and Allan, 313
Perseverance, as essential entrepreneurial skill, 21
Persistence
as essential entrepreneurial skill, 21
principle, 21
Personnel management
skills necessary, 144–145
See also Employees
Planning
for change, 24
scheduling time for, 43
See also Growing a business; Marketing plan
Positive attitude
and confidence, 20
and entrepreneurial success, 4–5
as essential entrepreneurial skill, 18, 20
and growing a business, 116
and overcoming obstacles, 11
towards change, 22–26
turning adversity into opportunity, 25
Profit margins
and efficiency, 90–93
and growing a business, 116
increasing, 82–83
reviewing, 288, 298–299
Promotion
combining techniques, 179
definition, 165
product displays, 173
sale and clearance items, 173
store appearance and organization, 172–173
window displays, 172
See also Advertising
Public speaking
becoming an "expert," 212, 230, 231
benefits, 230
body language, 215
"Five Ts" of terrific talking, 213–219
inspiring the audience, 215
need for speakers, 212

preparing presentations,
214–215
"Seven Cs" of a successful
speaker, 217
teaching adult education
classes, 231
technical preparation, 218
timing, 219
venues for, 213
verbal techniques, 217
workshops and seminars,
232–233
Publicity. *See* Advertising; Media
kits; Media releases; Promotion

Q

Questionnaires
communication
What is newsworthy about
your business, 235
employees
Am I ready to be an
employer?, 141
Are you a good boss – or a
bad boss?, 157–158
Ten key questions for
checking references, 151
financial management
Ten topical questions for
credit checks, 104–105
Thirty-question credit
questionnaire, 102–103
Twenty-question "Do I need
it?" checklist, 87
growing a business
Are you ready for exporting?,
130–131
Are you ready for growth
checklist?, 115
How will the business grow?,
121
Is my business growth out of
control?, 112–113
My go-getter goal-setter plan
of action, 120–121

marketing
Review of marketing
methods and messages,
166
Review of marketing
strategies, 166
Where and how can I use
low-cost marketing
magic?, 242–244
operating in a crisis
Am I committed to
continue?, 294
planning
"Where am I going?", 34–36
"Where am I now?", 12–16
selling
Can I improve my sales
skills?, 281
succeeding
I will feel successful when,
311
Quick Tax software program, 177
Quicken software program, 177

R

Radio advertising, 255–256
Real life examples
communication
Easy as pie, 201
Front-page news, 234
The too-big bank, 207
customer service
Coaxing in the chain store
customers, 250
WestJet: small airline – big
service, 6
employees
Friend or Foe?, 148
Having fun...and letting go,
156
No check – no money, 150
No management, no
motivation, no money, 140
Stealing with a smile, 160
financial management

Cutting off the credit, 106
growing a business
Tailoring the formula for
success, 125–126
inventory management
What's in a decimal point?,
98
marketing
Cleaning up their act, 171
Cooking up new customers,
228
Sewing up her USP, 168
Wonder-ful publicity, 196
See it, feel it, touch it, 236
operating in a crisis
Tackling a tax crisis, 291–292
planning meetings
Terrible timing, 51
positive attitude
Put on a smiley face, 26
public speaking
Be Aware of Your Audience,
218
selling
Filling a want and a need,
278
succeeding
Traveling back to success,
286–287
time management
No time for business, 42
The resurrected entrepreneur,
30–31
websites
From Russia with love, 254
See also Case studies
Reputation theft, by employees,
160
Résumés, reviewing, 148
Retail businesses
break-even point, 77
children's play area, 173
cleanliness, importance of,
172–173
location, selection of, 7

organization of store, 173
promotions, 173
staff appearance and manners, 171, 173
washrooms, 171–172
Retained earnings, 63
RPM (Review, Plan, Map your time), 40

S

Sales
analyzing, 71
commissioned employees, 143–144
invoices, filing, 46
over-projection, 9–10
six-step sales process, 268
skills, 8
See also Selling
Sales journal, 64
SCCOPPED (essential entrepreneurial skills), 18
Self-Employment Tax (IRS Publication 533), 143
Selling
"averting" sales technique, 277
closing or purchasing, 277–279
definition, 266
as everyday experience, 266
features versus benefits, 274
"feel, felt, found" technique, 276
filling the customer's needs, 267
"Five Ws," 268–270
high-pressure, 267
planning the approach, 273
presentation, 274
problems and objections, 275–276
prospect, 272–273
public relations after the sale, 280
relationship selling, 271–272
"Six Ps" of selling, 272–280
six-step sales process, 268
See also Sales

Service. *See* Customer service
Service businesses
break-even point, 77
catering to self-employed people, 9
Shareholder's loan
in bankruptcy of business, 297
definition, 82
Slogan, of business, 170
Small business owners, as potential market, 248–249
Snappy Lawn Equipment Services Inc.
balance sheet, 79–82
break-even point, 75
business analysis, 75–76
chart of accounts, 68–69
income statement analysis, 69–73
Spam, cutting down on, 48
Speakers. *See* Public speaking
Spoilage, inventory costing, 100
Stagen Leadership Institute, 39
Stagen, Rand, 39
Statement of income and expenses, 67
Success
definitions, 308–309
and "Five Fs," 309
and good business management, 318
and happiness, 308
inner rewards of, 308
meaning of, 308
and relationships, 313
requirements for, 319
Systems inventory
accounting system, 90
accounts payable, 91
billing and collections, 90
checks, 91
payroll, 91

T

Taxes

dealing with tax agencies, 290–292, 302
filing system, 46
tax deductions, for incorporated businesses, 133–134
Technical skills
and confidence, 19
learning, 8
Technology, and entrepreneurial success, 4
Telephone
assessing expenses, 93
cheap long-distance rates, 93
cold calls, 209–210
etiquette, 208
follow-up calls, 210–212
managing calls, 49
professional greetings and messages, 206–207
tackling tardy accounts, 211
use of, 206–207
See also Communication skills
Television advertising, 255–256
Testimonials
benefits, 240
letter of permission to use, 241
as marketing tool, 240
obtaining, 240
Thank-you letters, 247
Theft
by employees, 158–160
inventory costing, 100
Think group, 309
ThinkShift, 271
Time management, 38–44
meetings, 50–52
monthly routine, 50–52
telephone calls, 49
Time theft, 159
Time Zones Model, of time management, 39
Tips
communication skills
Ten tips for telephone etiquette, 208

Twelve tips for writing
winning letters, 189–190
customer service
Seven tips to build loyalty
and sales, 247–248
entrepreneurial skills
Seven tips for entrepreneurial
success, 4–5
financial management
Seven tips for successful
planning, 85–86
Ten tips for saving time and
money, 92–93
Ten tips for tidy accounting,
66–67
growing a business
Ten tips for expanding your
business, 122
inventory management
Ten tips for astute inventory
control, 95
marketing
Eight excellent trade show
tips, 237–238
Ten tips for sprucing up your
store, 172–173
men in business
Ten tips for, 317–318
operating in a crisis
Seven tips to speed up
collections, 293
organizing yourself
Ten tips to keep your day
organized, 55–56
selling
Ten tips for relationship
selling, 271–272
succeeding
Ten simple, happy tips to
"make your day," 310
women in business
Ten tips for, 313–315
See also Checklists
Trade shows
benefits, 236

conferences and seminars, 238
as market research, 175
selecting, 236
tips, 237–238
Trends
capitalizing on, 168
and entrepreneurial success, 5
potential longevity of trendy
business, 9
reevaluating, 168
researching, 25
Trial balance, 62, 63

U

Unique Selling Proposition
(USP), 167–168
U.S. Department of Commerce,
132
U.S. Export Assistance Centers,
132
U.S. Export-Import Bank, 132
U.S. Small Business
Administration
export assistance, 123, 131–132
loan programs, 123
USP (Unique Selling
Proposition), 167–168

V

Verbal skills. See Public speaking;
Telephone
Virus protection, of computer
files, 47
Volunteering
in the community, 226–228
for public speaking, 213
and time management, 53

W

"Wall of fame," 239
Washrooms, in retail businesses,
173
Waste, inventory costing, 100
Websites
advantages of, 251–253

of competitors, researching, 175
cost, 251
cross-linking with other sites,
254
designers, 251
designing for easy use, 251
domain names, 252
Internet Service providers
(ISP), 251
locating employees, 145–148
as marketing tool, 251–254
necessity for, 251
posting your published articles,
239
Weekly Time Planner, 40
WestJet, 6
White-collar crime, by employees,
160
Why Men Don't Listen and Women
Can't Read Maps, 313
Women, as customers
and appeal of retail stores,
172–173
as consumer decision-makers,
172
Women in business
in the boardroom, 311
challenges, 312
as different from men, 311–312
and "Five Fs," 309
ten tips for, 313–315
traits of successful women,
311–312
Word processing files, backing up,
47
Working capital, 82

Y

Year-end statements, 63
Yellow Pages advertising, 257–258
You are your business, 3, 5, 10–11